IN HOT PURSUIT
THE HIDDEN HISTORY OF THE UNDERGROUND RAILROAD IN LAWRENCE COUNTY, PENNSYLVANIA

Susan Urbanek Linville, PhD

Elizabeth Hoover DiRisio

IN HOT PURSUIT: THE HIDDEN HISTORY OF THE UNDERGROUND RAILROAD IN LAWRENCE COUNTY PENNSYLVANIA, SUSAN URBANEK LINVILLE & ELIZABETH HOOVER DIRISIO

Copyright 2016 by Susan Urbanek Linville & Elizabeth Hoover DiRisio. All rights reserved. Published by Pokeberry Press, a division of Pokeberry Exchange, LLC., www.pokeberryexchange.com. No part of this book may be used or reproduced in any manner whatsoever without written permission except in the case of brief quotations embodied in critical reviews and articles. For information, Pokeberry Press, 41 N. Mercer St., New Castle, Pennsylvania 16101

Pokeberry books may be purchased for book club, educational, business, and promotional use. For information, email editor@pokeberryexchange.com with your request.

ISBN 978-0-9972276-1-1

FIRST EDITION

Printed in the United States of America
Cover Art by Susan Urbanek Linville
Book Design by Stephen V. Ramey

Contents

Acknowldegements   i

Preface   iii

An Introduction to the Underground Railroad   1
- Early Resistance   2
- The Cotton Gin   3
- The Garrisonian Influence   3
- Voices of Vigilance   4
- Fugitive Slave Act and Dred Scott   4

Pre–Civil War African American Community   7
- 1790–1830   7
- 1830–1850   8
- 1850–civil war   10
- Other Notable Individuals   11

African Americans in the Civil War   21
- Elijah Jackson, Jr.   22
- Thomas W. Johnson   22
- George Washington Williams   23

Cloaked by the Cloth: Presbyterian Ministers & Their Congregations   25
- Early Years—American Colonization Society   25
- Later Years—Rebels & Infidels   25
- The Churches   28
- Incident at Iberia   33
- Firebrand   35
- Buttonwood   39
- Way Station   39
- Deep in the Backwoods   39

Print, Politics and Public Opinion   41
- Western Anti–Slavery Society and Lawrence County   43
- Political Parties mid–1800s   44
- Slavery Discussion in the News   44
- Responses to Newspapers   51

Abolition, Western Expansion and Bloody Kansas   53
- Western Pennsylvania Kansas Company: 1854   53
- New Castle–Kansas Aid Group: 1856   54
- Beecher's Bibles   55
- John Speer and the Kansas Pioneer   55
- Border Ruffians: 1855   55

The Speer Defy	56
The Topeka Constitutional Convention	56

Abolitionists and Conductors — 61
Abolitionism	61
Conductors	64

New Castle Borough — 65
Crawford White's Brick House	65
Covenanters Preached Against Slavery	66
Alvira Fights the Slave Catcher	67
Clendenin Looks the Other Way	68
Presbyterians Break Away	68
Judge Whippo Brings Speakers to the City	70
Merchants Store More Than Dry Goods	71

Hickory Township — 81
Eastbrook	82
Conductors	83

Little Beaver Township — 85
Ramage & McQuiston	86
Samuel Taylor Station	86
The Silliman Homestead	87
Old Covenanter Church	87
Home Guards	88
Conductors	89

Mahoning Township — 91
Wright Farm	93
Conductors	94
Abolitionists	95

North Beaver — 97
Abolitionists	99

Perry Township — 101
Portersville	102
Magee Farmhouse	102
A Close Call	103
African Perry	103
Three Runaway Slaves	103
Conductors	104

Plain Grove Township — 107
Conductors	108
Abolitionists	109

Pulaski Township — 111
New Bedford	112

A Ten-Sided House	112
Pulaski	113
The Alma Academy	113
Wanted: Dead or Alive	113
Conductors	114
Conductors (continued)	115
Abolitionists	116
Abolitionists (continued)	117
Free Presbytery of Mahoning	118

Shenango Township — 121

A Reminiscence	122
Conductors	124
Abolitionists	125

Slippery Rock Township — 127

Rose Point	128
Princeton	128
Conductors	129

Union Township — 131

Parkstown	132
An Ardent Abolitionist	132
She Often Baked Biscuits At Midnight	132
Conductors	134
Abolitionists	135

Wilmington Township — 137

New Wilmington	137
A Little Band of Noble Men	138
Conductors	139
Abolitionists	140

Slaves Who Traveled Through Lawrence County — 143

Lewis' Tavern Rescue	143
Slaves Riot & Escape to New Castle	143
A Ship's Carpenter	144
An Identified Escaped Slave	144
Millie Davis Escapes in Pittsburgh	146
Frederick Douglass	146
Frank Jackson Born a Freeman—Eight Years a Slave	148
Passmore Williamson	151
Portersville Posse	152

Ex-Slaves Who Came to Lawrence County — 155

Judge Makes a Home in New Castle	155
Virginia Slave Settles in New Castle	155
George Washington Kincaid School	156

First African American Westminster Grad	162
Old Mose, an Icon at McConnell's Mill	164

Other Ex–Slaves — 169

Simon Arnold	169
Isaiah Miller	169
Charles Tilden	169
Nancy Joiner	170
Alexander Oakes	170
John Joiner	171
Peter M. Doup	171

Myths & Legends — 175

Kurtz House	176
Christian Genkinger House	177
Courthouse	177
Euwer Building	178
New Wilmington Tavern	179
New Bedford's Second Many–Sided House	181
Mystery House	182

ACKNOWLDEGEMENTS

We are extremely fortunate to be able to include the faces of many of Lawrence County's Abolitionists from a glass slide collection prepared in 1901 by Charles C. Sankey and local photographer A. W. Phipps for the 50th Anniversary of the Central Presbyterian Church, originally the Free Presbyterian Church. Sankey, one of the church's eldest members, conceived the notion of putting together an Old–Timers Picture Show. Using his own negatives and copying photographs and portraits of other locals, Phipps created approximately 100 images on glass–plate slides to be cast on a screen by the use of a stereopticon or "Magic Lantern." The plates were donated to the Lawrence County Historical Society in the 1970s by Mr. Sankey's daughters. In 2010, Elizabeth Hoover DiRisio digitally copied and enhanced the plates. These images represent the vast majority of photographs contained in this book.

Special thanks to Mr. Roy McGee for his family information and the photo of the McGee house in Perry Township; to Kathyrn H. Willis for copies of the photos of Almira and Benjamin Ramage of Enon Valley; to Judy Foster, Enon Valley Historical Society, for providing information on the Silliman, Ramage and Bradford families; to Vince Shivers and the Mahoning Valley Historical Society for information and photos of P. Ross Berry; and to the Ashtabula Historical Society for the photo of Charles Garlick.

For help with editing and publication, we thank Alison McNeal, John Nichols, and Steve Ramey. Research for this book was partially funded by a grant from the Laurel Foundation, Pittsburgh, Pennsylvania.

PREFACE

From the address of Arthur B. Bradford, Enon Valley, Pennsylvania at the Reunion of the Old Abolitionists October 1, 1879, Alliance, Ohio:

"The crime of slavery consisted in the fact, that irrespective of color or blood, upon the legal principle partus sequitur ventrem—the child follows the condition of the mother—it converted millions of the American people into chattels personal to be bought, sold, or inherited as property. The outrage it inflicted on humanity was as great as the insult it offered to God who is the Father of us all. The National Constitution limited the slave trade on the coast of Africa to the year 1808, but the Inter-State slave trade was not prohibited, and men, women and children, of all ages and complexions, being in law only property, were exposed in the marketplace to all the incidents of property. Michael Reece, who died in California last year worth 13 millions, began his fortune by keeping three slave shambles in as many Southern cities—Washington, Baltimore and Richmond, where he traded in the flesh of Christians as the Christians had traded in the flesh of his Jewish ancestors centuries ago, and where his odious traffic was advertised in all the leading papers of those cities. Loving each other with all the tenderness we feel toward our relatives, the suffering of the slaves all over the South were inexpressibly great. My heart aches even now when I remember the scenes which I myself have witnessed, but I never saw the one-millionth part of the agony which was endured by the enslaved race. The Slave Power which embodied in the persons of not more than a quarter of a million of Slaveholders, all told, exercised absolute control over the Nation in both Houses of Congress, shaped its foreign and domestic policy, subordinated the Supreme Court itself, and made the President its willing tool in carrying out its plans. It reached the acme of its diabolism when, as one of the compromise measures of 1850, it enacted the Fugitive Slave Law. Up to this period the southern slaves alone were its victims; but this law made it a penitentiary offence in a northern man to aid or abet in the escape of a slave from his master. Worse than that, it converted us all, North and South indiscriminately, into two-legged blood hounds to go, at the word of the slaveholder, and chase down a fugitive slave, and return him to his bondage, or to submit to the fine and imprisonment. Mr. Mason, of Virginia, who originated the Bill in Congress, declared that his main purpose was to humiliate the abolitionists by compelling them to do this menial service to the slaveholding aristocracy or go to jail.

"Except the Quakers, and the Covenanters who were remarkable for the smallness of their numbers, all the churches of the country, Catholics, Presbyterians, Episcopalians, Methodists, Baptists, Congregationalists and every other sect, were on the side of the slaveholders, their members practicing, and their clergy defending the system by appeals to the Bible. It was at such a time as this, and under such circumstances, that the Abolitionists arose under the leadership of William Lloyd Garrison, and took the startling position that slavery was in itself a sin against God, and a crime against man, and that it should be immediately abolished."

1
AN INTRODUCTION TO THE UNDERGROUND RAILROAD

THE UNDERGROUND RAILROAD was neither underground nor a railroad. The origin of the name has been attributed to three sources. Wilbur Siebert quotes the Kentucky owner of slave Tice Davids as saying, "He must have gone off on an underground road."[1] R. C. Smedley suggested it was slavers in Columbia, Pennsylvania who surmised, "There must be an underground railroad somewhere."[2] Reverend Calvin Fairbanks related the story of Levi Coffin and his wife who hid many slaves, in which frustrated slave hunters supposedly said, "That old Quaker must have an underground railroad, for once a slave gets here, he is never seen again."[3]

From the late 17th century until shortly after the American Revolution the Underground Railroad was a loose network of routes running south to Florida, then a Spanish possession. The northern tier formed in the early 1800s and reached its apex between 1850 and 1860. This network featured Eastern routes through Philadelphia and New York to Boston, and Midwestern routes from Ohio, Illinois and Michigan to Canada via Detroit, Cleveland, Sandusky and Erie.[4]

Many assume the railroad was a well organized network of conductors and operators, but that was not the case. Conductors usually knew only of operators living nearest them, and never when an escaping slave might arrive. With secrecy paramount, few first–hand stories were shared.

One consequence of this lack of accurate record keeping is that many myths and legends have taken root concerning the Abolitionists who transported runaway slaves during the three decades preceding the Civil War. Storytellers breathlessly relate tales of underground hiding places, tunnels to nearby rivers, daring rescues, violent confrontations, and other high drama events.

The actual Underground was not nearly so glamorous. Most conductors did not build secret rooms, but housed escapees in cellars, stables, barns, even caves, and elaborate steps were taken to avoid interaction with slave hunters and the general public. This does not mean conductors and slaves were not heroic. The price of failure was as high as in any James Bond adventure. Lives were lost, Abolitionists jailed, captured slaves returned to their owners and whipped.

The Pennsylvania Railroad featured three escape routes. One branch traversed eastern counties of York, Lancaster, Chester, Delaware and Philadelphia. A second crossed central counties of Adams, Fulton, Cumberland, and Dauphin. A third operated in the western counties of Washington, Fayette, Allegheny, Beaver, Lawrence, Mercer, and Erie.

On this third route slaves proceeded northeast from Uniontown in Fayette County along the Monongahela River to Pittsburgh, or northwest to Washington, Pennsylvania. From either destination they could then travel west to Ohio, or north into Beaver, Butler, and Lawrence County toward freedom in Canada.[5]

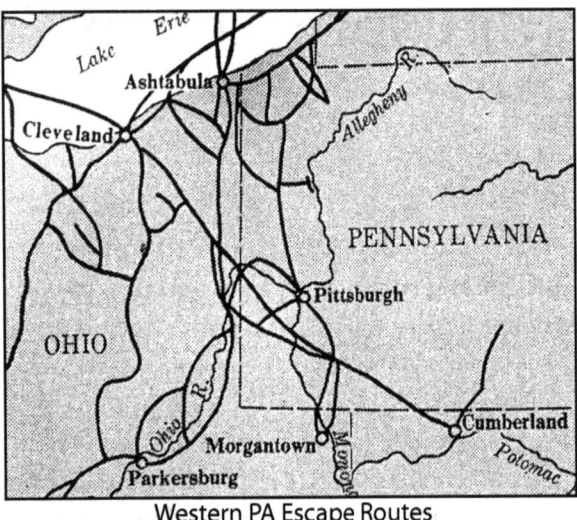

Western PA Escape Routes

EARLY RESISTANCE

SLAVERY WAS PERMITTED in the original 13 colonies, but the Quakers took an early lead in calling for elimination of the practice. In 1693, George Keith published a pamphlet decrying slavery.[6] By the 1770s, Quaker led organizations such as The First Abolitionist Society of America and the Pennsylvania Abolition Society had formed in Philadelphia.

Anti–slavery sentiment in Pennsylvania culminated with passage of the Gradual Abolition of Slavery Act in 1780. Drafted by a committee of new Revolutionary political leaders under the guidance of George Bryan, the Act begins with an expression of gratitude for deliverance from the "Arms and Tyranny of Great Britain," and goes on to state:

> "It is in our Power, to extend a Portion of that freedom to others, which hath been extended to us; and a Release from that State of Thraldom, to which we ourselves were tyrannically doomed, and from which we have now every Prospect of being delivered."[7]

Under the Act, no one could be

> "...deemed and considered as Servants for Life or Slaves; and that all Servitude for Life or Slavery of Children in Consequence of the Slavery of their Mothers, in the Case of all Children born within this State from and after the passing of this Act as aforesaid, shall be, and hereby is, utterly taken away, extinguished and forever abolished."

When released, all slaves were to receive the same freedom and privileges, "such as tools of their trade," as indentured servants. Current slaves were to be registered or set free. The bill passed the State Legistlature by a vote of 34 to 21.[8]

In 1797, Senator Charles Carroll introduced legislation in the Maryland Assembly proposing that the state purchase all female slave children, educate them, and free them at the age of 28. His thinking was that the men would become ready for freedom under the influences of their educated wives and sisters.

As one of the wealthiest men in the country, Carroll wielded considerable influence. He had served as a member of the Continental Congress, was the last living signer of the Declaration of Independence and the only Catholic signatory.

Ironically, Charles Carroll was also one of the country's most prominent slave owners. At any given time, he owned some 300–400 slaves on his Maryland plantations. Even so, he became an outspoken proponent of gradual abolition, recognizing slavery's evil, but believing it impossible to free all slaves at once. Such an action, he rationalized, would force an entire population to fend for themselves in a hostile society, without skills or education.

The bill did not pass. Undaunted, Carroll appointed teachers to instruct his slaves' children daily in the catechism and Christian morality. Without a plan for gradual abolition in the United States, Carroll believed the alternative was to prepare and return freed slaves to Africa.

In 1830 he became President of the American Colonization Society (ACS).[9][10]

THE COTTON GIN

DESPITE PROHIBITION of slavery in many northern states, the number of slaves in the country grew by 257% between 1820 and 1860, to nearly 4,000,000. This trend was fueled by invention of the cotton gin, which revolutionized the industry. Daily cotton processing increased 50–fold, resulting in huge demand for slaves in southern states. Manumissions decreased dramatically between 1830 and 1840, with approximately 250,000 slaves transported across state lines.[11] By 1860, nearly 400,000 Southern families, roughly one in four, held slaves. This amounted to 8% of all American households.[12]

The slave population fueled an economic boom in the South, but not without horrendous cost. Slavery was characterized by exhausting work, little food, brutal beatings, and failing health. Individuals became separated from family and clan, and were forced to cohabitate with people from different regions with different customs. Many ethnic Africans lost complete knowledge of their tribal origins.[13]

THE GARRISONIAN INFLUENCE

NO ONE HAD GREATER impact on the Abolitionist movement than William Lloyd Garrison. Victim of a broken family and abject poverty, the intensely curious Massachusetts-born Garrison was appointed to a seven year apprenticeship with Ephraim W. Allen, the editor of the *Newburyport Herald*, at age 13. This led to a series of newspaper jobs and a meeting with Benjamin Lundy, editor of the *Genius of Universal Emancipation*, who introduced him to the Abolitionist cause.[14]

William Lloyd Garrison

William Lloyd Garrison was born December 10, 1805 in Newburyport, Massachusetts. His father, Abijah, was a merchant marine, and his mother, Frances Maria Lloyd, a devout Baptist. Abijah abandoned the family when Garrison was very young, forcing his impoverished mother to place him with a Baptist Deacon.

At age 13, he was appointed to a seven-year apprenticeship with Ephraim W. Allen, editor of the Newburyport Herald. He became involved in the Abolitionist movement through the American Colonization Society (ACS), but eventually rejected its programs, and gained a reputation as a radical Abolitionist.

Garrison published an influential Abolitionist newspaper, The Liberator, and helped organize the New England Anti–Slavery Society and the American Anti–Slavery Society (AASS). He criticized the U.S. Constitution as a pro-slavery document in The Liberator as the Civil War broke out. Some were surprised when he professed support for Abraham Lincoln's policies, as he had always advocated for change through peaceful means.

William Lloyd Garrison died May 24, 1879 in New York City.[22]

William Lloyd Garrison became involved with the American Colonization Society (ACS), which advocated gradual freeing of slaves and establishing a homeland on their native continent, but eventually rejected its programs, believing that while some members were sincere in promoting the freedom and wellbeing of Blacks, most members merely desired to reduce the number of free Blacks in America through emigration. He left the ACS, called for immediate emancipation, and soon became known as a radical Abolitionist, though he advocated peaceful tactics.

Garrison published *The Liberator*, a widely read Abolitionist newspaper and helped organize the New England Anti–Slavery Society and the American Anti–Slavery Society (AASS).

He did not believe that the AASS should align itself with a political party and thought that women should be allowed to participate in the organization. These views led to internal rifts resulting in the creation of two splinter organizations, the Liberty Party (political) and the American and Foreign Anti–Slavery Society (men only). Garrison and his followers retained control over the AASS.[15]

His influence transcended his New England roots, to Lawrence County and beyond. An 1840's speaking tour with Frederick Douglass featured several Western Pennsylvania stops, and galvanized the Abolitionist movement in the region for decades to come.[16]

VOICES OF VIGILANCE

INSPIRED BY WILLIAM Lloyd Garrison and other powerful Anti-Slavery advocates, vigilance committees formed as early as the 1830's in Northern cities to prevent the return of runaway slaves.

The Abolitionist movement was further emboldened by Frederick Douglass, whose 1845 autobiography, *Narrative of the Life of Frederick Douglass, an American Slave*, was a bestseller. After escaping slavery in Maryland in 1838, Douglas went to Massachusetts to become an orator and journalist, and his published works greatly influenced Northern thinking of the time. Douglass remained an active campaigner against slavery even after the Civil War. In 1868, he spoke in New Castle.[17]

Harriet Tubman stoked the Abolitionist fires in Pennsylvania. Tubman first escaped slavery in Maryland in 1849, accompanied by her two brothers. When the men went back Tubman was forced to return with them. Having tasted freedom, however, she soon escaped again on her own. Traveling at night, guided by the North Star, Tubman reached Philadelphia safely. She became a leader in the Underground movement and would return to Maryland about 20 times, rescuing more than 300 runaways.[18]

FUGITIVE SLAVE ACT AND DRED SCOTT

DISAGREEMENTS OVER slavery reached a boiling point in the 1840s, resulting in passage of the Fugitive Slave Act of 1850. This law made any Federal Marshal or other official who did not arrest an alleged runaway slave liable for a $1,000 fine. Officials now had a duty to arrest anyone suspected of being a fugitive, and officers who captured a fugitive slave earned a bonus or promotion.

The suspect could not demand a jury trial or testify on their own behalf. In addition, any person aiding a runaway was subject to six months imprisonment and a $1,000 fine. These developments thrust Abolitionists into a difficult situation. They must either deny their beliefs and follow the new law, or stand firm with their conscience and defy a law they perceived to be unjust.[19]

Harriet Beecher Stowe responded to escalating tensions by writing Uncle Tom's Cabin, which first appeared as installments in 1851 in the Anti-Slavery newspaper, The National Era, and as a book in 1852. Stowe's vivid portrayal was based on freedom narratives and first-hand accounts. Uncle Tom's Cabin became a best seller in the United States, Britain, Europe and Asia.[20]

Another momentous event of the era was Dred Scott v. Sandford, 60 U.S. 393, a lawsuit in which Dred Scott, a slave transported by his owners to free states and territories, sued for his freedom. The resulting 1857 landmark decision by the U.S. Supreme Court held that African Americans could not be American citizens and therefore had no standing to sue in Federal court. The Federal Government could not regulate slavery in territories acquired after the creation of the United States. This decision spurred wide public debate and became an indirect catalyst for the American Civil War.[21]

Harriet Tubman

Harriet Tubman was born Araminta Ross, a slave in Dorchester County, Maryland around 1820. She began to work as a house servant at the age of five or six. By her early teens she was a field hand, but even then resisted her fate. She blocked a doorway to protect another slave from an angry overseer and was struck by two-pound weight in the head. From then on, she suffered from spells in which she would fall into a deep sleep.

About 1844, she married a free black named John Tubman. In 1849, in fear that she was to be sold, Tubman ran away. During a ten-year span she made 19 trips into the South and escorted over 300 slaves to freedom. She became friends with the leading abolitionists of the day and took part in antislavery meetings. Frederick Douglass said, "… I know of no one who has willingly encountered more perils and hardships to serve our enslaved people…." John Brown, referred to her as "General Tubman" and said she was "one of the bravest persons on this continent."

During the Civil War, Tubman worked for the Union as a cook, a nurse, and even a spy. After the war she settled in Auburn, New York, where she would spend the rest of her long life. She died in 1913.[23]

Chapter Notes

1. Siebert, Wilbur H. *The Underground Railroad from Slavery to Freedom*. McMillan and Co., New York, 1898, 44-45.
2. Smedley, Robert Clemens. *History of the Underground Railroad*. John Hiestand Printer, Lancaster, PA, 1883, 34-35.
3. Switala, William J. *Underground Railroad in Pennsylvania*. Stackpole Books. 2001, 12-13.
4. Siebert, 120-125.
5. Switala, 55.
6. Moore, George H. "The First Printed Protest Against Slavery in America," In *The Pennsylvania Magazine of History and Biography, Vol. XIII*. Philadelphia, 1889, 265.
7. The Pennsylvania State Archives Doc History Transcripts: An Act for the gradual Abolition of Slavery. http://www.portal.state.pa.us/portal/
8. Ibid.
9. McClanahan, Brion, T*he Politically Incorrect Guide to the Founding Fathers*. 2009, 199-208.
10. McDermott, Scott, *Charles Carroll of Carrollton: Faithful Revolutionary*. 2002, 210-211, 243.
11. Kolchin, Peter. *American Slavery, 1619-1877*. New York: Hill & Wang, 2003, 78-96.
12. Morgan, Marcyliena H. *Language, Discourse and Power in African American Culture*. Cambridge University Press. 2002, 20.
13. Kolchin, Peter. *American Slavery, 1619-1877*. 78-96.
14. Hinks, Peter & John McKivigan, eds. *Encyclopedia of Antislavery and Abolition, Vol. 1, A-I*. Greenwood Press, Westport, CT, 2007, 288.
15. Alexander, Leslie M. & Walter, C. Rucker, eds. *Encyclopedia of African American History, Vol. 1*, ABC-CLIO. Santa Barbara, CA, 2010, 304-305.
16. http://www.pbs.org/wgbh/aia/part4/4p1561.html
17. Trotman, James C. *Frederick Douglass: A Biography*. ABC-CLIO Publishers, Santa Barbara. 2011, 118-119.
18. Larson, Kate Clifford (2004). *Bound For the Promised Land: Harriet Tubman, Portrait of an American Hero*. New York: Ballantine Books, 72-100.
19. Fugitive Slave Law. Complete Text: http://www.usconstitution.net/fslave.html
20. Harriet Beecher Stowe Center. https://www.harrietbeecherstowecenter.org/
21. http://www.sos.mo.gov/archives/resources/africanamerican/scott/scott.asp
22. http://www.biography.com/people/william-lloyd-garrison-9307251
23. Larson, Kate Clifford, *Bound for the Promised Land: Harriet Tubman, Portrait of an American Hero*. Ballantine Books, New York, 2004, 72-100.

2

PRE–CIVIL WAR AFRICAN AMERICAN COMMUNITY

RECORDS OF BLACKS LIVING in Mercer and Beaver Counties, parts of which were to become Lawrence County, are scant before 1800. While Pennsylvania made slavery illegal in 1780, census and archival records show that most Black residents in Western Pennsylvania were slaves owned before the Gradual Abolition of Slavery Act. These men and women were to be freed over a period of time.

1790–1830

Mercer County

TWO SLAVES WERE BROUGHT to the area by William Morehead from Westmoreland County as early as 1790. An elder in the First Presbyterian Church, Mr. Morehead settled between the Mahoningtown and Oakland areas of New Castle.[1]

In the 1800 Mercer County census, Joseph Axtell, John Colvin, Sr., Samuel McBride, Robert Wallis, and John Littleford owned one slave each.[2]

James Fullerton brought his wife and "a colored girl" from Cumberland County, Pennsylvania, in the spring of 1801. They settled on a farm in North Beaver Township.[3]

In the fall of 1802, Walter Clarke from what is now Lewisburg, Snyder County, Pennsylvania, arrived with an extensive family and workers that included "a colored girl."[4]

John Calvin of Salem Township bequeathed a mulatto girl to his wife in 1804. The same year, John Sheakley moved from Gettysburg to Sandy Creek Township, bringing with him four "Negro slaves."[5]

But it was another man who made the biggest splash. Arthur Chenowith moved to New Castle from Virginia and built the Old Stone Corner in 1812, a hotel located on Jefferson Street at the Diamond.[6] He was said to have brought the "first colored man ever seen in the place."

> "Many of the little folks believed for a time that 'Black Jack,' as he was called, was a white man painted black. For many years he was the only colored man in town. When he attended the Methodist Church, as he was in the habit of doing, he attracted more attention on the part of the young folks than the minister himself."[7]

In 1818, a Black freeman named Richard Travis paid two dollars for 150 acres along Sandy Lake shore, establishing a safe harbor for fugitive slaves and Native American families.

John Young, Sr., who lived on Indian Run in Springfield Township, also owned slaves. One of them, Peggy Johnston, was welcomed into the Neshannock Church congregation, which was unusual at the time. Her children, Bob and Sally, became free at the age of 28.

7

"Bob was given the usual schooling that boys received in his day, and had the same religious training. In manhood, his fine moral and other qualities made him well known to a large community and brought him the inconvenient notoriety of being an example of what freedom would do for the slave. This notoriety purchased for him his deepest humiliation. He happened innocently to enter a wrong pew one Sunday morning in the Neshannock Church, and was promptly ordered out by its owner. Of course he never returned to the church–nor did certain white men, his friends."[8]

In his will of April 20, 1825, John Young, Sr. stipulated:

"I do will that Peg, the old wench, is to be supported out of my farm, left to John and David."

Peggy died in 1850.[9]

According to Mercer County record books, George Mitchell, a colored man of Butler County, left a parcel of New Castle City land to his friend, Nellie, a slave woman. As a slave, she was only empowered to own property by an act of legislature on April 16, 1829. That plot was transferred to John Wilson in 1836 for the sum of $100. The deed was signed by two witnesses and the mark of the grantor, Nellie. This represents one of the very rare transfers of property of that period in which a Negro was the grantor.[10]

Beaver County

The 1800 Beaver County census listed four slaves. By 1810 there were eight, and in 1820, five. All had been liberated by 1830.

James Nicholson, a farmer in Big Beaver, willed his farm to three former slaves, Pompey and Tamar Frazier and Betsy Matthews. After the Fraziers died, Betsy took possession of the farm and married Henry Jordan in 1840. She sold the majority of the land, which later became the borough of New Galilee.[11]

1830–1850

Boom Times

THE 1830S WERE A TIME of rapid development for the area that would become Lawrence County. Roads were improved and bridges constructed. The Erie Canal Extension was completed in 1833, extending about five miles above New Castle, and the Cross–Cut canal was finished and opened for traffic in 1838.

The first boats were constructed for both freight and passengers, allowing produce to be transported south to Beaver in exchange for other merchandise. New Castle, which became a borough on March 25, 1825, doubled in population, reaching 611 by 1840.[12]

An 1840 business directory listed carpenters, coopers, nail rollers, milliners, shoemakers, physicians, blacksmiths, tailors, hatters, merchants and attorneys. Names on the list associated with the Abolitionist movement included Samuel Alexander, carpenter, Reverend W. Bushnell, Presbyterian clergyman, S. C. Euwer & Co., merchants, White McMillen, merchant and hatter, C. T. Whippo, physician, and Crawford White, farmer.[13]

Liberia

By 1840 there were more than two dozen Black residents in the safe harbor established by Richard Travis near Sandy Lake. This Underground Railroad station became known as Liberia, and it existed until the early 1850s when passage of the Fugitive Slave Act hastened the departure of fugitives to Canada.[14, 15, 16]

African Americans in the Census

Free African Americans in the 1840 Mahoning Township census, with the exception of John Sawer's family, lived with white landowners

Samuel Mitchell, Peter Smith, Elijah Satterfield, and Hugh Cotton. In Shenango Township, one young black woman resided with the M. H. Gold family. North Beaver Township was home to the Barzeal and William Ormes families. Others resided with white landowners John Neil and Robert Gaily. The John and Anges Lightner families lived in Big Beaver Township. Others lived with Bump Yrajer. New Castle was home to Levi Davis and his wife, the Henry Johnston Family, and an older man, Daniel Jackson.[17]

Saint Luke's African Methodist Episcopal Church

Saint Luke's African Methodist Episcopal (A.M.E.) Zion Church is the earliest Black congregation and one of the oldest churches still operating in Lawrence County. As early as 1837, most of the free Blacks, not feeling as free as they desired in the white churches, began hosting their own services in the home of Isabelle Taylor. They moved from house to house until the school board gave the congregation permission to use the basement of the New Castle Academy on North Jefferson Street.

In May 1844, John Norman, Isaac Baker, Daniel Starks, Thomas Hall, John Harris and Elijah Jackson organized a new congregation, known as the M.E. Church.[18, 19] Their numbers increased and they attracted some white families as well. The church secured a structure on North Shenango Street in Snake's Rest, an area tucked into a ravine near West Wallace Avenue.[20]

Land for the building was reportedly donated by the Honorable Thomas W. Phillips. The church had a seating capacity of 125. After a few years of operation, the land title was disputed. Phillips sold the property, purchased a site on Elm Street, and deeded it to trustees of the A.M.E. Zion Church of America. The old building was physically moved to the new site.[21]

Fanny Wilson

Fanny Wilson's identity remains a mystery. She was born in Virginia about 1800 and was likely a freed slave.

The 1850 Census reveals that Fanny had opened her home to Lewis Davis and his wife, Marie, their two sons, John and David, ten-year-old Robert Wilson, and two of Henry's children. Oscar Johnston was nine years old, and Frances, eight.

In 1860, Oscar Johnston and John Davis were still with her, and two additional young people had joined them, V. Madoline of Ohio, and David Hall.

Henry Johnston

Henry Johnston is listed in the 1840 census with a wife and five children. By 1850, Henry was 60 years old, working as a hostler with Lewis Davis, and living with Innkeeper Peter Shoemaker. Two of Henry's children, nine-year-old Oscar Johnston, and eitght-year-old Frances, lived with Fanny Wilson.

> **Elijah & Sarah Jackson**
>
> In the 1840 census, the Jacksons resided in Lackawannock Township in Mercer County, a Free Black man with his wife and son. They lived near the David Young family, and Elijah was one of the founders of the Saint Luke's A.M.E. Church. By 1850, Elijah was a laborer in Neshannock Township, and a neighbor to Reverend Wells Bushnell.
>
> Their son, Elijah Jackson, Jr., fought in the Civil War.

1850–CIVIL WAR

Lawrence County Is Formed

BY 1850, NEW CASTLE had become a converging point for roads and canals and was rapidly expanding. This caused difficulty for residents, as the existing county line passed directly through the borough. Some citizens were forced to travel south to transact legal business in Beaver County while others went north to the Mercer County seat.

The creation of a new county from portions of Mercer, Beaver and Butler Counties had been discussed as early as 1820, but did not come to fruition until the spring of 1849. This led to a need for new governing bodies and a courthouse. For this purpose, County Commissioners purchased land on June 18, 1850, and signed a contract for the courthouse and jail with Hamilton, Craig and Company.[22]

Work commenced in the fall of 1850, and was completed in 1852, using locally quarried stones and brickwork laid by an African American, P. Ross Berry.[23]

African Americans of the Time

In 1850 the African American population of Lawrence County numbered 132, with 51 residing in New Castle.[24] Biographical information included in the census suggests that Black Americans had made strides in terms of contributing to, and being accepted by their communities.

Neshannock Township and New Castle were home to the largest number of African Americans. Some individuals resided with white families, including John Snowdon, laborer, living with the Robert Peebles family. Diana Cowens was a part of William Carey's household. James Davis and Harry Johnson, hotel workers, were listed at the residence of P. Shoemaker, innkeeper. Theodore Potter resided with cabinetmaker Robert McGuffin, and John Leonard and David Robison lived with Richard Craven, brick mason.

Other African American community members lived with families of their own. Examples include John Harris and Daniel Starks, co-founders of Saint Luke's A.M.E. Church, Thomas Fitzhugh, a blacksmith, James Hale, Peter Logan, James Fitzhugh, George Anderson, and Peter Gordon.[25]

In Shenango Township, David Hall, farmer, resided with daughter, Sarah, son, Lewis, a boatman, and John, also a farmer. Their real estate was listed at $2,000.

Big Beaver Township was home to the farming families of Rachel and John Lightner. William Arnold, blacksmith, and Julia A. Homer also lived in Big Beaver with their families.

Mahoning Township lists Peter Smith, laborer, and Lawden Curtis, potter. Each had a sizable family.

Ned Burk was a twelve year old boy living in Wilmington Township with J. S. Johnston. Samuel Wright, 14, lived in Perry Township with George Magee, a member of the Underground Railroad.[26]

Passing Through to Pandenarium

In 1854, a large group of African Americans arrived by packet boat at the canal wharf in New Castle.[27]

> "On the 12th of November a party of fifty-two colored people passed through New Castle, on their way from Virginia to Mercer, where they had concluded to settle."[28]

These were the freed slaves of Dr. Charles D. Everett of Charlottesville, Virginia, who had served as the physician to Thomas Jefferson and the private secretary to James Monroe. Having become convinced that slavery was sinful, he determined to free his slaves.

His first thought was to send them to Liberia, West Africa, but he decided to explore closer options as well. He briefly considered Canada, but finally asked his nephew to go to Pennsylvania and seek a location suitable for a colony of freedmen.

In Mercer, the nephew met William F. Clark, editor of the *American Freeman*, ardent Abolitionist, and conductor on the Underground Railroad. Clark introduced him to John Young, a conductor at Indian Run.[29] Young offered his property to create the new settlement.

Dr. Everett died before his plans were completed but his will provided for the release of his slaves and their maintenance and support. He not only freed his slaves, but gave them money to buy freedom for their family members. Wives bought husbands from slavery and vice versa. It was estimated that the cost to Everett was in excess of $26,000, which would be the equivalent of roughly $700,000 in 2015.

Each family was provided with a plot of land, cabin, clothing and supplies. Unfortunately, Pennsylvania winters proved difficult to endure, and the community was overcome with tuberculosis. Two families moved to Tennessee, five moved to Mercer, and others returned to the South.

Even so, the community endured into the 1890's.[29] By 1900 there were only two individuals left in Pandenarium.[31] Today, nothing exists of the settlement.

OTHER NOTABLE INDIVIDUALS

ALTHOUGH THE HISTORIES of many individuals are unknown, some African Americans in the New Castle area prior to the Civil War achieved noteworthy careers. A few are memorialized below.

A Tonsorial Bazaar

According to the *New Castle News*, Thomas D. Berry was

> "…one of the most respected citizens in New Castle… [H]e was a man of fine appearance, and was noted for the intense interest he took in the education of his children."[32]

Thomas and Mary Ann Berry arrived in New Castle with their children in the early 1840s, and Thomas wasted no time in making his presence known.

> "The first barber who succeeded in making a living in New Castle is said to have been Thomas D. Berry, a colored man, who opened a 'Tonsorial Bazaar' a few doors west of the Mansion House (later the Leslie House), in 1844."[33]

J. S. Smiley related a tale about the city's early days when it was not unusual for rough crowds to gather in the taverns and spend the night howling and singing.

> "At that time, Tom Berry's barber shop was a sort of symposium where the business men got together when trade was dull. A group had gathered in Berry's shop on this particular day when a stranger arrived. Berry was out at the time, so when the stranger started to deride the condition of the city, the men couldn't help but take advantage of the situation.

The Berry Family

Thomas D. Berry

Thomas D. Berry was born about 1813 in Ohio.

The family lived in Bridgewater and Mount Pleasant before moving to New Castle in 1841, and Thomas became one of the city's first barbers. They built a two–story brick house on the west side of North Jefferson Street, today 305 North Jefferson Street.

In the 1850 census, Thomas was a 37 years old mulatto barber with $1,000 in assets. He lived with wife, Mary, and children, Ross, Mary, Emma, and Thomas. Other household members included a son–in–law, John Norman, a steward, and their elder daughter, Margaret Norman.

In 1852 Berry moved his barbershop from Cochran House to the rear of Meckling's Store at the southeast corner of Washington and Mercer Streets.[47] A local newspaper stated: "Mr. Berry, who has been indisposed for some time, in consequence of which his shop has been closed, is now open again for the accommodations for his friends and customers."[48]

Thomas D. Berry died at the age of 40 on May 29, 1853.[49]

Mary L. (Johnson) Berry

Mary L. Berry was born in 1839[50] in Bridgewater, Pennsylvania. She was a resident of New Castle for more than 60 years, and appears in the records as attending the New Castle Academy in 1851–1852.

She attended Central Presbyterian Church, and married Thomas W. Johnson before 1860.

Thomas W. Johnson

The 1860 census listed, Thomas and Mary in Mary Ann Berry's household. It also included Emma, Thomas, P. Ross, his wife, Mary and two children, and son–in–law Thomas Johnson with his wife and two children.

Johnson may have taken over Thomas Berry's barbershop after Thomas' death.

Margaret Berry

Margaret Berry was born in 1832, birthplace unknown. She married John H. Norman before 1850, and they lived in New Castle with the Berry family. The couple moved to Newark, Ohio before 1863. Their six children were Mary, Mariah, Frank, Oliver, Fremont, and Lizzie.

John H. Norman

John Norman was born in the District of Columbia, but moved to New Castle early in his life, where he co–founded Saint Luke's A.M.E. Church in 1844. In the 1850 census John is listed as a steward. The family moved to Newark, Ohio in the early 1860's and John became a barber.[51]

Thomas Berry

Thomas Berry was born in 1845 in New Castle. In the 1872 census, he was a barber on North Street. The rest of his life is undocumented.[52]

# of New Castle

Mary Ann Berry

Mary Ann Berry was born in Blairsville, Pennsylvania in 1810.[53] After Thomas' death, she remained in the house until 1857, when she bought a house owned by Joseph S. White on East North Street, near Apple Alley.

In 1860, Mary lived with P. Ross Berry and his family. By February 1869, she and her daughter–in–law, Mary M. Berry, purchased a second house on North Street from Joseph and Adaline White for $500. In 1870 Mrs. Berry owned $2,000 in real estate and $100 in property. Living with her were daughter, Emma Davis, and grandsons, Alexander Davis and Evan Norman. Mary Ann died on January 22, 1900, at the age of 90. "She was a lady highly respected by many who knew her, and among the older families of the city there were many who regularly visited her for many years past. Her mental faculties were well preserved and her memories of early events clear. For 50 years she had been a member of the First Methodist Episcopal church, and she died secure in the faith she had cherished for half a century."[54]

Emma Berry

Emma Berry was born in 1850 and was a devoted member of the Central Presbyterian Church her entire life. She died in December 1920 at the age of 58. Her niece, Ida G. Johnson was appointed executrix. A lawsuit followed, husband William insisting he was due $5,000 under an 1909 act of Congress. The house was sold in 1917 at a sheriff's sale, but it's unclear whether William received his money.[55]

William Curry

William Currie was born about 1839 in English Canada (many escaping slaves formed communities in Ontario). He immigrated to the United States in 1870, through Buffalo, New York, married Emma Berry in 1872 and became a New Castle barber. He and Emma had no children.

There is no record of William's death.

Plympton Ross Berry

Plympton Ross Berry was born in 1834 in Mount Pleasant, Pennsylvania, and moved with his family to the New Castle area before 1840. By 16 he was a trained bricklayer and stonemason.

At six and a half feet tall and well known for his skill and honesty, P. Ross became a leader in Youngstown's African American community after the Civil War. Berry's company was responsible for many major building projects, including banks, schools, hotels, factories, and churches.

After a half–century of bricklaying, designing and building, P. Ross Berry died in 1917. He was laid to rest in Oak Hill Cemetery, Youngstown, Ohio.[56]

Mary (Long) Berry

P. Ross married Mary Long in 1857. In 1861 they traveled by canal boat to Youngstown, where they would settle. They had four sons.[57]

> "The stranger wanted them to know that he came from a real city, and called New Castle a one–horse town. He harassed them, 'Why, there ain't a decent store in town! You don't have any stores where dry goods or groceries or hardware are sold exclusively, but just one–horse stores, where you sell everything from a bunch of onions to a coffin. Say, can't a man get shaved here.'
>
> "Alex Cameron, who owned a general store on the northwest corner of Washington and Mercer, had been sitting in a corner listening to the man. 'Why certainly,' he said. His face as impassive as a sphinx. 'Sit right down in this chair.'
>
> "Supposing Cameron to be the barber, the stranger obeyed, and Cameron, with an expression like a Scotch elder, mixed up a large mug of lather. Then he liberally bathed the face of the stranger, not being all that particular to keep it out of his eyes and mouth. This done, he deliberately strolled over to his corner and coolly sat down.
>
> "'Here barber, ain't you going to finish shaving me?' called the stranger. 'Not much,' said Cameron, 'we only lather you here; you get shaved down the street.'"[34]

The Berry family lived in a brick house along North Jefferson Street near the base of the North Hill on the upper part of the lot now known as 305 N. Jefferson (formerly 155 N. Jefferson).[35] Various sources state that Thomas built the house.

Since Thomas was a barber, his involvement in the actual bricklaying is unknown. His teenaged son, P. Ross Berry, was an accomplished brick mason, suggesting that Berry was familiar with local masons. In any case, the secret cellar constructed in this home at the time was part of the Underground Railroad.[36] There is no record of Thomas purchasing this land from Joseph S. White, and it appears the men enjoyed a measure of friendship based upon subsequent real estate trades between them.

Berry paved the way for future generations of respected Black barbers, including Charles Nighten, who billed himself as a "Tonsorial Professor" in the 1860s, and T. A. Dennison,

---

Charles Nighten

Charles Nighten was born in Virginia about 1822. He and wife, Ariana (Ann), and four children moved to New Castle prior to 1860. Nighten was listed in the census as a barber with $300 in property. His barber shop was located on the south side of the Diamond, one door west of the Leslie House.

By 1870, the Nightens had six children and were sharing their home on the east end of North Street with two young barbers, their nephew, Charles Berry, and William T. A. Dennison. In the 1872 New Castle Directory, four other barbers, Thomas Berry, William S. Carlisle, Edward Cuff, and Jacob Hill, resided on North Street.

Nighten may have mentored these young men, since he referred to himself as a "Tonsorial Professor." Nighten died in February 1874 at the age of 49 years of stomach cancer.[60]

T. A. Dennison

William T. A. Dennison was a barber and political activist.[61] He became assistant state organizer of the Colored Voters' League in 1898 and that same year was appointed a vice–president from Lawrence County at a mass meeting of the Republican League of Allegheny County.[62]

William married Charles and Ariana Nighten's eldest daughter, Sarah.

The Dennisons were members of the Saint Luke's A.M.E. Zion Church, and had 14 children.

The Stewart Family

Lemuel B. & Margaret (Rouse) Stewart

Lemuel B. Stewart was a highly respected laborer in New Castle. Born in Westmoreland County, Pennsylvania, about 1809, he married Margaret Rouse in 1830 and moved to Mercer County four years later. In 1849 they settled in New Castle and raised seven children: Mary (Margaret), William A., Lemuel A., Samuel, Roberta, Zachariah, Charles, George and Henry.

In 1870, Lemuel was a widower living with his daughter (Mary) Margaret. By 1880 he was with a second wife, Eliza, 20 years younger. Stewart was a member of the Baptist church for 64 years. His children were prominent members of the New Castle and Youngstown communities. His grandson, George Washington Williams, became a member of the Ohio Legislature and a political leader in Cincinnati, then a lawyer in Boston, where he wrote a history of the Negro in America that received favorable press and public attention.

Lemuel B. Steward died in 1893 at his residence on W. Falls Street.

William A. & Isabelle (Berry) Stewart

William A. Stewart was born about 1834 in Mercer County. The second child of Lemuel B. and Margaret Stewart, he married Mary Berry's younger sister, Isabelle, and sired two children, Eugene and Emma.

Isabelle was born in Blairsville, Pennsylvania and lived in New Castle since girlhood. She attended the Park Christian Church and was a prominent member of the community.

A photograph of William's barbershop shown in the background.[58]

Lemuel A. Stewart

Lemuel A. Stewart was the third child of Lemuel B. and Margaret Stewart. A bricklayer and building contractor, he moved to the Mahoning Valley during the Civil War to partner with P. Ross Berry.

The Stewart and Berry families were connected by friendship and marriage, and their sons continued their building dynasty in the Youngstown area. The next generations produced doctors, dentists, attorneys, musicians and leaders.

One son, William R. Stewart, was admitted to the Ohio bar in 1888 and became the first colored representative from Mahoning County, elected to the 72nd general assembly as a Republican. He was instrumental passing anti–lynching legislation and sponsored bills providing pensions to civil servants.[59]

who would become an assistant state organizer of the Colored Voters' League in 1898.

A Visionary Builder

In 1850, Thomas Berry's eldest son, P. Ross Berry, was hired to lay brickwork for the Lawrence County Court House. When construction was completed in 1852, the New Castle Gazette stated that the courthouse "will stand for ages as a monument of youth, vigor and taste."[37]

In 1861, P. Ross and his wife, Mary, relocated to Youngstown, Ohio, where he would partner with Lemuel A. Stewart, son of New Castle natives, Lemuel B. and Margaret Stewart. As a businessman, Berry provided training and jobs to members of the U. S. Colored Troops and hired white workers as well as Black. As activist, he organized the 1867 Emancipation Ball and Dinner which attracted African Americans from across eastern Ohio and Western Pennsylvania. As philanthropist, he contributed a large sum to Youngstown's courthouse construction.

Berry laid brickwork for the original Rayen School, the Homer Hamilton & Company, the Parish of Saint Columba Church, Youngstown City Jail, William Hitchcock Mansion, First Presbyterian Church, Governor David Tod's Mansion, Baptist Temple, Youngstown's Grand Opera House, and Tod House Hotel. In 1865 he returned to New Castle to build the Disciple Church.

His four sons were trained as brick masons and became union organizers for Brick Masons Local #8.[38]

The New Castle Academy

The New Castle Academy was founded in 1849 as a successor to the New Castle Female Seminary, founded 1838. It was a private school that admitted both male and female students, Black and white. About 100 families patronized the school and

> "...the liberality and promptness which they show in the payment of tuition is a clear index to the intenseness of their feeling in regard to this subject..."

Among known graduates were William Patterson, noted banker and Industrialist, who completed his Accounting education in a two year program. An African American resident of New Castle, Mary L. (Berry) Johnson, the daughter of Thomas D. and Mary Ann Berry, was also listed in the Academy rolls for 1851-52.[39]

The Color Line Is Drawn

William A. Stewart was a respected New Castle barber, and well-known in the area. In the 1877 Republican Party convention he edged out six white men for his party's nomination for Associate Judge.[40]

Some Republicans were reportedly dissatisfied. Stewart was qualified to sit at the side of the Judge, and was learned in the law, but "the color line was drawn and not by the Democrats."[41]

The Stark County Democrat described the situation this way:

> "[Stewart was] one of the most intelligent men of this city during his prime. During the late sixties (sic), he was nominated by the Republican Party for associate judge of this county and came within a few [174] votes of being elected to the bench. None doubted his ability or capability, but racial prejudice was so strong, he being a colored man, that many Republicans refused to support the party nominee, and he was defeated. The campaign is remembered by all the older residents of the county. William Stewart, in spite of his accident of birth, associated with the leading intellectual men of the city and was a member of the Symposium, an organization formed by lawyers, doctors, teachers, and other professional men and flourished here many years, the meetings being held for intellectual profit of its organizers."[42]

European Tour Disaster

In the late 1870s, Oscar L. Johnston, a prominent New Castle barber, and his wife, Melissa, left the city to tour Europe. Their daughter had become a popular lecturer, and Oscar planned have her speak in principle Old World cities. Things did not go as planned.

In 1881, Melissa sent a letter from Glasgow, Scotland to William Stewart with the following:

> "My husband died on the 16th of December last, of broncho–pneumonia. He had been ailing for some time and had intended going home in the Spring, but he took very bad on Friday, and Sunday following had three fits, which left him unconscious, so that he was unable to tell us anything about his business. He had a large hair–dressing and perfume shop on one of the principle streets in Glasgow. He died Thursday morning. We thought that when the business was settled that we would have money enough left to take us home, but we were mistaken. The people here are so crafty and penurious that when all was over we had nothing. Anna and I are both well, but we cannot get along in this country, and believing you to be a friend we appeal to you for help. Any assistance we may receive towards getting home we will gladly repay after we get there. We have no one here whom we can call a friend and are very lonely."

Melissa and her children did return home.[43]

A Map Sponsor

Isaac Baker was a mulatto barber and livery merchant living in New Castle in his early career. He was successful enough that he became a business sponsor for the city map published in 1855. Isaac was also one of the founders of the Saint Luke's A.M.E. Church.[44]

He Owes Me Money!

Another colorful character of the time was Tyrone Landrum. An 1887 newspaper article reported that he was a brake–man on the first train in Pennsylvania.[45]

Oscar L. & Melissa Johnston

By the 1870s Oscar Johnston was a well–known New Castle barber in the Leslie House on Mercer Street. He and his wife Melissa lived on North Street with two children, Anna and Robert.

They shared their home with David Hall who had been living with Oscar at Fanny Wilson's. Hall was also a barber.

Oscar died on December 16, 1880, while touring Europe with his family.

Melissa died unexpectedly in 1900 at the age of 64 years. She belonged to the Central Christian Church.[63]

Issaac and Frances Baker

Isaac Baker was born in Pennsylvania about 1825. In the 1850 census he is listed as a mulatto barber living with wife, Frances, an 80 year old white man, George Taylor, 54 year old mulatto, Elena Taylor, and a 14 year old mulatto boy also named George Taylor. The elder George, Frances and Elena Taylor were born in Virginia. It is likely that George was Frances' father.[64]

His obituary stated:

"Isaac Baker, a former resident of this city, and well known among the colored citizens of this community, died at Youngstown Friday night. He had a number of relatives here and the remains will be brought to this city for interment. The deceased was engaged in the livery business some years ago in this city and left New Castle for Warren, O., where he lived until recently, when he became quite ill and he was removed to Youngstown, where his relatives, of which he had a number at that place, could care for him. His wife passed away about 15 years ago."[65]

Tyrone Landrum

Tyrone Landrum was born in 1829 in Donnegal Township, Butler County, Pennsylvania.

In the 1870 census, he is listed as a laborer. He and his wife, Sarah, had eight children and lived at the corner of Mercer and Grant Streets in New Castle.

According to his obituary:

"Tyrone Landrum has been a well–known character on the streets of this city for many years. At the time the Indian, Sam Mohawk, was hung for killing the Wiggans family, near Butler, Landrum had the honor of conducting the burial rites of the murderer, whom he interred in a field.... [Tyrone was] not without his vices, from which he himself was always the greatest sufferer. His last words were to the effect that he was going away and some white man owed him $3.50."[46]

Chapter Notes

1. "Mrs. Belinda Clendenin Dead," *New Castle News*, April 29, 1907, 1, 10.
2. Johnson, Hubert Rex, *History of the Neshannock Presbyterian Church, New Wilmington, Pennsylvania : together with some account of the settlement of that part of northwestern Pennsylvania in which the church was organized*. 1925, 219.
3. Durant, S. W. and P. A., *History of Lawrence County Pennsylvania*. 1770-1877, 69.
4. Durant, 65.
5. Burns, Edward M. "Slavery of Western Pennsylvania," in *Historical Magazine, Volume 8, Number 4*, October 1925, 208.
6. Hazen, Aaron L. *20th Century History of New Castle and Lawrence County, Pennsylvania*. Richmond-Arnold Publishing Co. Chicago 1908, 60.
7. *New Castle News*, December 19, 1918.
8. Johnson, *History of Neshannock Presbyterian Church*. 219.
9. Burns, Edward M. *Slavery in Western Pennsylvania*. 208.
10. *New Castle Herald*, July 17, 1923.
11. *Daily Times*, June 27, 1912.
12. Hazen, 63-69.
13. Hazen, 256.
14. Barksdale-Hall, Roland, *African Americans in Mercer County*. Arcadia Publishing. 2009, 8.
15. White, John G. *A Twentieth Century History of Mercer County, Pennsylvania*. Lewis Publishing Company. 1909, 140.
16. *History of Stoneboro* at http://www.Stoneboropa.com
17. United States Census: Pennsylvania, Lawrence County 1840.
18. *New Castle News*, November 29, 1927.
19. *New Castle News* May 29, 1943.
20. *New Castle News*, May 27, 1944.
21. "Rallying Altar for Race," *New Castle News*, March 13, 1917, 10.
22. Jesse Hamilton Obituary, *New Castle News*, March 26, 1902.
23. Hazen, 75-76.
24. United States Census: Pennsylvania, Lawrence County 1850.
25. Ibid.
26. Ibid.
27. *The Lawrence Journal*, November 18, 1854.
28. Hazen, 79.
29. Seibert, Wilbur H. *The Underground Railroad from Slavery to Freedom*. The Macmillan Company. New York. 1898, 433.
30. Barksdale-Hall, *African Americans in Mercer County*. 8, 23.
31. "Be That As It May," *The Record-Argus* (Greenville, Pennsylvania), October 20, 1942, 4.
32. Mary Berry Obituary, *New Castle News*, October 10, 1900.
33. Durant, 28.
34. "In Youthful Days," *New Castle News*, April 7, 1897, 1.
35. Shivers, Vincent Ajamu. "Plympton Ross Berry (1834-1917)" in *African American Architects: A Biographical Dictionary 1865-1945*, ed. Dreck Spurlock Wilson. Routledge. New York. 1904, 33-34.
36. "Glimpses into the Past of New Castle and Lawrence County," *New Castle News*, March 6, 1914.
37. Durant, 32.
38. Shivers, "Plympton Ross Berry (1834-1917)," 33-34.
39. *The Learner, Volume 1, Issue 1*. New Castle, Pennsylvania. Published by The Pupils.
40. *Elk County Advocate* (Ridgway, Pennsylvania), September 6, 1877, 3.
41. *Stark County Democrat* (Canton, Ohio), November 15, 1877, 4.
42. Mrs. Isabella Stewart Obituary, *New Castle News*, April 18, 1906.
43. "Oscar Johnston," *New Castle News*, December 3, 1881.

44 "Saint Luke's A.M.E. Church Observes 99th Anniversary," *New Castle News*, May 29, 1943.

45 *New Castle News,* July 20, 1887.

46 "Poor Old 'Ty'," *New Castle News*, February 18, 1891.

47 "Barber Shop Removed," *Lawrence Journal*, May 22, 1852.

48 *Lawrence Journal*, September 18, 1852.

49 Thomas Berry Obituary, *Lawrence Journal*, June 4, 1853.

50 Mrs. Mary L. Johnson Obituary, *New Castle News*, December 6, 1905.

51 "Saint Luke's A.M.E. Church Observes 99th Anniversary," *New Castle News*, May 29, 1943.

52 *New Castle City Directory*, 1872.

53 Shivers, Vincent Ajamu. "Plympton Ross Berry (1834-1917)," 33-34.

54 Mary Berry Obituary, *New Castle News*, October 10, 1900.

55 Mrs. Emma J. Currie Obituary, *New Castle News*, December 27, 1910.

56 Shivers, 33-34.

57 Shivers, 33-34.

58 Mrs. Isabella Stewart Obituary, *New Castle News*, April 18, 1906.

59 "Atty. William R. Stewart, 91, Dies; Dean of City's Lawyers," *Youngstown Vindicator,* April 5, 1958.

60 Charles Nighten Obituary, *Lawrence Journal*, February 28, 1874.

61 "The Opening Gun of the Republican Campaign about to be fired," *New Castle News*, September 7, 1898.

62 *New Castle News*, June 15, 1898.

63 United States Census: Pennsylvania, Lawrence County 1850,

64 United States Census: Pennsylvania, Lawrence County 1850

65 Isaac Baker Obituary, *New Castle News*, April 23.

3

AFRICAN AMERICANS IN THE CIVIL WAR

BY 1860 THE ERIE CANAL had connected Beaver to Erie through New Castle, and the Cross–cut Canal linked New Castle to Akron and Cleveland. Even rail travel required a canal trip to the station at Enon Valley.

With such a well–established and versatile delivery network, industry flourished. The Cosalo and the Orizaba Iron works operated at full capacity, their furnaces, rolling–mills and nail factories consuming ore, coal and limestone from neighboring hills to manufacture anything and everything made of iron. Croton Glass supplied a steady stream of windows to the west, and several flouring–mills, two foundries, a number of machine and engine shops, and numerous smaller manufactories employed a growing population. The public schools accommodated nearly 600 pupils in one large three–story brick building.[1]

John W. Forney described New Castle at that time as

> "...a city of broad streets, large brick dwellings, noble schoolhouses, comfortable residences and immense manufactories. It is beautifully located, reminding one of Pittsburg in its abundance of coal and iron and in its swarthy complexion. Yet it is fresher far than its dusky neighbor. There is an air of health in all natural surroundings. In its romantic streams and the lovely valley in which it lies embosomed it possesses advantages of which Pittsburg cannot boast."[2]

This peaceful prosperity was short–lived. In January, 1861, political differences incited national turmoil that led to the Southern states seceding from the Union. The first armed conflict broke out at Fort Sumter in April. The Civil War had begun.

During the war, the Union instituted four military drafts. The following eligible Lawrence County African Americans registered between 1863 and 1865:[3]

(name, age, occupation, b. = born; m. = married)

William Curtis: 43, b. Virginia

Thomas Hall: 25, m., b. Ohio

William Hamilton: 40, b. Virginia

Thomas Johnston: 33, barber, m., b. Kentucky

Oscar Johnston: 22, barber, m., b. Pennsylvania

Tyrone Landrum: 40, b. in Pennsylvania

Samuel Matthews: 33, m., b. Virginia

James Michaels: 44, wagon maker, b. Virginia

Chas W. Nighten: barber, b. in Virginia

William A. Stewart: 20, barber, m., b. Pennsylvania

Leonard A. Stewart: 27, barber, m., b. Pennsylvania

Samuel Stewart: 21, barber, b. in Pennsylvania

William Strongfellow: 21, blacksmith, b. Pennsylvania

Robert Wilson: 24, laborer, m., b. Pennsylvania

Three Lawrence County African Americans are known to have participated in the Civil War.

ELIJAH JACKSON, JR.

ELIJAH JACKSON, JR. enlisted at age 19 on December 28, 1863, in Cleveland. He was a private in Company K, 5th Regiment of the U.S. Colored Infantry, which formed as the 127th Ohio at Camp Delaware, Ohio, but was re–designated the 5th Regiment and moved to Norfolk, Virginia in November 1863.[4]

The regiment served in several states and saw a variety of action including the capture of Point City, Virginia, the attack against Fort Converse, the Richmond–Petersburg Campaign, Battle of Fort Fisher, and Sherman's Carolinas Campaign. The 5th was mustered out on September 20, 1865, having lost a total of 249 men, 81 killed or mortally wounded and 168 dead by disease.[5]

THOMAS W. JOHNSON

DURING THE CIVIL WAR, individuals could receive payment for enlisting in another's slot. Thomas Johnson enlisted October 5, 1864 in Warren, Ohio, in place of a white 35-year-old Youngstown father of five named Thomas Crowley.[6]

Johnson was part of the 15th Regiment U.S. Colored Infantry, Company G. The 15th was organized at Nashville, Tennessee, December 2, 1863. It was attached to the Post of Springfield District of Nashville, Department of the Cumberland, from August 1864 to March 1865 and the 5th Sub–District, District of Middle Tennessee, Dept. of the Cumberland, until April 1866. The regiment served at Nashville,

127th Ohio Volunteer Infantry

Columbia and Pulaski, Tennessee, guarding the railroad, public property, and commissary depots. They were on duty at Springfield, TN, and in District of Middle Tennessee until they mustered out April 7, 1866.[7]

GEORGE WASHINGTON WILLIAMS

ACCORDING TO SOME biographies, in the summer of 1864 George Washington Williams tried to join the Union Army in Pittsburgh at the age of 14, but they would not take him. Williams was quoted as saying his

> "hart[sic] burned with eager joy to meet the planter on the field of battle to prove our human cheracter [sic]."[8]

Williams traveled to Meadville, Pennsylvania, falsified his age, and enlisted under an assumed name. He may have used the name William Stewart or Charles Stewart, both of whom are recorded in the rolls of the Second Division of the 25th Army Corps, where he claimed to have served.

Williams reenlisted under his own name in 1867. An enlistment paper read,

> "3rd Enlistment, last served in Co. C., 41st U.S.C. Infantry, discharged December 7, 1868."[9]

There is also an enlistment record on August 29, 1864 for a George W. Williams in Pittsburgh, serving under Captain Haymond for a term of five years. He was listed as a 22 year old barber, born in Bedford, Pennsylvania, and was discharged for disability on September 5, 1868 at Fort Arbuckle.

Williams spoke of participation in battles near Richmond and Petersburg, Virginia. In his book, History of the Negro Race in America, he wrote a great deal about the Civil War, its causes and aftermath.

George Washington Williams

George Washington Williams was born in Bedford Springs, Pennsylvania, son of free Blacks Thomas and Ellen Williams, and lived with his family in Johnstown, Pennsylvania in 1850. By 1860, his father's search for better paying work brought the family to New Castle.[10]

After the war, Williams wrote History of the Negro Race in America, a treatise on the Civil War, its causes and aftermath. After the book's publication, Williams graduated from Newton Theological Institution and entered the ministry at the Twelfth Baptist Church in Boston, then the Union Baptist Church in Cincinnati.

In Cincinnati, Williams studied law at the office of Alphonso Taft, the father of President William Howard Taft. He was elected to the Ohio House of Representatives in 1879, and traveled widely in Europe and Africa.[11]

Williams is considered one of the first African American investigative journalists, traveling to Congo in 1890 to expose King Leopold II as a human rights violator. Unfortunately, Williams succumbed to an early death in 1891 at the age of 41.

Chapter Notes

1 Hazen, Aaron L. *20th Century History of New Castle and Lawrence County, Pennsylvania.* Richmond-Arnold Publishing Co. Chicago. 1908, 81-85.

2 Forney, John W. "New Castle," *Philadelphia Press*, June, 1858.

3 U.S. Civil War Draft Registrations Records, 1863-1865 [database on-line]. Provo, UT, USA: Ancestry.com Operations, Inc., 2010.

4 U.S. Colored Troops Military Service Records, 1863-1865 Ancestry.com

5 "5th Regiment, United States Colored Infantry",Civil War Soldiers and Sailors System, National Park Service. http://www.nps.gov/civilwar/soldiers-and-sailors-database.htm

6 U.S. Colored Troops Military Service Records, 1863-1865 Ancestry.com

7 "15th Regiment U.S. Colored Infantry, Company G", Civil War Soldiers and Sailors System National Park Service. http://www.nps.gov/civilwar/soldiers-and-sailors-database.htm

8 Reeves, Frank, "He Told a Vital Story," *Pittsburgh Post-Gazette*, February 22, 2015.

9 Franklin, John Hope , *George Washington Williams: A Biography.* Duke University Press, 1998.

10 United States Census: Pennsylvania, Lawrence County, 1850 and 1860.

11 Frank Reeves, "He Told a Vital Story."

4

CLOAKED BY THE CLOTH: PRESBYTERIAN MINISTERS & THEIR CONGREGATIONS

EARLY YEARS—AMERICAN COLONIZATION SOCIETY

THE AMERICAN SOCIETY for colonizing the Free People of Colour of the United States, or American Colonization Society (ACS) as it came to be known, formed in 1817 as a natural outgrowth of Pennsylvania and other Northern states enacting laws to encourage the freeing of slaves. The Society's original constitution stated:

> "The object to which its attention is to be exclusively directed, is to promote and execute a plan for colonizing (with their consent) the free people of colour, residing in our country, in Africa, or such other place as Congress shall deem most expedient. And the Society shall act, to effect this object, in co–operation with the General Government, and such of the States as may adopt regulations upon the subject."[1]

In 1822, the Society, with the assistance of the U.S. Government, established a colony on Africa's west coast that would later become the independent nation of Liberia. (By 1867 the ACS had assisted some 12,000 Blacks to emigrate to the new colony.)[2]

From the beginning, colonization of Africa by free Blacks was a subject that divided both races. A segment of Black society supported emigration because it believed it would never receive justice in the United States. Another maintained that free Blacks should remain in the United States and continue the fight for full rights.

Some whites saw themselves as genuine allies of free Blacks and hoped that colonization would eradicate slavery. Others viewed colonization as a way to rid America of Negroes or suggested they would be happier in Africa where they would be free of racial discrimination. Still others believed that Black American colonists could play a central role in Christianizing Africa.[3]

Presbyterian ministers such as Robert Sample and Elder William Cairns played a significant role in the early Abolitionist movement in the area that would become Lawrence County. At least three pastorates—the Presbyteries of New Castle, Slippery Rock (Wayne Township) and New Bedford—supported ACS efforts in the early years of the Abolitionist movement. From these church pulpits and pews came many of the county's Abolitionists and Conductors of the Underground Railroad.

LATER YEARS—REBELS & INFIDELS

REBELLIOUS PRESBYTERIAN ministers and their congregations were almost solely responsible for the Abolitionist movement and Underground Railroad in Lawrence County, although a few Covenanters and Methodists were also involved. The years from 1839 to 1844

Reverend Robert & Ann (Kirkpatrick) Sample / Semple

Reverend Robert Sample, (often spelled Semple) was an early pioneer and settler of what would become Lawrence County. He was born in North Carolina, August 31, 1775, lived in Beaver Township, Allegheny County, in 1800. He was licensed to preach in 1810, and ordained over the congregations of New Castle and Slippery Rock (Wayne Township) Presbyterian Churches on April 10, 1811.

At the time of Sample's accession, Crawford White, was clerk of the Session. The other ruling elders at that time were William Moorhead, Joseph Pollock, William Raney, James McKee, and Samuel Wilson. David White, David Somerville and Thomas Hanna were ordained ruling elders on April 16th, 1820.[26]

He served the First Presbyterian Church of Slippery Rock through 1835, and the First Presbyterian Church of New Castle (originally Lower Neshannock) through 1838. He subsequently served in Pulaski for a year, and in Brookfield, Ohio for a year or two. Sample's Slippery Rock and New Castle congregations supported the efforts of the American Colonization Society (ACS) as early as 1831, and records of contributions were found through 1834.

He married Ann Kirkpatrick and had ten children. Samuel, studied law in New Castle and moved to Meadville, Crawford County. Martilla married Moses Elliot of Slippery Rock, Angeline married John Breckenridge of New Castle, Philo M. became a Presbyterian minister, Florinda remained unmarried, Nancy married Lawrence L. McGuffin, Kirk became a doctor in Ohio, Eliza married William Pomeroy, Zenesta married a Mr. McCready in New Wilmington, and Manurva died in her youth.[27]

After his wife's death, Sample married the widow of Henry Rhodes of Scott Township, Lawrence County. In 1840, Sample had a residence at the corner of Washington and Mill Streets.[28]

Sample was described as a man of respectable talents and great amiability who was faithful and laborious in his pastoral work. It was noted in a 20th Century Lawrence County history that the only of his descendants "left among us" was his granddaughter, Mrs. Gennie V. Morrow, born in 1843 to Judge Lawrence L. McGuffin.

Robert Sample died on April 11, 1847. He is buried in Greenwood Cemetery in 'the old graveyard'.[29]

---

marked some very turbulent times in the area's Presbyterian Churches. Differences of opinion and bitter arguments regarding the slavery question led to dissention and division.

In 1844, at a height in the Anti–Slavery discussions, local clergy filed 20 Memorials (or requests) with the General Assembly of the Presbyterian Church in the USA—the governing body of the Presbyterian Church—requesting action and guidance. Previous guidance of 1818 had declared slavery to be

> "…a gross violation of the most precious and sacred rights of human nature, utterly inconsistent with the law of god, and totally irreconcilable with the spirit and principles of the gospel of Christ,"

and it was

> "…manifestly the duty of all Christians to use their honest, earnest, and unwearied endeavors to efface this blot on our holy religions, and to obtain the complete abolition of slavery throughout Christendom, and if possible throughout the world."[4]

By the late 1840's, however, the sitting Assembly appeared to be turning a blind eye to the slavery issue. Memorials were tabled without action.

This prompted a group led by Reverend Wells Bushnell to file a protest for the Assembly's failure to act upon requests signed by eight ministers, about 50 elders, and nearly 1,000 private members.

In his protest, Bushnell argued,

> "...slavery, is not only a political, but also a great moral question, which is extensively agitated at the present day, in which both the church and the world are beginning to take a deep and still deeper interest, and in regard to which many of the people in our communion anxiously desire to understand their duty."[5]

The document was signed by ministers Wells Bushnell, J. M. Stone, William McCandlish, Robert B. Dobbins, W. S. Rogers; and elders John Hannen (Bushnell's father-in-law), and William M. Francis.

Pressured to respond, the Presbyterian General Assembly ruled on June 22, 1847 that slavery was a fixed institution and that nothing better could be promised the slave at the time beyond a gradual abolition of the practice. They further declared that slaveholding was not a bar to Communion.

Many in the congregations were outraged by this profession of tolerance. Seven Presbyterian Churches eventually broke away from the main body to form Free Presbyterian Churches under the Presbytery of Mahoning. These churches were located in Darlington (Beaver County), Mount Jackson, New Castle, New Bedford, and New Wilmington, (Lawrence County) and Mercer and Clarksville (Mercer County).

Free churches also sprang up in Ohio communities frequented by Lawrence County residents. As the Republican Party was a political protest against slavery, so the Free Church became a religious protest against the iniquities of American slavery. One very active group led by John Young, Jr. broke away from the Presbyterian Church completely and formed an independent religious organization housed in the White Chapel.

These men of faith, leaders of their congregations—pastors and elders—were the

---

William & Nancy Cairns

Born in 1765 in County Derry, Ireland, William Cairns came to the US in 1790 and settled first in Delaware. He was married there in 1792, and shortly after removed with his wife, Nancy, to Westmoreland County, Pennsylvania. Sometime in 1796, Cairns moved his family, including two children, to Shenango, where he made a clearing, built a cabin, and set to work cultivating the land. Cairns planted the first orchard not long after his arrival.

It was a rugged frontier, and Mrs. Cairns was the only female settler seen in the area for two years. A third child, a daughter named Rachel, came into the world on July 19, 1798, becoming the first white child born in the township.

Cairns served in various public offices while the township was part of Beaver County, becoming a county commissioner from 1810–1811, and sheriff from 1815–1818. In 1815 Cairns owned 200 acres, three cows, a horse, a distillery, a weave shop, and a store that supplied cloth for the locals. The latter two were referred to as his "post of profit" in filed documents.

He was one of the first Abolitionists in the area, and an elder in the Slippery Rock Presbyterian Church in Wayne Township led by fellow Abolitionist, Reverend Robert Sample. A zealous advocate of the American Colonization Society from its 1817 inception, Cairns contributed sums over the years amounting to $4,000, an astonishing amount of philanthropy for the time. He believed the ACS was the most useful society on Earth, and would result in abolition of slavery in America and civilization and Christianizing of Africa.

Cairns died on April 7, 1854, and was buried in a family plot. His remains were later relocated to Oak Park Cemetery in New Castle.

cogs in the wheels and the fuel in boilers that moved the Underground Railroad in and out of Lawrence County. No story of the Abolitionist movement would be complete without them and their parishes.

THE CHURCHES

Free Presbytery of Mahoning

ON OCTOBER 20, 1847 at a meeting in New Athens, Ohio, Ministers Arthur B. Bradford and Samuel A. McLean, having declined the jurisdiction of the General Assembly, united with Joseph Gordon, recently dismissed and certified in good standing by the Presbytery of Ripley, in the formation of a Presbytery. The focus of this endeavor was to create a congregation free in all respects from the sin of slavery. Elders from other churches joined their cause, including John Boggs of New Athens, Daniel Boyd of Darlington, Samuel D. Clark of Westfield, Nathaniel Porter of (New) Bedford, and Josiah Cotton, of Clarksville.[6] The basis of the new organization included the following Declaration:[7]

1. God has made of one blood all nations of men; consequently, all human being, endowed with rationality, have an equal right to freedom.

2. The holding of human beings as property, is destructive of all the ends for which man was created and endowed with rational powers, and consequently one of the greatest evils that can be inflicted upon human nature; highly immoral, and entirely inconsistent with Christian character and profession.

3. No person holding slaves, or advocating the rightfulness of slaveholding, can be a member of this body.

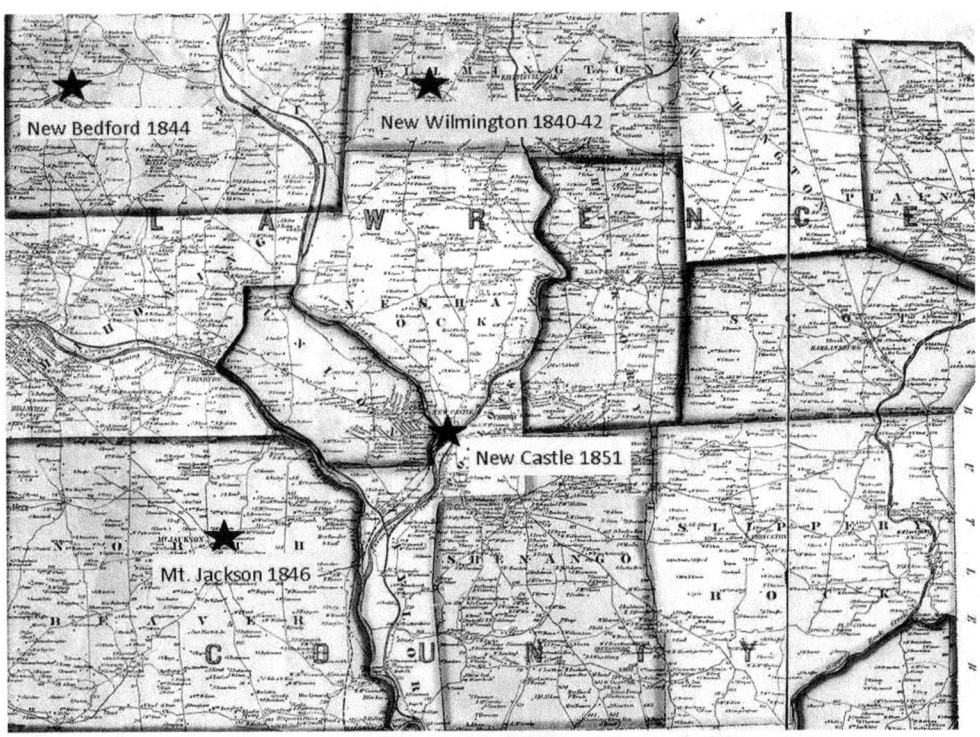

Map of Free Presbyterian Churches in Lawrence County

4. No Church, Presbytery, or Synod, tolerating slaveholding or the advocates of slaveholding in its communion, can be a constituent part of this body.

This small body of churches soon grew. Minutes of the Presbytery show ministers forming new free churches and bringing established churches under its care.[8]

Participation reached a high point by 1858. Arthur Bradford was then in New Castle, Wells Bushnell in Mount Pleasant and New Bedford, J. C. Bigham in New Wilmington, Samuel A. McLean in Clarksville, and J. W. E. Torrence at Mercer.

Free Presbyterian Synod

The Free Presbyterian Synod was founded in 1847 to govern the Free Presbyteries. The Synod was mostly confined to Ohio and Western Pennsylvania and included the Presbytery of Mahoning.[9]

On October 25, 1855, the Synod met in New Castle with Reverend John Rankin providing the sermon. Rankin was one of Ohio's first and most active conductors on the Underground Railroad, and his writings and works influenced prominent pre–Civil War abolitionists William Lloyd Garrison, Henry Ward Beecher and Harriet Beecher Stowe. At this meeting, Wells Bushnell was elected moderator, and Joseph Gordon and John D. Whitham as temporary clerks. George Gordon also attended.[10]

A need for a college and theological institution had been expressed (primarily for the education of slaves), and the Free Presbyterian Synod responded, establishing Iberia College at Iberia, Ohio. Reverend George Gordon was urged to become its president and instructor for divinity students.[11] Elected as trustees for Iberia at the 1855 Synod meeting were George Gordon, James Auld, D. Carnahan, V. M. King, and Samuel Boyd.

An article appearing in the Anti–Slavery Bugle regarding the new facility seemed almost an invitation for safe haven in the North.

> "The main object of this communication is to apprize your readers that the College at Iberia is one of the very few institutions in the North that will cheerfully receive young men and women of color without making any degrading distinction. Iberia is a pleasant and healthful location and accessible from all points of the compass. The moral atmosphere of the place is good also, and all things combined, the Institution has great claims upon the patronage of the Anti–Slavery public."[12]

Neshannock Presbyterian, New Wilmington, Lawrence County

Neshannock Presbyterian Church was located in New Wilmington within the present confines of Lawrence County. Its parish boundaries covered a vast area beyond New Wilmington, however, including parishioners from both Lawrence and Mercer Counties.

Very few churches had to face the slavery issue from so many angles as did Neshannock Presbyterian. For many years anti–slavery sentiment had been building in the Neshannock

Neshannock Presbyterian Church

Presbyterian Church, resulting in an aggressive movement that continued through the Civil War.

Piece by piece, the church's traditional support eroded. The Free Presbyterian Church broke away in one direction and White Chapel, an independent Anti–Slavery church in another. Additional fracturing came from the creation of a colony of liberated slaves (Pandenarium infra.), and a branch of the Underground Railroad aided by Neshannock Presbyterian members and operated by former members.

White Chapel

John Young, Jr., described as a faithful supporter of the Neshannock Presbyterian Church and a young man of unwavering conviction, was one of the first Anti–Slavery leaders in the area.

According to an account by H. U. Johnson, Young's animosity began when he inherited a Virginia Plantation in the James River Valley along with a large number of slaves. His "soul revolted" at the idea of holding them in bondage. He did not relish the idea of living amid the

White Chapel, October 13, 1900

withered and blighted scenes of slave labor and slave traffic, so he found a purchaser for his many acres. Before disposing of his plantation, he made a trip to Mercer County and purchased an extensive tract on the rich bottoms of Indian Run.

His friends were amazed at him becoming a "Pennymite" farmer. His slaves panicked, expecting to be sold on the auction block. Young allayed their fears by presenting them with their freedom papers. Amid excited cheers he told them he was moving north where it was respectable for a white man to labor, and should they ever come his way, they would find him chopping his own wood and hoeing his own corn.

> "Though foreign to the purpose of Mr. Young, he yielded to the importunity of those he had manumitted, and soon there appeared on the Pennsylvania purchase a spacious residence, built rather in the Virginia style, and around it were grouped numerous cabins occupied by the sable colony that had followed the Caucasian proprietor. The family equipage was brought along, and Alexander Johnson always persisted in being Massa's coachman and driving him in state."

The home site improved quickly, aided by paid labor and it became known as a hospitable home and to none more so than to the fugitive from bondage, "for he early became an influential agent on the great thoroughfare to Canada."[13]

Joseph White took issue with the above account and wrote "[n]ow John Young never was a slaveholder; his father may have been."[14]

Regardless of its genesis, Young was so filled with indignation over the inhumanity of slavery and at the apparent disinterest of his fellow Christians that he seized every opportunity to debate the subject. His chief supporters were Joseph Kirk and James Minick, though many shared his views.

In June 1835 after a speech by a visiting minister, Young and his associates decided to form an Anti–Slavery society in Mercer County as a platform from which to rail against the sinfulness of slavery. They gradually separated themselves from the Neshannock Presbyterian Church, severing the relationship entirely between 1840–1842, building an independent church known as White Chapel on John Young's land.

Free Presbyterian of Neshannock, New Wilmington, Lawrence County

Abner Gibson was a devout parishioner of the Neshannock Presbyterian Church, a ruling elder, and a man beyond reproach. Frustrated by the inactions of the General Assembly, and considering the church to be pro–slavery, he declared he would no longer share in its guilt. In 1850, he set out to build a new one.

Reverend A. B. Bradford advised Gibson and his group to join with the newly formed Free Presbyterian Church of New Castle rather than organizing independently as White Chapel had done. Gibson agreed, and in 1851, Bradford arranged for Pastor William Lumsden of the Free Presbyterian Church at New Bedford to split time between that church and Gibson's congregation.

The new church enrolled in the Presbytery of Mahoning and the Free Presbyterian Synod headquartered in Cincinnati. Their parting was not without vitriol, and the preamble to the resolutions of organization for the new Free Church contained these words:

> "Whereas the wicked Absalom McCready, pastor of the Neshannock Presbyterian Church, has by his pro–slavery attitude made it necessary for certain members to renounce the jurisdiction of his church…"

Gibson died in 1852 before the building could be finished, but made provision for its construction in his will. Reverend Wells Bushnell became the church's second pastor while also serving New Bedford and Mount Jackson, but his term did not last long. The congregation did not keep pace with Bushnell's "radical Anti–Slavery" views, and he resigned in June 1853, and became a pastor at the Free Presbytery of Mahoning in April 1854.

Construction of the Free Presbyterian Church of Neshannock was completed in 1854, one mile south of the old church. Reverend J. C. Bigham, a Conductor in the Underground Railroad, became pastor when Bushnell left and served for twelve years, until December 16, 1867. Bigham would subsequently minister at United Presbyterian in Plain Grove, Lawrence County.

Known members of the Neshannock Free Presbyterian Church included: T. M. Best, John Burgess, William Cotton, William Cozad, John Donaldson, Cordon Elliott, Abner Gibson, Charles Gibson's family, Francis Gibson, Hiram Gibson, Isaac M. Gibson, William M. Gibson, William Wiley Gibson, James W. Hopper, James R. Johnston, William J. Johnston, James Y. Kirk, Robert McCrumb, William Mercer, Nancy Miller, John Minick, Wilson Mitchell, Mary H. Porter, John E. Robinson, Alexander Shaw, William Shields, J. M. Sterling, Mrs. Stewart, B. C. Trotter, William Watson, Hiram Watson, John R. Wilson, Sarah Williamson, and James H. Woods.[15]

New Bedford Presbyterian—New Bedford Free Presbyterian, Lawrence County

In 1843, Reverend John Knox was "the supply" or minister assigned to supply services for Hopewell Presbyterian Church. A devout adversary of slavery, he encouraged a group of like–minded men to present a Memorial to the Presbytery of Beaver, and they did so in January 1844.

A committee of three was appointed to answer the Memorial, which explored the propriety of New Bedford Presbyterian withdrawing from the jurisdiction of the Presbyterian Church. Two of the three committee members were Reverend John Knox himself, and Reverend Arthur B. Bradford, men considered to be the most radical Anti–Slavery men in the Presbytery.

They, of course, brought back a favorable report, but the third member's minority report was the one adopted, and that action revealed the fact that the Presbytery would never forsake their General Assembly. Consequently John Knox withdrew from the Presbytery to organize the New Bedford Presbyterian Church. Three years later, in 1847, the New Bedford Free Presbyterian Church branched off, and Knox and his congregation joined it.

New Bedford Free Presbyterian Church 1844

Reverend J. C. Bigham

Reverend J. C. Bigham, supply minister for Lowellville Free Presbyterian Church, was the son of Ebenezer Bigham, a Conductor on the Underground Railroad who owned a farm near Millersburg, Holmes County, Ohio. Ebenezer and his sons, J. C. and William, aided some 200 slaves from 1842–1860.[30, 31]

By 1859 J. C. Bigham was ministering in New Wilmington, Lawrence County. After the war, he joined the U.P. Church at Plain Grove,[32, 33] Lawrence County.

Mount Jackson Free Presbyterian Church, Lawrence County

The Mount Jackson Free Presbyterian Church was organized in 1846 by members of the Westfield Presbyterian Church in North Beaver Township. Reverend Wells Bushnell served as pastor from 1854–1863.

Free Presbyterian Church, Darlington, Beaver County

On June 22, 1847, Reverend Arthur B. Bradford of Mount Pleasant Presbyterian and Reverend Samuel A. McLean of Hubbard, Ohio notified the Presbytery at Beaver of their withdrawal. Two days later the Presbytery struck their names from the roll, declaring that they "have greatly erred and greatly sinned." The two men founded the Free Presbyterian Church at Darlington.

Lowellville Free Presbyterian, Trumbull County, Ohio

Lowellville Free Presbyterian, established in the summer of 1848, was the first congregation of that denomination organized near Lawrence County. The congregation comprised Anti–Slavery parishioners from Mount Jackson and New Bedford in Lawrence County, Poland and Coitsville in Ohio and the intermediate countryside. Early meetings were held in the old McGillsville schoolhouse on Jackson Street, and presided over by Reverend John D. Whitham, a resident of Mahoning Township, Lawrence County.[16]

In the winter of 1848 meetings were moved to Liggett's warehouse on Canal Street, and early in 1849 the church was organized. Reverend John D. Whitham became the first minister. James S. Moore and John M. Porter were the first elders, and Elias King, John McFarland and James S. Moore, the first trustees.

On February 5, 1850, the congregation purchased land from James Duncan, and the church building was raised on May 9, 1850. Reverend Whitham continued as pastor from 1849 to 1857 after which time Reverend Wells Bushnell was instated as supply for six months, succeeded by Reverend J. C. Bigham from October, 1858 to December, 1864.

Frankfort Presbyterian, Beaver County

Reverend George Gordon, Hookstown, Beaver County, withdrew from Frankfort Presbyterian and joined his brother, Reverend Joseph Gordon, and others on April 22, 1850, to found the Free Presbytery of Mahoning.

Free Presbyterian, New Castle, Lawrence County

Early church records indicate dissatisfaction among the Presbyterians of New Castle with the General Assembly decision of 1845 that slaveholding was no bar to communion, but the congregation did not act until President Fillmore signed the Fugitive Slave Bill in September 1850. It became intolerable to many that their church, and now their government, had failed to take a stand against the status quo of slavery.

On the 15th day of February, 1851, the Reverend George Gordon of the Free Presbytery of Mahoning moderated a secession meeting at the Reformed Presbyterian Church, and the Free Presbyterian Church of New Castle was formed. Reverend brothers George and Joseph Gordon, and Reverend A. B. Bradford, among others, supplied the newly formed congregation with services until a permanent pastor could be installed.

In February 1854 Reverend A. B. Bradford, previously of the Darlington Free Presbyterian Church, accepted a call to become pastor.

INCIDENT AT IBERIA

IN MAY 1860, REVEREND George Gordon, was serving as the Principal of the Iberia College in Iberia, Ohio when he encountered a large group of fugitive slaves. Their masters, with the aid of some "lick–spittles," were in the process of taking them back to Kentucky.

As one of the slaves was being dragged away, a Black youth at the College tried to help and was fired upon and wounded. A group of students sprang to his aid, fighting off the slave catchers with whips and sticks. Little did they realize that a Deputy U.S. Marshall was among the slave catchers. As principal, responsibility for the events fell upon Reverend Gordon. When

Reverend George & Mrs. Gordon

George Gordon was born near Washington, Pennsylvania, on January 8, 1806. The son of a Scotsman, Alexander Gordon, and Eva Fisher, George graduated from Washington College in 1832 and from Western Theology Seminary in Pittsburgh in 1835.

From 1835 to 1843, Gordon was Pastor at Millersburg and Hopewell Presbyterian, Holmes County, Ohio. From there he moved to Frankfort Presbyterian Church in Hookstown, Beaver County.

Sometime before 1855 his brother, Joseph, was censured for Anti–Slavery views. Joseph withdrew from the Presbytery and helped to form a Free Presbyterian Church. Two years later, George transferred his own church membership to the Free Presbyterian Church and began his successful pursuit to lead New Castle Presbyterians to secession.

George's other brother, John, was a frequent visitor of Abolitionist and Underground Railroad Conductor Daniel Hise of Salem, Ohio. It is likely that John introduced George to Hise, leading to numerous meetings between the two men. Many slaves who traveled through Lawrence County would make their way to Salem.

In 1861, Gordon was tried and convicted for his part in an uprising at Iberia College, when he was its president. Gordon fought the charges, but was ultimately sentenced to a fine and six months imprisonment. After a short, but brutal, stay in the Cleveland jail, he accepted a general pardon from President Lincoln.

Before his incarceration, Reverend Gordon had been a large, rather stout man. Imprisonment rendered him frail, however, and he never recuperated from his sicknesses and suffering. In September 1867 he was carried onto the train and delivered to his brother, John's, home in Salem, Ohio. He died on December 11, 1867.

---

he did nothing to stop the students, a warrant was issued for his arrest for interfering with the enforcement of the Fugitive Slave Act.

Gordon, fleeing arrest under President Buchanan's Pro–Slavery administration, arrived in New Castle and spent an afternoon and night with Joseph S. White, before fleeing to Canada. White described him as "a noble white fugitive."

When Abraham Lincoln took office in March 1861, Reverend Gordon returned to Iberia and turned himself over to the Federal authorities. On November 6, 1861 he was indicted and tried in the U.S. District Court for the Northern District of Ohio for "resisting a process in the hands of a Deputy Marshal in his attempt to arrest a fugitive slave."[17]

This is Gordon's actual testimony:

> "My arrival on the ground was not ten minutes before the whole thing was over. One of our colored young men had twice been shot at, and wounded by them, or part of their company. One claimed as a slave had been seized and violently dragged away. Under all the provocation a company [of students] acted. When I arrived, I was told they had received a few stripes. Some ten or fifteen more were laid on, whilst I was present and with my consent. The men begged forbearance and the matter ceased. I handed no one a stick with directions to lay on more—told no one to suppress my name—struck no one myself—nor did I administer an oath to any. I did stand by with consent whilst ten, perhaps fifteen lashes were laid on. I did not know whether they were slaveholders, marshals, deputies, or assistants, and it is but candid to say, I did not care. I then told one of them that the chastisement he had received had been inflicted by some of the best men in the

community, men who would not hurt a hair of his head, but protect him to the fullest extent, in any business. But the slave catching we would not tolerate. His reply was 'this will be a lesson to me. I knew it was a mean business when I went into it, but that I could not well help it. I will go home and resign my office, and never do so again.'"

Gordon was convicted, fined $300, and sentenced to six months imprisonment in the Cleveland jail. The severity of the sentence was considered by many to be an act of cruelty and vindictiveness on the part of the presiding Judge, who had it within his power to set a more lenient sentence.

Reverend Gordon addressed the court:

> "Some things in my situation would seem to command silence—The form of a trial has been passed—my counsel has been heard in defence (sic) of marked ability—a verdict of guilty has been brought in by the jury. Nothing, therefore, remains for me but to receive my sentence and endure it to the bitter end. I cannot say anything that will modify or mitigate its severity. Yet I stand before the court in the full confidence of rectitude, without any sense of guilt or abasement. I utter no apologies, make no confessions. Why then do I stand branded as a criminal before the court, and yet enjoy feelings of innate rectitude? ...my conduct was guided by the express will of God as revealed in the Scriptures, a standard clearly opposed to the fugitive slave enactments, and not recognized by this tribunal."

A man of principle, Gordon was strong in his faith and just as strong in his abolitionist views. Even faced with imprisonment, he stood erect and defiant, a martyr for his anti–slavery convictions.

In closing he told the court:

> "And now, sir, apart from the defence (sic) of the rectitude of my conduct, I have no favors to crave– no mercy to implore. I stand erect, in conscious integrity and manhood. My house has been a home for the fleeing fugitive, and shall be so still. If my dwelling be reduced to a cabin, he shall be welcome to a corner. All the devils in hell and slave catchers out of hell shall not close my door against him. I cannot repress the hope that, in this line of persecution I may be the last victim of the slave power. Whether this be so or not, I wish when 'all that's mortal' of your humble prisoner shall be in its last resting place it may be with truth written on my gravestone, 'here lie the remains of one who in life was faithful to God's poor.'"[18]

When first incarcerated, Gordon was treated humanely and given leave to walk the corridors unsupervised. But when another prisoner took advantage of his situation, wore his clothing, and made an escape, Reverend Gordon was blamed for assisting. Subsequently, the jailor was no longer so accommodating, and treated Gordon cruelly. Visits from his wife, who had taken up her residence near the jail, were limited, and he found himself confined to a damp basement cell with only a gas lamp for light. Here he contracted sciatic rheumatism, which caused severe suffering.[19]

Gordon's attorney filed an appeal, which was denied, and then requested a pardon from President Lincoln on the grounds that the laws of Congress under which Gordon was convicted were utterly null and void because they ran contrary to the United States Constitution. So strong was Gordon's conviction that his lawyer stated in the pardon request that his client did not desire a pardon on any other grounds. Lincoln was sympathetic, but could not justify a pardon on Gordon's terms. The sentence, while severe, he admitted, was legal at the time, and Gordon had atoned.[20]

At the urging of his lawyer and his friends, Gordon reluctantly accepted a general pardon. After three months' imprisonment he was freed and his fine remitted. He returned to Iberia, where he remained until 1867.

FIREBRAND

REVEREND JOHN KNOX and his wife, Elizabeth, were financial supporters of the

Anti–Slavery Bugle, and his wish was that the Church not sugar coat his life in its writings. As a consequence, the history of Neshannock Presbyterian Church published in 1925 states:

> "John Knox, like John Young of White Chapel, withdrew from the church he had founded and proclaimed himself an infidel. He became an almost sullen recluse, and even withdrew his children from the public school. They returned, however, after his death, which occurred at his home near Pulaski. Such men seem to live in vain, but after all, their extreme views and actions are undeniable factors in human progress. When they are stoned let it be done along with the stoning of that larger group who never trouble the world with either views or action. John Knox publicly renounced the Bible because slavery founded itself upon it, and because the Church was content to stand with slavery on the same foundation."[21]

Abolitionist W. W. Walker of Pulaski wrote:

> "Knox was formerly a minister in the Old School Presbyterian Church, and held in high estimation as such, especially by those of reformatory tendencies. In the Fall of 1843, he became convinced, after a thorough examination of the whole question, that a church, which according to facts, and the declaration of its own highest tribunal, retained, approvingly, within its membership, eldership and ministry, men whom it declared to be the 'highest kind of thieves' –'sinners of the first rank'—even, 'manstealers,'—That, a Church, whose approved members were living in the daily perpetration of what its highest court declared to be, a 'gross violation of the most precious and sacred rights of human nature,' and 'totally irreconcilable with the spirit and principle of the gospel of Christ'—&c, was not a fit organization for decent, honest man, to say nothing of a Christian minister, to be conected (sic) with, and when the Beaver Presbytery, of which he was a member met in Hopewell Church, at New Bedford in January 1844, Mr. Knox, in opposition to the entire Presbytery, made a triumphant, and unanswerable defense, of the duty of secession; and though he had not the least assurance of 'material aid' in his new position, and, with a dependent family without fortune, himself unused to labor, he 'conferred not with flesh and blood,' but determined to secede though it should reduce him to beggary, preferring to be alone in the right, rather than to enjoy ease, affluence, and honor with a guilty multitude. However, about 60 of the members of Hopewell congregation, seceded with him, and formed the first Free Presbyterian Church that was ever organized in the United States. He then continued to preach, and organize Free Presbyterian Churches, in various places, for about two years, when, coming in contact with some of the agents of the American Anti–Slavery Society, he made, (as was his custom) an honest effort to defend his principles, but, having, in his own opinion failed, and deeming his connection with the government of the United States indefensible, he determined, once more, cost what it might, to secede, and abandon his voluntary support, of a Pro–Slavery Constitution and Government, and thenceforth, he became a disunionist. From that time he was compelled by necessity, almost entirely to abandon public life, and he betook himself with most untiring industry to the improvement on his farm, in which effort, he was eminently successful. He was most pointed in his rebukes, having the misfortune of being always understood. For this, he was hated, and maligned, by cowardly hypocrites, and persistent transgressors, to an extent seldom equaled in the history of the most unyielding reformers. For acting out his convictions on the Sunday, and other questions, his property was repeatedly sacrificed, by fine, or otherwise. He had however before his death, by a persistent course of independent integrity, and uprightness, so disarmed public prejudice, and bigotry, that he was permitted to carry out his convictions without molestation. His views of consistent Anti–Slavery action, forbade him to use the products of slave labor. He held it to be extremely inconsistent, to profess Anti–Slavery sentiments, and yet, by the purchase

---

Reverend John & Elizabeth (Gordon) Knox

John Knox, born in Ireland, accompanied two brothers to America when he was 17. He married Elizabeth Gordon, sister of Reverends George and Joseph Gordon (all born in Washington County, Pennsylvania), and for a number of years she and her husband resided in Mahoning County, Ohio before moving to Pulaski Township, Lawrence County, Pennsylvania.

John Knox died on July 6, 1857 at his farm.

Reverend Arthur B. & Elizabeth (Wicks) Bradford

Reverend Arthur B. Bradford was born in 1810, a direct descendant of Governor William Bradford of the Plymouth colony pilgrims. As a young man in Washington, DC he witnessed a mother being separated from her children and auctioned into bondage. In that moment, he committed himself to the struggle against slavery.

He attended Lafayette College, became a student at West Point, then changed his mind and decided to become a Presbyterian minister. During his time at Princeton Theological seminary he preached to Blacks and subscribed to an Anti-Slavery paper, acts that caused problems at the college and within his family. Despite pressure, Bradford refused to rescind his Anti-Slavery views, leading his uncle to disinherit him from a fortune.

After graduation, Bradford preached in Philadelphia, Baltimore and Clinton, New Jersey, before marrying Elizabeth Wicks, daughter of Captain Wicks of the Philadelphia Navy Yard. They moved to Darlington, Beaver County, Pennsylvania, and he took charge of Darlington Presbyterian Church.

Frederick Douglass spoke at the Presbyterian Church in Darlington, most likely during his mid-August, 1847, speaking tour with William Lloyd Garrison. That same year, Reverend Bradford led a contingent of members to break away and form a new Anti-Slavery church. Bradford preached at the Free Presbyterian Church in Darlington for 14 years. In February 1854, he accepted a call to pastor the Free Presbyterian Church in New Castle.

In the mid-1850s, Bradford was a member of New Castle's Kansas Aid Society, collecting and sending aid to the Kansas Anti-Slavery settlers emigrating from Western Pennsylvania. A learned and powerful orator, he became nationally known, speaking at conferences and publishing Anti-Slavery articles in Abolitionist papers such as the New Castle Courant.

Prior to the War, he actively campaigned for Abraham Lincoln and worked so hard for Lincoln's election that his health suffered, leaving him unable to enter service when the war began. His relationship with New Castle's Free Presbyterian Church continued until the summer of 1867, with the exception of one year when Lincoln appointed him United States consul to China.

In his later years, Bradford renounced his Presbyterian religion. As he studied other creeds, he pronounced them all false. Having observed so-called heathen in foreign lands, he deduced that

> "…the sentiment of justice, honor, chastity, benevolence and self-respect were as noticeable among them as among those at home."

After much study and trepidation he embraced agnosticism and rejected his former title of Reverend. He died in 1899.

of slave grown products, hold out to the slaveholder, the most efficient bribe possible, to induce him to continue his villainous plunder, and to carry out their convictions on the subject, he, and his family, for the last 20 years, made sacrifices, such as are rarely made, to carry out a principle. He was led, by various circumstances, to examine, thoroughly the whole subject of Theological Orthodoxy, and the result was, that he discarded almost the entire system of popular religion, viewing it, for the most part, as a degrading, and demoralizing imposition, of which, good men ought to try to rid the world, as its tendency was, as it always has been, to retard all radical reformation. He died a Spiritualist, and what the church calls a thorough Infidel, and his life, and the manner of his death, triumphantly, refutes, the oft repeated declaration of the priesthood, that faith in the inspiration of the Bible, the atonement of Christ, &c., was essential to a calm and peaceful death. For while he rejected, almost entirely the Christian system of Theology, no Christian ever yielded up his spirit, more calmly, peacefully, or

Reverend Wells & Eleanor (Hannen) Bushnell

Reverend Wells Bushnell was born on the east end of Long Island, New York, on April 25, 1799. His parents, Alexander and Sarah (Wells) Bushnell, were New England natives, and professors of Christianity.

In 1816, Bushnell resided in Pittsburgh, and made a public profession of religion, connecting himself with the First Presbyterian Church. In 1817 he began working as a blacksmith, assisting the chief blacksmith at the Allegheny Arsenal. In a short time he was able to take charge of a fire and was considered a fair workman.

Encouraged by his minister to become a minister himself, he attended Jefferson College, and graduated in 1823. His theological education was completed at Princeton Theological Seminary. In 1825 he entered the Presbytery of New Brunswick, New Jersey, and became licensed to preach the gospel.

In April 1826, Bushnell married Eleanor Hannen, eldest daughter of John and Elizabeth (Richards) Hannen. From 1827 through 1839 Bushnell answered various calls from Presbyteries in Pennsylvania, Indiana and Kentucky. He also spent 18 months ministering to Indians in Kansas, but ill health necessitated a return east. For a time, he ministered in Louisville, Kentucky, but his views on the subject of slavery were so strong that he could not long tolerate living in a slave state.

On April 18, 1839 he received a call and was transferred to the Presbytery of Beaver, Pennsylvania. He served as a pastor in the New Castle Presbyterian Church for more than 15 years, and purchased property on the Public Square in West New Castle. His home was located on the west side of Center Street, now Greenwood, near the corner of West North Street.

During his tenure in New Castle, Bushnell experienced a change of heart. An honest and sincere man, he reached a point where he could no longer, in justice to his feelings regarding slavery, remain with the Presbyterian Church.

He severed ties with the Beaver Presbytery and united himself with the Free Presbyterian Church. In his remaining years, he accepted calls from the Free Presbyterian Churches of New Castle, Mount Jackson, and New Bedford.

Bushnell was described as possessing a warm heart. One of his elders said of him,

"He was courteous and affable in his general intercourse as a Christian. He was zealous and sincere as a minister. His sermons were written carefully, and delivered with a force that carried conviction to the minds of his hearers."

On July 16, 1863, Reverend Wells Bushnell died at the age of 65 of cholera morbus (acute gastroenteritis) in Mount Jackson, Pennsylvania. He is buried at Mount Jackson Battery B. M. E. Cemetery.

with a more rational, or satisfactory faith in his future, eternal felicity than he did. And he said that all he asked of the Church, concerning himself, was, that she would not lie respecting him as she had done of those Infidels who had gone before him." (W. W. Walker, *Anti–Slavery Bugle*. (New–Lisbon, Ohio), August 1, 1857).[22]

BUTTONWOOD

As in most places at the time, tension existed within Western Pennsylvania congregations regarding slavery. Some did not consider it a great evil, while others bitterly opposed the practice.

Reverend Arthur B. Bradford held strong views on the subject, and did not hesitate to express them from the pulpit. This caused a rift in the congregation, and led to Bradford withdrawing to form a Free Church. He would go on to preach in Free Presbyterian churches for many years.

Bradford owned a farm near Darlington, about one and a half miles from Enon Valley, Pennsylvania, where they established an Underground Railroad station known as Buttonwood. Fugitives were sent to him from Quaker settlements at New Brighton, and he was charged with getting them to Salem, Ohio. The Bradfords were also known to have brought slaves to Lawrence County and across the Mahoning River at Covert's Crossing in Mahoning Township to David Young.

Buttonwood became an active link in the route from New Brighton and Beaver Falls to Enon Valley in Lawrence County, and west through Salem, Ohio, then north to Canada. Bradford's son, O. B., would assist him in transporting escaping slaves to the next station.

Fearing confiscation of his property under the Fugitive Slave Law, it is reported that Bradford transferred ownership to a friend in the event he was caught in the act of assisting escaping slaves. The deed transferring his property does not, however, appear to have been recorded in the courthouse records in Beaver County.

Many Abolitionists visited Buttonwood. Abby Kelley, founder of the *Anti–Slavery Bugle*, and Sara Jane Clark spent a summer there. Others included Joshua R. Giddings, Wendell Phillips, and William Lloyd Garrison.[23]

WAY STATION

In 1843, Charles A. Garlick escaped to Pittsburgh from Virginia and travelled to the home of Samuel Marshall, the keeper of a Way Station in Butler County. Garlic stayed two weeks before being forwarded to

> "[a] haven kept by John Rainbow, a relative of Mr. Marshall, living in Beaver, Pa. Here he stayed only one night and the next morning started for New Castle. He stopped there with a Mr. Bushnell, and the next night made Brookfield."

Reverend Wells Bushnell was an avid Abolitionist in the New Castle area and a well respected figure in the Free Presbyterian movement.[24]

DEEP IN THE BACKWOODS

Reverend John D. Whitham operated an Underground Railroad Station in the deep backwoods of North Beaver Township.

> On the farm of good old John Davidson, in the backwoods on the banks of Hickory creek, was a station of the 'Underground Railroad' in charge of Reverend Whitren (sic Whitham) of the 'Free' Presbyterian church, where the poor colored people were assisted on their way across the boarder (sic) into Canada and freedom. This religious community along in the '40's heard the whisperings of a new doctrine—that of 'universal salvation,' and many were the long and ardent petitions to the Divine Master that this direfnt (sic) heresy might be spared to them; the idea that everybody was to be saved was not to be tolerated by these people, who had become steeped and saturated from further generations with the Presbyterian and Covenanter doctrine of 'predestination'…[25]

> ### Reverend John D. Whitham
>
> Reverend John D. Whitham was living in Hanover Township, Beaver County, Pennsylvania, at the time of the 1840 Census. Ordained by the Philadelphia Presbytery on October 10, 1841, he was installed at Unity and Wolf Run Churches in Green County, Pennsylvania, through April 18, 1843. By October, 1843, he was aligned with the Presbytery of Wooster and was reporting to the Synod of Ohio Coshocton in 1845.
>
> In 1848, Whitham broke from the Presbyterian Church and organized the Free Presbyterian Church at Lowellville, Ohio, about four miles west of the Pennsylvania border. By 1850, he was living in Mahoning Township, Lawrence County, Pennsylvania.

Chapter Notes

1. Proceedings of the American Colonial Society at their Sixteenth Annual Meeting in *The Annual Report of the American Society for Colonizing the Free People of Colour of the United States, Vol. 16*. Printer: James C. Dunn. Washington. 1833.
2. *Encyclopedia of African American History, 1619-1895: From the Colonial Period to the Age of Frederick Douglass, Vol 2*. ed. Paul Finkleman. Oxford University Press, USA. 2006, 57-59.
3. http://www.pbs.org/wgbh/aia/part3/3p1521.html
4. Presbyterian Church in the U.S. General Assembly, *Minutes of the General Assembly of the Presbyterian Church in the United States: 1840-51*. Philadelphia.1841, 15.
5. *Minutes - United Presbyterian Church in the U.S.A*, 1842, 376.
6. *Minutes of the Free Presbytery of Mahoning*. Dr. Isaac Ketler Collection, Grove City College.
7. *The United Presbyterian and Evangelical Guardian, Vol. 2*. 1848, 42.
8. *Minutes of the Free Presbytery of Mahoning*. Dr. Isaac Ketler Collection, Grove City College.
9. Velde, Lewis George Vander, *The Presbyterian Church 1861-1869*. 1932, 124.
10. *Notes from the Free Presbyterian, Vol. 4*, 144. Wooster College Free Presbyterian Church Collection.
11. Crist, Rev. A. C. *History of Marion Presbyterian*. 1908, 248.
12. *Anti-Slavery Bugle*, January 31, 1857, 2.
13. Johnson, H. U., *From Dixie to Canada, Romance and Realities of the Underground Railroad, Vol. 1*. Charles Wells Moulton. Buffalo. 1894, 64.
14. White, Joseph S. Letter to Wilbur H. Siebert, January 1897, p.3. The Wilbur H. Siebert Underground Railroad Collection, State Library of Ohio.
15. Johnson, *History of the Neshannock Presbyterian Church*, 222-224.
16. *20th Century History of Youngtown & Mahoning County*. ed. Gen. Thos. W. Sanderson. Biographical Publishing Co. George Richmond Press. Chicago. 1907.
17. White, Joseph S. Letter to Wilbur H. Siebert.
18. *Holmes County Republican,* December 19/20, 1861.
19. Crist, Rev. A. C. *History of Marion Presbytery*, 249.
20. *Anti-Slavery Bugle* (New-Lisbon, Ohio), May 4, 1861.
21. Johnson, *History of Neshannock Presbyterian Church*, 227-228.
22. Walker, W. W. *Anti-Slavery Bugle*, August 01, 1857.
23. "Recalls Another Station on Underground Railway," *New Castle News*, March 13, 1925.
24. Garlick, Charles A. *Life Including His Escape and Struggle for Liberty of Charles A. Garlick*. Jefferson, Ohio. 1902, 6.
25. *New Castle News*, August 20, 1902.
26. *Lawrence Guardian*, October 9, 1875, 3.
27. http://archiver.rootsweb.ancestry.com/th/read/SAMPLES/2002-07/1026171315
28. *Biological Sketches of Leading Citizens Lawrence County, Pennsylvania*. Biographical Publishing Company, Buffalo. 1897, 589.
29. Hazen, 207, 314, 359.
30. Siebert, 423.
31. Stallman, David A. *Our Home Town Holmesville, OH*. Stallman. 2001, 19.
32. *The Presbyterian Historical Almanac and Annual Remembrancer of the Church, 2nd Vol*. 1860, 213.
33. *1876 City Directory*, New Castle, Pennsylvania.

5
PRINT, POLITICS AND PUBLIC OPINION

ALTHOUGH MANY Lawrence County newspapers and newsletters from the early to mid–1800s are lost to history, those for which copies have survived give us a window into the past. Where modern news publications typically claim to be unbiased, newspapers of the time were often named after their political views, such as the *New Castle Democrat*. These periodicals were a reflection of local and national sentiment and did not hesitate to express opinions on slavery and abolitionism.

Before 1838 newspapers came and went in the New Castle area, but no single paper gained prominence. In fact, from December 1838 to August 1839 New Castle readers had no newspaper at all to provide news and opinions to the growing community. In 1839, the *Mercer and Beaver Democrat* began publication as a four–page, five–column sheet supported by the newly powerful Whig Party. Whigs avoided the slavery issue in favor of state's rights and congressional versus executive power concerns. Deep internal divisions over slavery, however, would lead to the party's demise in the 1850's.

The *New Castle Democrat* was the first Democratic newspaper in the area. Published in July 13, 1844 by George F. Humes and J. N. Hallowell, it consisted of four pages, five columns per page, and lasted about a year.[1] The *Lawrence Journal* began publishing May 26, 1849 as a Democratic–Free Soil newspaper.[2] James M. Kuester was editor and proprietor, with assistance from James Telford. *The Gazette*, published by Shaw and Craig, also made its inaugural appearance before 1850.

The Promulgator, a Free Soil paper, made its first appearance on December 20, 1853, published by Mr. Blanchard from Washington DC.[3] In May of 1854, Blanchard sold the paper to William F. Clark of Mercer, who merged it with *The Mercer Freeman*, and changed the name to *Promulgator and Freeman*. A year later he changed the name again, to *American Freeman*, and branded it as an anti–slavery paper.[4] Colonel Daniel Leasure, who formed the infamous 100th Pennsylvania Volunteer Regiment (Roundheads) in Lawrence County, was an associate editor of *American Freeman* in 1856.[5] The paper later became the *Courant*.

William F. Clark published several Abolitionist publications, including the Mercer–based *Free Presbyterian*,[6] a similar New Castle-based newspaper, and an 1850 pamphlet by George Gordon entitled, "Secession From a Pro–Slavery Church a Christian Duty: A Sermon."[7] Though Clark was an ardent Abolitionist and one–time Conductor for the Underground Railroad, editorial work for the *Free Presbyterian* was performed by Reverend Joseph Gordon.[8]

The *Anti–Slavery Bugle*, a regional Abolitionist newspaper, began publication in 1845 in Lisbon, Ohio with the motto: "No Union with

> ### William F. Clark
>
> William F. Clark was an ardent Abolitionist, a Conductor on the Underground Railroad, and an elder in the Free Presbyterian Church of Mercer. He is best known, however, for his work as a newspaperman.
>
> In 1833, Clark purchased the Anti-Masonic Mercer paper, *Luminary*, from New Castle residents William and James Moorhead, and kept it alive through a constant shifting of allegiances. When the Anti–Masonic party dissolved, the paper continued in support of the Whig party, and later the Liberty and Free Soil Democratic parties.
>
> Around 1850, Clark retitled the *Luminary* as the *Free Presbyterian* and shifted the paper's focus to religion and slavery. Clark also published a pro-Abolition paper in New Castle and founded the *Mercer Dispatch*.
>
> He was the oldest newspaper man from the county when he died in Indianapolis at the age of 88.[50]

Slaveholders." It did not align itself with any one party, but published for those who shared their principles regardless of political affiliation.

The paper moved to Salem, Ohio after six issues, probably because that city was more welcoming to Garrisonian views that included abandoning churches viewed as corrupted by slavery. The paper printed letters and speeches, including Sojourner Truth's 1851 "Ain't I a Woman" speech, along with calls for meetings and editorials. The paper supported women's rights and involved itself in a peace movement opposing the Mexican War.

The *Anti–Slavery Bugle* was unique, extreme, and loud in contrast to other papers representing Whigs, Republicans, Democrats, Independents, and even Pro–Slavery, temperance, and labor factions. Despite inadequate funding, the Bugle lasted more than 18 years.[9]

The *Free Church Portfolio* was published in New Castle, Pennsylvania from 1859 to 1861 by editor, Reverend A. B. Bradford.[10] By 1860, it was a four page, six column weekly. The paper's motto was as follows.

"There is neither Jew nor Greek, neither bond nor free, for ye are all one in Christ."

According to an editorial,

"Our position, as an Anti–Slavery body of Christians, requires of us that we use all our efforts for the exposition and advocacy of the principles we hold in common with other Free Churches in our land– the complete triumph of which is necessary to our continued existence and prosperity as a Nation; and, above all, the honor of the Church of Christ."[11]

WESTERN ANTI–SLAVERY SOCIETY AND LAWRENCE COUNTY

IN 1840 THE OHIO STATE Anti–Slavery Society was debating entry into the political arena, and the issue of women's rights within the Society itself. They decided to remain neutral on women's rights and severed their connection to the American Anti–Slavery Society (AASS) controlled by William Lloyd Garrison and his followers, which included women's rights in its platform.

Some members wanted to reconnect with the AASS in 1842, but agreement could not be reached. Impatient for resolution, a portion of the membership broke away and became The Ohio American Anti-Slavery Society of New Lisbon. This group re-affiliated with Eastern Garrisonian Abolitionists, condemned churches for neglecting the Abolition cause, and requested speakers from the AASS to support their efforts.

William Lloyd Garrison agreed to assist with funding and to provide speakers. When he sent Abby Kelley, a Quaker Abolitionist and feminist, to New Lisbon for a three day speaking tour, she arrived in her "most aggressive attitude." Radical anti-slavery resolutions and denouncements of the Constitution of the United States as a "covenant with death and an agreement with hell" were proposed, discussed and adopted, notwithstanding strenuous opposition from some members.[11]

Many moderate Abolitionists, while supporting women's rights in the abstract, scorned the public role of women and believed they should not vote nor speak at American Anti–Slavery meetings, much less take part in decision-making. As a result of Kelley's strident goading and resulting resolutions, John Rankin and his radicals moved to Salem, wherein a large number of sympathetic Anti–Slavery Quakers resided. The group established the *Anti–Slavery Bugle* newspaper and changed its name to the Western Anti–Slavery Society.[13]

The Bugle adopted the Garrisonian disunionist motto "No Union With Slaveholders," which appeared under its header in every edition. Abby Kelley helped to raise funds for the *Bugle* and recruited Benjamin S. Jones and J. Elizabeth Hitchcock Jones to serve as editors.[14]

Members of the Western Anti–Slavery Society gave many lectures in the area. The first in New Castle took place at the old Presbyterian Church just north of County Line Street, near Shenango River,[15] and was headlined by Abby Kelley and her husband Stephen Symonds Foster, a man considered to be one of Garrison's most radical colleagues.[16]

Other known meetings included:

October 13 and 14, 1845 – J. Elizabeth Hitchcock and Benjamin Jones[17]

January 17 and 18, 1846 – Foster and Kelley[18]

September 18, 1851 in Pulaski – C. C. Burleigh[19]

January or February, 1853, in New Bedford and New Castle at the Court House – Charles S. and Josephine Griffing[20]

October 1853 at Pulaski – John F. Selby[21]

September 7th and 8th, 1854 at New Castle – C. C. Burleigh and others.[22]

The *Anti–Slavery Bugle* found many supporters in Lawrence County and the city was home to a variety of views concerning slavery.

POLITICAL PARTIES MID–1800s

THE DEMOCRATIC AND Republican Parties trace their roots back to the 1800s, but a number of other parties existed at various times throughout that century. Some even launched candidates to the White House.

The Federalist Party is considered the first American political party. The party's defeat in the 1800 election led to its decline, and it ceased to be a national party after 1816.

The Jeffersonian Republican Party, which supported Thomas Jefferson, James Madison and James Monroe, formed in opposition to the Federalists.

The Democratic Party was founded around 1828. It backed 15 Democratic presidents over the years, the first being Andrew Jackson.

The National Republican Party supported John Quincy Adams in 1828 and Henry Clay in 1832. It combined with the Whig Party in 1834 to oppose Andrew Jackson.

The Liberty Party was organized in 1839 by Anti–Slavery activists who wanted to make Abolition a political movement. The party ran a presidential ticket in 1840 and 1844 with James G. Birney, a former slaveholder from Kentucky, as their candidate. The Liberty Party only accounted for two percent of the vote in 1844.

The Free Soil Party formed in 1848 to oppose slavery. Their motto was "Free Soil, Free Speech, Free Labor and Free Men." The party nominated Martin Van Buren for president, and while he lost the election to Zachary Taylor of the Whig Party, the Free Soil Party did place two candidates in the Senate and 14 in the House of Representatives. The party did not last long, and its members were absorbed into the Republican Party.

The Whigs remained a major party throughout the 1840s, but split over the issue of slavery. Some Whigs joined the new Republican Party, while others opted for the Know–Nothing Party.

The Know–Nothing Party arose in the late 1840s as a reaction to immigration. After success in local elections, former president Millard Fillmore ran for president in 1856 as their candidate. Fillmore's campaign was unsuccessful, and the party dissolved.

The modern Republican Party, or Grand Old Party, formed in 1854 to combat the Kansas–Nebraska Act which threatened to extend slavery into the territories. The Party enlisted former Whigs and Free Soil Democrats to form majorities in nearly every Northern state.

In 1860 Democrats split along Northern and Southern lines over the choice of a successor to President James Buchanan. As the Civil War began, Northern Democrats further divided into War Democrats and Peace Democrats. Most War Democrats sided with Republican President Abraham Lincoln in his 1864 re–election.

With the election of Abraham Lincoln and the abolishment of slavery, Republicans dominated the political scene until 1932.[23]

SLAVERY DISCUSSION IN THE NEWS

ALTHOUGH NOT MANY area newspapers from the time exist, a number of articles about the slavery debate survive. Below, we present excerpts from publications covering public opinion and events of the day.

While these stories cannot possibly provide a comprehensive representation of the opinions of Lawrence County citizens, they do indicate that a vigorous discussion took place.

Anti–Slavery Meeting: 1837

"According to notice given, the Mercer County Anti–Slavery Society met at the courthouse in the borough of Mercer, and on the 22nd alt., and was opened by the Reverend Mr. Wilson of West Greenville."[24]

Anti– Negro Sentiment: 1838

"When Pennsylvania's Abolition hall was burnt to the ground Gov. Ritner offered the extravagant reward of $500 for each of the actors. This was done to convince Abolitionists that he was opposed 'to the base bowing of the knee to the dark spirit of slavery.' Since which time, two white men have been murdered by Negroes in Philadelphia and yet his Abolition Excellency has not thought proper to offer a reward for the Black rascals. In his opinion the burning of a Negro Hall is a much greater outrage than the murder of two white men by several Blacks! Need the public hear anything more to convince them that Ritner is an Abolitionist? We think not."[25]

Thomas Sample's treatment of the Negro

Thomas Sample was a prominent figure in early Allegheny history, and served as its second mayor. What follows is an account of his bizarre actions while a justice of the peace sometime before 1843.

A farmer had been murdered by a Negro tramp on the Beaver road below Economy, his head bashed in with a rock, and his body hidden in a culvert. The victim was soon discovered and parties in the vicinity trailed the fugitive to Allegheny. Before they could arrest him, however, he fled across a frozen river, broke through the ice, and drowned.

His body was recovered and laid out for the coroner, but mysteriously disappeared. Sample was the culprit.

> "The boldness of the transaction created quite an excitement at the time; and it continued without abatement until it leaked out that the object in surreptitiously removing the body was to skin it, and tan the hide, in order to solve the problem as to the quality of material manufactured out of the cuticle of the 'genus homo'. Razor–strops and watch–guards were fashioned out of the novel leather, and distributed among the curious. Sample was considered somewhat of a genius in his way. To his insatiable disposition to solve the various

Thomas Sample / Semple

Thomas Sample (also spelled "Semple") was born on January 8, 1791 in Girty's Run, Allegheny County. He was described as a man of sterling character, but rather eccentric habits.

As a young man he and his cousin, Judge William Hays, started a tannery. After marrying, he opened his own business, Sample Tannery, served as a justice of the peace for 20 years, and was elected the second mayor of Allegheny as a Whig.

In 1843 Sample bought a 100 acre farm in Lawrence County. Parts of the farm later housed the American Tin Plate Company of New Castle. He died at his home in Mahoningtown in August 1876.

problems of law, physics, and mechanics, may be attributed this seeming violation of the laws of humanity and good order. It was generally conceded that he was actuated by no other motive than the one above indicated. In view of the high estimation in which he was held by the citizens generally, he was unmolested."[26]

Sample was not alone in dehumanizing the Negro. A report from the time period tells of a boatman in Wesleyville, Pennsylvania, north of Erie, telling slaves fleeing to Canada:

> "You better go back d'ye hear! They'll make your Black hide into razor strops 'nless than a week. I paid a dollar for one made from a Black nigger. They're sending hundreds of them across the sea every week."[27]

Mrs. Clendenin Remembers

Mrs. Clendenin was born in Cumberland County in 1800 and moved to New Castle in 1839. She stated that,

> "New Castle then was the quietest and most respectable town I have ever seen. There was no drunkenness here at all, though there were three taverns here."

Of the political situation she said:

> "There were not many Democrats here then either. When I came here I was the only woman in town who was a Democrat. Everybody around this section was a Whig or Abolitionist, even my father was, and I got many a scolding for my views. David Tidball was a Democrat too, and he and I used to fight the whole town, but he is changed now. I do want to see another Democratic President. It used to make Mr. J. N. Euwer so mad to think that I was raising my boys to be Democrats."[28]

Anti–slavery Convention: 1844

February 23, 1844 a convention of the Anti-Slavery party of Pennsylvania was held at Pittsburgh and adopted their ticket. Amzi Semple of Mercer and William Scott of Beaver were among the Congressional Electors.[29]

Locals run for state Abolitionist positions: 1844

American Intelligencer, a Philadelphia abolition paper, published an electoral ticket recommended in support of the Abolitionists of Pennsylvania, which included James G. Birney of Michigan for President and Thomas Morris of Ohio for Vice President. Francis J. Lemoyne of Washington County was listed for Governor, and William Larimer, Jr. of Allegheny County for Canal Commissioner. Electors for President included Amzi Semple and Robert Stewart of Mercer and William Scott of Beaver.[30]

In October 1844 an electoral ticket appeared in a Philadelphia paper with the names of Electors of President and Vice President to be supported at the Presidential Election. The Liberty Nomination for President was James G. Birney of Michigan and for Vice President, Thomas Morris of Ohio. Amzi C. Semple and William Scott were listed as Electors.[31]

A Black at School: 1846

In January 1846, an ex–slave named John Girley arrived in Quakertown (Mahoning Township) to lecture on slavery. Girley had been a slave for nineteen years, and free for eight. Since being freed, he had been sponsored at school by Garrett Smith of Peterborough, New York, and gone on to lecture in nearly every Free State of the Union.[32]

After several lectures in Quakertown in which he gave an account of the cruelties and outrages to which he was subjected by Southern tyrants, he decided "to stop and go to school awhile." Whether this statement was meant to provoke reaction or an expression of a desire to gain additional education we may never know, but we do know that two local men, Joseph Cadwallader, a Democrat, and Samuel R. Bailey, a Whig, were offended enough to remove their children from school and coerce others in the area to do the same. Ironically, Joseph Cadwallader's brothers, Septimus and Eli, and brothers–in–law, Talbot Townsend and Benjamin Sharpless, were all Underground conductors in Mahoning Township.[33]

The law at the time allowed for a committee of three to govern local school affairs provided that the board of six township directors gave them leave to do so. A majority of Quakertown directors believed that all men should enjoy the privileges of education and were not inclined to grant such leave. Undaunted, the offended parents enlisted an ex–justice of the peace to write the following notice:

> "To the School Directors of Mahoning Township, Mercer County. You are hereby noticed that certain persons in school district No. 29 at Quaker town have put teacher and pupils into our public school contrary to our wish, and contrary to the act of assembly in such case made and provided. We therefore pray your honors to remove the nuisance, and pay no public money to any Teacher who is not examined and appointed according to Law."

A meeting was called in an attempt to elect a Pro–Slavery school committee to defy the township directors. The election, however, resulted in a board consisting of two Abolitionists and one slaveholder "in heart" who refused to serve. The election was said to have cooled the rebels' enthusiasm.

William C. Alexander, secretary of the Eastern District Anti–Slavery Society and a traveling teacher[37] brought this account to the attention of the *Anti–Slavery Bugle*.[35, 36]

Anti Slavery Meeting: 1849

> "A meeting of all persons irrespective of party connection will be held in the lecture room of the Associate Reformed church on Jefferson Street in New Castle on the evening of the 8th, inst., for the purpose of interchanging opinions respecting ways and means for protecting our newly acquired territory from defilement of slavery."[37]

Free Soil Nominations for Mercer County, in conjunction with the Mercer portion of Lawrence County: 1849[38]

Gentlemen for Assembly: Warren Carpenter, New Castle and George Lodge, Salem

Commissioner: Marcus H. Rose, Wolfcreek

Auditor: Jesse R. Perrine, Sandy Lake

Treasurer: Joseph L. Sykes of Mercer

Trustees: Reverend D. H. A. McLain and R. Hanna

Free Soil Convention: 1849

> "The friends of Free Soil should endeavor to have every district fully represented at said convention. Though our county be an infant, let us show to the world that Lawrence County is fast arriving at maturity in its appreciation of Human Rights.

> "The citizens of Lawrence County opposed to the extension of Slavery and not in favor of such action by the National Government as well, divorce from the guilt of sustaining this institution, are requested to meet at the usual places holding township elections on Saturday, July 13, between the hours of 3 and 5 o'clock, and appoint delegates to meet in County Convention, at the Town Hall in New Castle, on Tuesday the 16th day of July next, at 11 o'clock, A.M., to nominate a county ticket, and to appoint Congressional, Senatorial and Representative conferees, to meet with those who may be appointed in the other counties composing these districts. By order of the County Committee, J. C. White, president. R. W. Cunningham, Secretary."[39]

On August 21st, 1849, the Free Soil Central Committee of Lawrence County convened a meeting of delegates from the different townships at the Protestant Methodist Church in New Castle. The following were elected to manage the conference:

President: John Wright, Mahoning

Vice Presidents: John Carson, North Beaver and L. Carman, Wilmington

Secretaries: A.S. Hawthorn, Neshannock and Josiah C. White, New Castle

Other committee members: Reverend Whitham, Thomas Silliman, J. N. Phillips, Mr. Porter, William Allsworth

> "Whereas American Slavery, the curse of our continent, whose overthrow our organization was effected to consummate, still exists, and, with an affrontery peculiar to itself, has raised the issue of slavery or disunion, and proclaimed in tones of defiance its fell purpose of desecrating our newly acquired territory with the foot prints of slavery and its civil code; and Whereas, its uniform history and settled policy continues to be what it ever has been that of arrogance, encroachment, and haughty dictation."

The following were put into nomination:

Prothonotary: James Gilleland, New Castle

Treasurer: White McMillen, New Castle

Commissioner: Samuel D. Clark, North Beaver

Auditors: Thomas Silliman, Little Beaver and James Moore, Shenango

Coroner: James Shaw, Slippery Rock[40]

Anti–slavery Meeting: 1850

> "A meeting of all persons, irrespective of party connection, will be held in the Lecture room of the Associate Reform Church on Jefferson Street, in New Castle, on the evening of the 8th, for the purpose of interchanging opinions respecting ways and means for protecting our newly acquired territory from the defilement of Slavery."[41]

The meeting was called to order by Chairman John P. McGlathery of North Beaver Township. Josiah C. White of Neshannock and George Henderson of New Castle were appointed as Secretaries. Resolutions were drafted by Mr. Clark, Mr. Moore, and Mr. Kuester.

Free Soil Convention Delegates: July 20, 1850

Senate: Samuel D. Clark, North Beaver

Assembly: John McNickel, Neshannock

Commissioner: James Aiken, Perry

Auditor: L. Carman, Esq., New Wilmington

Indignation Meetings in Response to the Fugitive Slave Bill: 1850

New Castle

According to the announcement, many of the citizens of this county, without distinction of party, assembled at the First Presbyterian Church in New Castle for the purpose of expressing their sentiments in relation to the late act of Congress on the Fugitive Slave Law. The meeting was organized by calling C. W. McCulhan, Esq, of Slippery Rock Township to the chair and appointing James Dickson and Thomas Alford Vice Presidents, and Warren Carpenter and J. S. White, Secretaries.

A committee was appointed to prepare resolutions expressive of the sense of the meeting. The committee consisted of Reverend Josiah Hatchman, James B. Clark, John Reynolds, Joseph Emery, and Lot Watson, Esqrs. The meeting called for censure of all who participated in passage of the law. Other attendees wanted to censure members of Congress, and some wanted to include the President as well.[42]

New Bedford

An indignation meeting was held in New Bedford at the Free Presbyterian Church October 15th, 1850. The meeting was called to order by J. P. Cowden, Chairman, and R. K. McBride, Secretary. In their resolution, they claimed,

> "...the return of the fugitive slave is a direct opposition to the law of God whether we appeal

for it in the Old or New Testament, or to the law written on our hearts, by the spirit of God."

And,

"...come life or come imprisonment—come fine—or come death, we will neither aid nor assist in the return of any fugitive slave, but on the contrary, we will harbor and secrete, and by all just means protect and defend him and thus give him a practical God speed to liberty."[43]

Pulaski

A public meeting was held near Pulaski for citizens to express their opinions in relation to the Fugitive Slave Act. Jacob Book, President, and Alex Anderson, Secretary, created a preamble and resolutions that were nearly unanimously passed. These stated that the law was

"...unprecedented in the history of human legislation; not only violating the fundamental law of this nation, but outraging every principle of republicanism, humanity and sound morality."

And that the law should be

"...[t]otally disregarded by every true Republican."[44]

Croton

"The citizens of Croton met for the purpose of taking into consideration the propriety of resisting the late Fugitive Slave Law."

They concluded that the law was unjust and should be repealed, that it was of the "darkest nature and wicked in all its forms," that members of Congress who voted for it were unworthy.

"We as citizens of Croton, Lawrence County, Pennsylvania cannot, nor will not, supinely submit to any law or laws, made by any man or combination of men, that is so direct a violation of the constitution and infringement upon us."[45]

Anti–slavery Convention, New Castle: 1851

According to a *New Castle News* article in May 1851, an Anti-Slavery Convention took place in New Castle that year. The following details were provided.

John Clark, Esq. , President, Reverend David Goodwillie and Reverend Samuel Patterson, Vice Presidents, William F. Clark and Reverend Josiah Hutchman, Secretaries. Also attending were Reverend R. A. Browne, Associate Reformed Church, Reverend A. C. Kirk, Regular Baptist, Reverend D. R. Barker, Congregational church, Reverend A. B. Bradford, Free Presbyterian Church, Reverend J. W. Plannett, Free Will Baptist Church, Reverend David Goodwillie, Associate Church, Reverend Josiah Hatchman, Reformed Presbyterian. Others mentioned included Reverend George Scott, R. W. Oliver, and Mr. McClintock.

The Business Committee consisted of Reverend J. D. Wolf, Reverend R. A. Browne, Reverend A. G. Kirk, John Young, Reverend J. W. Plannett, Reverend Joseph Gordon, Freeman Dunn, Matthew Stuart, and William Scott.

Reverend Richard Gardiner gave his account of being captured as a fugitive slave, his redemption and return to his family in Beaver. Gardiner had been arrested in Bridgewater, Beaver County, Pennsylvania, and claimed as property by Miss R. Byers of Louisville, Kentucky. Judge Irwin of the United States District Court "remanded the fugitive back to his owner."

Gardner was afterwards bought for $600 and brought into a free State.

Adopted resolutions:

1. The system of American Slavery is a heinous sin against God. Its evils are not merely incidental but inherent. Under solemnity of law it institutes a title to property, by which man, designated by the Divine as an owner, is degraded to the position of a thing; and men of one race are tolerated and defended in the

possession as chattels of men of another race, without crime alleged–against the enslaved. The wrongs of cruelty, murder and lust, the debasement of the understanding, the repressing forever of the nobler instincts of mankind, and the withholding of the word of life and salvation, in order to hold him more securely as a brute, are its evils to the slave; enervation, licentiousness, pride and tyranny, the vices it fosters in the master, and discord and natural weakness, the injuries it entails upon the state; these are only the evil fruits of a tree essentially corrupt, which can never be improved by topping off the branches, but which must be hewn down and cast into the fire.

2. That we held the provisions of the Fugitive Slave Bill as having no binding obligation upon us, that they are utterly opposed to the word of God—and that when these come in contact, we are bound to obey the injunction of the "Higher Law."

3. That we view with profound interest the alarming increase in slavery influences in this land, in church and state. Not content merely to sit by sinful influence, as heretofore, beneath the churches shadow; now seeks to control her actions, and trammels the consciences of Christians to make them subserve its ends. Not satisfied to enjoy, merely, by unrighteous toleration, the shelter of the state, it now brooks nothing less than complete dominion, and not only holds the slave in bondage, but claims all new territories for its area, and seeks to make freemen its minions. Thus like a cancer it eats the vitality of religion and freedom; and it is made manifest that the preservation of all that is most precious to us depends upon its complete destruction.

4. That it is the duty of Christians to feel for those in bonds as bound with them,—and that we ought to labor and pray for the emancipation of the slave, as we would if we ourselves, or our families, were held in his condition; that it is the duty of the Christian Church to exercise discipline on slaveholders, and the justifiers of slavery, the same as on persons guilty of other scandalous sins, and therefore; that those churches which receive and retain the slaveholder, and the defender of slaveholding, in their communion, are the bulwarks of American Slavery, and responsible before God for all the evils flowing legitimately there from.

5. That the duty of Christians to honor God's ordinance of civil government, by choosing righteous men—"such as fear God and hate covetousness," and therefore, that those professing Christians who vote for slaveholders, duelists, and other gross offenders against the law of God, act inconsistent with Christian character.[46]

Free Soil Convention: 1854

A mass meeting of Free Soilers in Lawrence County was held at the New Castle County Courthouse in June 1854. They nominated the following:

Congress: Hon. John Allison, Beaver County

Assembly: J. D. Bryan, Shenango

Commissioner: Robert Reynolds, New Castle

Auditor: Dr. J. Randolph, Wilmington

The Whigs were becoming Free Soilers: 1854

> "It is somewhat amusing to see how the Free Soil party, in this country, is swallowing up the Whig party. They are cordially invited to step into the Free Soil ranks! A party having some eight or ten hundred majority in Lawrence County have been taken in by the great minority—the free soil abolition party—because the Whigs have lost their power and become obsolete!"[47]

RESPONSES TO NEWSPAPERS

According to the *Lawrence Journal*, an 1854 paper named the *Western Star* had published an article critical of Reverend Arthur B. Bradford coming out to make a political stump speech

> "...to a lot of men, women, niggers and ruffians, in the woods, through the darkness of night."

This elicited an article by the *Greenville Argus* newspaper.

> "Verily, the editors (of the *Western Star*) possess a nice sense of proprieties of ministerial life. . . . Our objection is to such men coming out on the stump, as have evidence to believe that they have been called of God, and set apart for the work of the ministry. They bring disrepute upon the cause of religion, not by doing that which is, in itself wrong, but that which is manifestly unwise. . . . When they leave the pulpit... to argue politics in the barroom and from the stump—then away with all such priests from the altar."[48]

In response to the Abolitionist movement: 1862

W. D. Clark wrote the following to the *Lawrence Journal*, published verbatim.

> "Mr. D G Kuester
>
> Sir
>
> I have been Tyred [sic] of your Slang in reading the journal. I do not lend my aid To a man that is Opposed To the abilision [sic] of Slavery in this Time of Peril when it appears the only remedy To Save our county. Men Professing Godliness and Still Go in for Opresion [sic] that Must have strange harts [sic] that is what I gather from your Sheet By upholding the Democratic Party. Excuse this and Stop the Journal and Believe Me. Your friend. W. D. Clark"[49]

Chapter Notes

1. Hazen, Aaron L. *20th Century History of New Castle and Lawrence County, Pennsylvania*, Richmond-Arnold Publishing Co. Chicago 1908, 72.
2. *Lawrence Journal*, June 30, 1849.
3. McCleary, T. Jefferson, *Early History of New Castle, Part XVI.*
4. "History of Herald Most Interesting," *New Castle Herald*, April 20, 1917, 18.
5. Leasure, D. "Letter from Pennsylvania," *The Kansas Herald of Freedom* (Wakarusa, Kansas), March 22, 1856, 3.
6. Johnson, *History of Neshannock Presbyterian Church*, 227-228.
7. Gordon, George, *Secession From a Pro-Slavery Church a Christian Duty: A Sermon.* William F. Clark. 1850.
8. *Minutes of the Free Presbytery of Mahoning*, p.8. Dr. Isaac Ketler Collection, Grove City College.
9. http://chroniclingamerica.loc.gov/lccn/sn83035487/
10. Johnson, T*he History of the Neshannock Presbyterian Church*, 227.
11. *The Free Church Portfolio, Vol. II, No. I*, January 19, 1860.
12. *History of Columbiana County, Ohio* excerpt: "History of the Anti-Slavery Movement," p. 4. Ohio Historical Society, State Library of Ohio.
13. *Encyclopedia of African American History, 1619-1895: From the Colonial Period to the Age of Frederick Douglass, Vol. II.* Leslie M. Alexander & Walter C. Rucker, eds. Oxford University Press. 2006, 39.
14. *Encyclopedia of African American History, 1619-1895: From the Colonial Period to the Age of Frederick Douglass, Vol II*, 334.
15. "Tells of Early Days of New Castle Churches," *New Castle News*, February 19, 1923, 12.
16. *Anti-Slavery Bugle (Lisbon, Ohio)*, Anti-Slavery Meetings October 10, 1845, 3.
17. *Anti-Slavery Bugle*, Conventions, January 2, 1846, 3.
18. Ibid.
19. *Anti-Slavery Bugle*, Anti-Slavery Convention, September 13, 1851, 3.
20. *Anti-Slavery Bugle*, Letter from Crawford County.

21 *Anti-Slavery Bugle*, Letter from John F. Selby, October 1, 1853, 2.

22 *Anti-Slavery Bugle*, Anti-Slavery Meetings, September 2, 1854, 3.

23 Nichols, Roy Franklin, *The Invention of the American Political Parties*. Macmillan. 1967.

24 *Western Press* (Mercer, Pennsylvania), March 4, 1837.

25 "Ritner's Love for Negros," *Western Press*, August 24, 1838.

26 Parke, Judge John E. *Recollections of Seventy Years and Historical Gleanings of Allegheny, Pennsylvania.* 1886.

27 Johnson, Homer Uri, *From Dixie to Canada: Romance and Realities of the Underground Railroad.* Charles Wells Moulton. Buffalo. 1894, 147.

28 "Grandma Clendenin," *New Castle News*, October 29, 1884.

29 *New York Daily Tribune*, February 28, 1844.

30 *Tioga Eagle*, July 10, 1844.

31 *Public Ledger*, October 31, 1844.

32 Clark, Reverend Rufus B. "History of South Ridge (Farnham) Conneaut Township, Ashtabula County, OH," In the *Conneaut Reporter*, January 22, 1880, part XII. http://www.geocities.ws/conneautohio/southridge/southridge.html

33 *20th Century History of New Castle and Lawrence County Pennsylvania and Representative Citizens*, 1908, 579.

34 *Anti-Slavery Bugle*, District Meetings, October 17, 1845, 3.

35 Alexander, William C. "Proscription." *Anti-Slavery Bugle*, Mahoning, January 28, 1846.

36 Letter to the Editor, *Anti-Slavery Bugle*, February 20, 1846.

37 *Lawrence Journal*, January 5, 1849.

38 *Lawrence Journal*, July 7, 1849.

39 *Lawrence Journal*, August 25, 1849.

40 *Lawrence Journal*, September 8, 1849.

41 *Lawrence Journal*, January 26, 1850.

42 *Lawrence Journal*, November 2, 1850.

43 *Lawrence Journal*, November 2, 1850.

44 *Lawrence Journal*, November 9, 1850.

45 *Lawrence Journal*, November 19, 1850.

46 *Lawrence Journal*, May 3, 1851.

47 *Lawrence Journal*, June 24, 1854.

48 *Lawrence Journal*, October 7, 1854.

49 "Abolition Fanaticism," *Lawrence Journal*, November 22, 1862.

50 William F. Clark Obituary, *New Castle News*, June 9, 1897

6

ABOLITION, WESTERN EXPANSION AND BLOODY KANSAS

BY THE 1850S, ABOLITION had moved front and center in American politics. In 1854, Congress passed the Kansas–Nebraska Act, which stipulated that settlers in the new Kansas Territory would decide by popular vote whether Kansas would be a Free or Slave state. Prior to this, Kansas Territory was directed by the Missouri Compromise Act of 1820, which admitted Missouri as a Slave state and Maine as a Free one. The Act provided that there would be no slavery in lands north of an imaginary line, an area which included Kansas Territory.

The Kansas–Nebraska Act negated the Compromise, and the North was outraged. Pro- and Anti–Slavery settlers flocked to the state in an effort to determine its political future. This resulted in a bitter and violent conflict replete with open warfare and mass murder by both sides. "Bloody Kansas" was born.

WESTERN PENNSYLVANIA KANSAS COMPANY: 1854

ONE GROUP THAT FLOCKED to Kansas from Western Pennsylvania was a Free–Soiler and Anti–Slavery group known as the Western Pennsylvania Kansas Company, formed on September 16, 1854. Led by their President, George Washington Brown from Conneautville, Crawford County, 200+ members set out on October 27, 1854 to settle the Kansas Territory.

G. W. Brown passed through New Castle on his way to Kansas and was probably joined by New Castle residents who had joined the cause, such as brothers James R. and William A. Stewart.[1]

Daniel Leasure, a prominent New Castle doctor, presented Brown with a "Bible" on behalf of local citizens, and Brown, who had founded the Conneautville Courier in Crawford County, told of his plans to publish an Abolitionist Free paper in Kansas. Leasure promptly purchased a year's subscription to what would become the *Herald of Freedom*, the first newspaper published in Kansas.

Daniel Leasure clearly held Abolitionist views, being an Associate Editor of New Castle's Anti–Slavery paper, the *American Freeman*. He also attended Greersburg College in Darlington where Abolitionist John Brown studied.

G. W. Brown arrived in Kansas City a day or two behind his group only to discover that the members had already scattered. Disgruntled over a lack of accommodation, the rainy and snowy weather they encountered, and apparent mismanagement of their affairs, they had disbanded. Some went to new towns like Lawrence and Topeka, some remained in Kansas City, and some apparently returned to Pennsylvania.

Brown set up press in Lawrence, near the western border of the Pro–Slavery state, Missouri.

Lawrence would become the center of Kansas' Anti–Slavery movement.

NEW CASTLE–KANSAS AID GROUP: 1856

IN LAWRENCE COUNTY, Pennsylvania, a New Castle–Kansas Aid Group Meeting took place on February 23, 1856, and Daniel Leasure was able to obtain 22 subscriptions to assist the *Herald*. Subscribers included Dr. D. Leasure, J. Kissick, John R. Richardson, Henry C. Falls, Reverend R. A. Browne, John N. Euwer, J. L. McMillan, Jas. Moorhead, David Crawford, Adam Moore, John N. Emery, John A. Stewart, William McClymonds, Reverend A. B. Bradford,

Dr. Daniel & Isabella W. (Hamilton) Leasure

Daniel Leasure was born in Westmoreland County in 1819 and married Isabella W. Hamilton in September 1842. Isabella was the daughter of the Honorable Samuel Hamilton of Beaver County, Pennsylvania.

Leasure graduated from Jefferson Medical College in 1846, and in 1849, the family settled in New Castle where he practiced medicine. In 1850 his family consisted of Isabella, Samuel (or George), James, Rachel, and Mary. Three more children, Milo, Edith, and John, had joined the family by 1855.[21]

Leasure was Associate Editor for the *Coal City Chronicle* and for an Abolitionist paper entitled *American Freeman*. He was a member of the Free Presbyterian Church, and a New Light Covenanter. In 1858, he served as County Coroner.

When word came that Fort Sumter had been attacked, Leasure dropped his medical practice and immediately set up a recruiting station at White Hall. He organized two military companies in the area. The first served 90 days without action. The second was the infamous 100th Pennsylvania Volunteer Regiment, "the Roundheads."[22]

Leasure's son, George, served with the Roundheads and was killed at Petersburg, Virginia. Daniel lost another son to sickness during the war, and his wife, Isabella, died in 1865. When the war ended, Leasure practiced medicine in Darlington and became a trustee of Greersburg Academy.

He moved to Saint Paul, Minnesota in 1878, and died eight years later, on October 10, 1886. His body was returned for burial in New Castle.

John & Catherine Emery

John Emery was a 59 year old man residing in New Castle at the time of the 1850 census. He lived with his wife, Catherine, and three children, Emily, Jeremiah, and Luke. John was elder in the New Castle Free Presbyterian church.

Robert Gilliland, Dr. A. T. Davis, Samuel Montgomery, E. W. Cunningham, Ebenezer Wilder, John Vogan, Joseph S. White, and Robert Glenn (Slippery Rock, Pennsylvania). Later supporters (January 1857) included James Donaldson, New Castle, William and James Cotton, Pulaski, and G. Allen New Wilmington.

In a letter dated March 4, 1856 published in the *Herald of Freedom*, Leasure stated that he felt a deep and at times painful interest in Brown's welfare, paper, and cause.

> "May you thus live, and print and if need be fight for the good time is coming and when it does come, millions of hearts will throb in unison with yours, with the free State men of Kansas, with the advanced guards of freedom's cohorts. Yours for a Free State."
>
> D. Leasure

Fear for Brown's safety was well founded. Elijah P. Lovejoy, a former Presbyterian minister and publisher of an Anti–Slavery paper had been murdered in 1837 in Illinois by a Pro–Slavery mob that destroyed his printing press and Abolitionist materials.

At the February meeting, the New Castle–Kansas Aid group resolved to set up a fund to defray the costs of actual settlers who might desire to preempt land claims and to

> "equip them as may be needed for the defence of their rights as American citizens."[2]

Dr. Leasure, William McClymonds, J. Reynolds, R. W. Stewart and William H. Shaw were appointed to receive contributions and collect names of emigrants to report at a subsequent meeting. Reverend R. A. Browne, J. Reynolds, Reverend A. B. Bradford and others unanimously adopted the measure. S. Robinson, S. D. Doulton and D. W. Freemen entered their names as volunteers for Kansas. In April 1856 a party of 21 persons left New Castle for Kansas, Lawrence County residents Henry Williams and Dr. William Shaw among them.

BEECHER'S BIBLES

MUCH OF THE "defence" referred to above took the form of Sharpe's rifles. It is quite possible that Leasure's reference to his gift of a "Bible" to Brown was not typical scripture, but a breech–loading Sharpe's rifle. "Beecher's Bible" was the name given to Sharpe's rifles by Abolitionists.[3,4]

Henry W. Beecher, New England minister and Abolitionist, believed the Sharpe's Rifle was a

> "truly moral agency, and that there was more moral power in one of those instruments, so far as the slaveholders of Kansas were concerned, than in a hundred Bibles…they have a supreme respect for the logic that is embodied in Sharp's(sic) rifle."[5]

JOHN SPEER AND THE KANSAS PIONEER

G. W. BROWN WAS NOT the only local journalist to go to Kansas. Another was John Speer, the fearless champion and acknowledged leader of the Free–State movement.

Speer and his brother Joseph L. settled in Lawrence, Kansas, on September 27, 1854. They published the first issue of the *Kansas Pioneer* shortly afterward. The *Pioneer* thus became the second newspaper published in Kansas, both supporting the Anti–Slavery cause.[7]

Despite numerous threats to his safety as a reult of his fearless advocacy, he remained steadfast in his desire to make Kansas a free state.

BORDER RUFFIANS: 1855

THE FIRST KANSAS territorial elections in March 1855 were fraught with fraud. "Border Ruffians" came by the thousands from Missouri, overran every election precinct but one, replaced legally appointed election judges with their own, and drove away legal voters.[8]

The Pro–Slavery movement won a majority of seats and sent a Pro–Slavery delegation to Congress. The first act of the Council and House of Representatives was to deny seats to Free–State men who had legally won election, filling their positions with Pro–Slavery opponents.

This Kansas legislature passed a number of pro-slavery statutes which were commonly referred to as "bogus statutes passed by a bogus legislature." The outrageous laws against would-be emancipators included one with three provisions prescribing death, three requiring imprisonment for not less than ten years or death at the jury's discretion, three mandating imprisonment for not less than five years, and

John Speer

John Speer was born in Kittanning, Armstrong County, Pennsylvania, on December 27, 1817 to Captain and Mrs. Robert Speer. He owned the Mercer and the Beaver Democrat published in New Castle, Pennsylvania, which supported the principles of the Whig party.

In 1853, Speer declared that the Whig party had outlived its usefulness and severed his connection. When the Nebraska–Kansas Act passed, he joined the Free–State cause and left for Kansas.

Speer was a member of the first free-state Territorial Legislature and introduced the first bill to establish a civil code in Kansas.

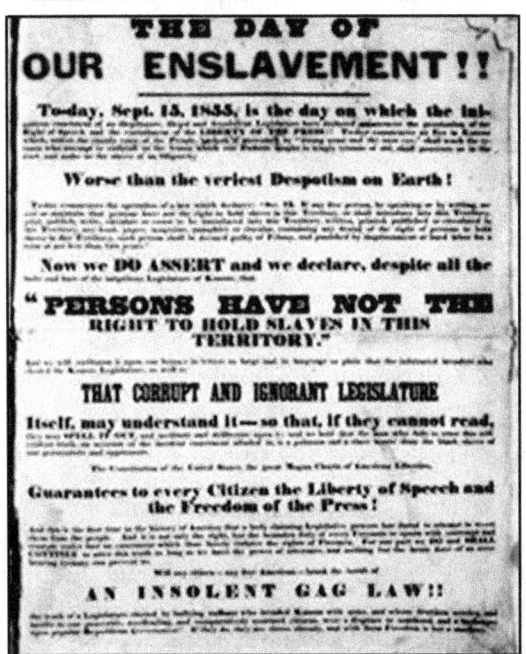

The Speer Defy

two authorizing imprisonment for not less than two years.[9]

The legislature also restricted citizens' constitutional right to free speech, providing that any person who spoke or wrote against the right to own slaves in Kansas were guilty of a felony punishable by imprisonment and hard labor for two years minimum.[10]

THE SPEER DEFY

IN REACTION TO THIS power grab, John Speer published what has come to be known as the *Speer Defy*:

> "We assert and declare despite all the bolts and burrs of the iniquitous legislature of Kansas, that persons have not the right to hold slaves in this territory, and for our part we shall utter this truth, so long as we have the power of utterance, and nothing but the brute force of an overbearing tyranny can prevent us."[11]

THE TOPEKA CONSTITUTIONAL CONVENTION

ANTI–SLAVERY SETTLERS largely ignored the Territorial government. The Topeka Constitutional Convention met and drafted the Topeka Constitution and established its own provisional government. James H. Lane was made President. The new Free State Executive Committee appointed G. W. Brown, editor of the *Herald of Freedom* newspaper, as its agent to pursue immediate admission of Kansas under the provisions of the Topeka Constitution.[12]

On February 11, 1856, President Pierce and his Pro–Slavery administration denounced the convention and the government it formed, and declared it was insurrectionary, revolutionary and treasonous. He ordered its leaders to be arrested and punished.[13]

"Prison" illustration showing George W. Brown (far left) next to John Brown, Jr.

G. W. Brown was charged with high treason and jailed in May. A week later, on the morning of May 21, 1856 a *posse comitatus* of some 800 Pro–Slavery Border Ruffians led by a U.S. Marshal descended upon Lawrence.

The mob proceeded to systematically destroy the town. Lawrence with its Free presses had become the capital of the Anti–Slavery state of Kansas, and a target. The town's printing presses were destroyed. The *Herald of Freedom's* offices being among them, its types were thrown into the river, all printing machinery and supplies were destroyed.

The following speech given to Border Ruffians by David R. Atchison, Acting Vice President pro tempore of the United States, *during* the raid, provides a window into the times:

> Boys, this day I am a Kickapoo Ranger, by God! This day we have entered Lawrence with "Southern Rights" inscribed upon our banner, and not one damned Abolitionist dared to fire a gun. Now, boys, this is the happiest day of my life. We have entered that damned town, and taught the damned Abolitionists a Southern lesson that they will remember till the day they die. And now, boys, we will go again, with our highly honorable Jones, and test the strength of that damned Free–State Hotel, and teach the Emigrant Aid Company that Kansas shall be ours. Boys, ladies should, and I hope will, be respected by every gentleman. But when a woman takes upon herself the garb of a soldier by carrying a Sharp's rifle, then she is no longer worthy of respect. Trample her under your feet as you would a snake. Come on, boys. Now do your duty to yourselves and your Southern friends. Your duty I know you will do. If one man or woman dare stand before you, blow them to hell with a chunk of cold lead.[14]

With this act, the town of Lawrence became the first casualty in America's Civil War that would not officially be declared until five years later. This attack sparked a bloody guerrilla war in Kansas that lasted for months.

The soon–to–be infamous Abolitionist John Brown, once a resident of Crawford County, Pennsylvania, had a number of sons that answered the call and moved to Kansas with their families. Brown received word sometime prior to the raid that the families there were completely unprepared to face attack, and that Pro–Slavery forces there were militant. Determined to protect his family and oppose the advances of slavery supporters, Brown left for Kansas, enlisting a son–in–law and making several stops just to collect funds and weapons.

In response to the sacking of Lawrence, John Brown led a small band of men to Pottawatomie Creek on May 24, 1856. The men dragged five unarmed men and boys, believed to be slavery proponents, from their homes and brutally murdered them. Afterwards, Brown raided Missouri–freeing eleven slaves and killing the slave owner.

George W. Brown was imprisoned along with John Brown's son and held on charges of high treason. John Brown, Jr. was released the following June.

Excitement rose to a great pitch during the time the Kansas–Nebraska bill passed Congress back home in Lawrence County, Pennsylvania. Old John Brown's famous midnight raid at Harper's Ferry took place on October 17, 1859. He was tried and found guilty of treason and hanged on December 2, 1859. The excitement at the time of his hanging was also quite intense. There were times when the few southern sympathizers in New Castle were in danger.[15, 17]

On April 12, 1861 the Confederate forces fired upon the US Army installation at Fort Sumter in Charleston Harbor, South Carolina. Civil war had officially begun. Shortly afterwards, on April 28, 1861 in Youngstown, Ohio two separate canal boat operators reported that John Brown, Jr. had encamped near Beaver Creek mid–way between New Castle and the Ohio river and was training several hundred negro troops in military drill. It was further rumored that they were destined for Virginia for vindication of their race and in support of the Union.[16] It should be noted that Blacks were not permitted to serve in the Federal service until July 1862 and not permitted to serve in combat until January 1863 when Lincoln signed the Emancipation Proclamation.

Meanwhile, in the pre–dawn hours of August 21, 1863, while its inhabitants slept, guerrilla forces led by William Quantrill entered Lawrence, Kansas with bloody intent. By 9 A.M. a city of 3,000 was burned to the ground and nearly 200 civilians massacred.

John Speer witnessed the destruction and sought refuge for his family in a cornfield. Rebels stole his horses and set fire to his home. When they moved on, Mrs. Speer and her youngest children were able to extinguish the fire. Three of their boys had stayed overnight at the downtoan offices of the *Journal*, the *Tribune*, and *Lawrence Republican*, all owned by Speer.

John Speer, Jr., aged 19, started home from his *Tribune* office when the rebels arrived. A printer tried to induce him to hide in a nearby well, but the Junior Speer insisted on returning to defend his family. He was stopped and his money demanded.

He handed over his wallet and was immediately shot by Reverend Larkin M. Skaggs of Cass County, Missouri, a Baptist minister who had taken an active part in numerous and the May 1856 sacking of Lawrence. As Speer lay in pain a few feet from a burning house, the heat became so intense he asked one of the guerrillas to move him. The man shot him through the head.

Robert Speer, aged 18, and another printer were asleep in his *Republican* office when the raid began. The building was burned and no trace of two boys' bodies was ever found.

Mrs. Speers gave her 15 year-old son, William, a rifle and told him to go out and shoot some rebels. The boy hid behind some bushes and, as Skaggs walked past, shot him in the shoulder. An Indian friend who accompanied Willy followed up his shot with another, killing Skaggs.

The crimes committed that day were horrendous. Pro-Slavery forces entered a recruit camp and murdered 18 of 23 unarmed boys, many still in their tents. Some of Quantrill's men rousted a local boarding house's residents and were about to set fire to it when they were informed a Negro baby was in the house. Their response was, "we will burn the G__d d___d little brat up," and they did.[18, 19, 20]

Quantrill's would later claim that his attack was retaliation for an unauthorized Union attack on Osceola, Missouri in September 1861. That attack had been led by Colonel James H. Lane. Nine men were court martialed and executed, the town plundered, and hundreds of slaves emancipated.

Chapter Notes

1. "Diary of James R. Stewart," *Kansas Historical Quarterly, Vol. 17 No. 1*, February 1949. www.kshs.org
2. Fear for his safety was well founded. Elijah P. Lovejoy, a former Presbyterian minister and publisher of an Anti-Slavery paper was murdered in 1837 in Illinois by a Pro-Slavery mob that destroyed his printing press and abolitionist materials.
3. *Biographical Sketches of Leading Citizens Lawrence County*, 17.
4. "The Reverend Dr. Browne Goes to His Reward," *New Castle Weekly Herald*, May 21, 1902, 2.
5. "The Sharps Rifle Episode in Kansas History," *The American Historical Review, Vol. 12*, April 1, 1907 (quoting from the *New York Tribune*, February 8, 1856, 6), 547.
6. Hazen, 70.
7. *Garnett Journal*, Dec. 21, 1906; Collections of the Kansas State Historical Society, Volume 10, By Kansas State Historical Society, 480-484 (1907-1908).
8. Brown, G. W., "The Truth at Last: History Corrected" *Reminiscences of Old John Brown* (1880), 15.
9. Chiorazzi, JD, MLL *Pre-statehood Legal Materials: A Fifty-State Research Guide, Vol. 1*, (2013) 411-412.
10. Speer, John, "Life of Gen. James H. Lane", *Liberator of Kansas*, 1896, 21.
11. *The Kansas Tribune*, September 15, 1855.
12. Certificate of appointment of G.W. Brown as agent for the Kansas Executive Committee, December 10, 1855 (TerritorialKansasonline.org); "Life of Gen. James H. Lane, Liberator of Kansas," By John Speer (1896) 47-48.
13. History of the State of Kansas, Territorial History, Part 30 (Kansas Collection books at www.kancoll.org)
14. Speer, John, *Life of Gen. James H. Lane, Liberator of Kansas*, J. Speer, Printer. Garden City, Kansas. 1896, 24.
15. *New Castle Daily News*, March 5, 1897, p. 5-6. The Wilbur H. Siebert Underground Railroad Collection, State Library of Ohio.
16. "John Brown, Jr., Preparing for an Irruption upon Virginia" *The Cass County Republican* (Dowagiac, Michigan), May 9, 1861 (from the *Cleveland Herald*, April 28, 1861).
17. "John Brown, Jr.," *Raftsman's Journal* (Clearfield, Pennsylvania) May 8, 1861, 2.
18. "Saw Fiery Times John Speer, Pioneer, Talks of Quantrell and Lane," *The Topeka Daily Capital*, September 3, 1901
19. "Lawrence in Ashes," *The Emporia Weekly News*, August 29, 1863
20. Connelley, William Elsey, *Quantrill and the Border Wars*. Torch Press. 1910, 355, 381.
21. United States Census: Pennsylvania, Lawrence County, 1850, 1860.
22. *History of New Castle and Lawrence County Pennsylvania and Representative Citizens, 1908*, 42, 164, 194-196.

7
ABOLITIONISTS AND CONDUCTORS

ABOLITIONISM

FROM THE 1830s through the American Civil War, the Abolitionists' goal was to achieve immediate emancipation of slaves and an end to racial segregation. The sentiment was nothing new, having been voiced since the American Revolution in the North, and in the Upper South during the 1820s, but the 1830's saw a coalescing of anti-slavery factions into a militant crusade.

The previous decade had seen the advent of manufacturing and commerce, which displaced many workers and tempted citizens with soulless consumerism. Evangelical movements arose to guide society through these morally troubling times. Preachers such as Lyman Beecher, Nathaniel Taylor, and Charles G. Finney gave rise to what would be called the Second Great Awakening. Religious revivals incited rebellion against the dehumanization of workers while generating reform sentiment in the areas of temperance, pacifism, and women's rights.

The movement also poured fuel onto the Abolitionist flame. By the early 1830s, prominent preachers Theodore D. Weld, William Lloyd Garrison, Arthur and Lewis Tappan, and Elizur Wright, Jr., had rallied to the cause of "immediate emancipation."

Historians debate the extent of Abolitionist political influence, but the movement's impact on northern culture is clear. The impassioned speeches of Frederick Douglass, Wendell Phillips, and Lucy Stone, the poetry of John Greenleaf Whittier and James Russell Lowell, and the autobiographies of fugitive slaves such as Douglass were particularly strong influencers of the mentality of the time.

Abolitionists were particularly important to the religious climate of the time, tearing apart the Methodists and Baptists while birthing a number of independent Anti-Slavery "free churches." Abolitionists founded racially integrated Oberlin College, the Oneida Institute, and Illinois' Knox College.

In Pennsylvania, passage of the 1780 Gradual Abolition of Slavery Act fomented anti–slavery sentiment. As Southern slavery increased, God–fearing Lawrence County citizens took to the pulpits to speak out against the practice.

In 1847, Western Pennsylvanian and Eastern Ohio Presbyterians broke from parent churches and formed the Free Presbyterian Synod to govern the new Free Presbyteries.

Political parties, such as the Free–Soil party also formed in protest to slavery. The political agenda differed from religiously motivated movements, but the two prongs of attack worked to bring issues of slavery and equality to the forefront of national discussion throughout the 1830's, 40's, and 50's.[1]

Underground Railroad Routes

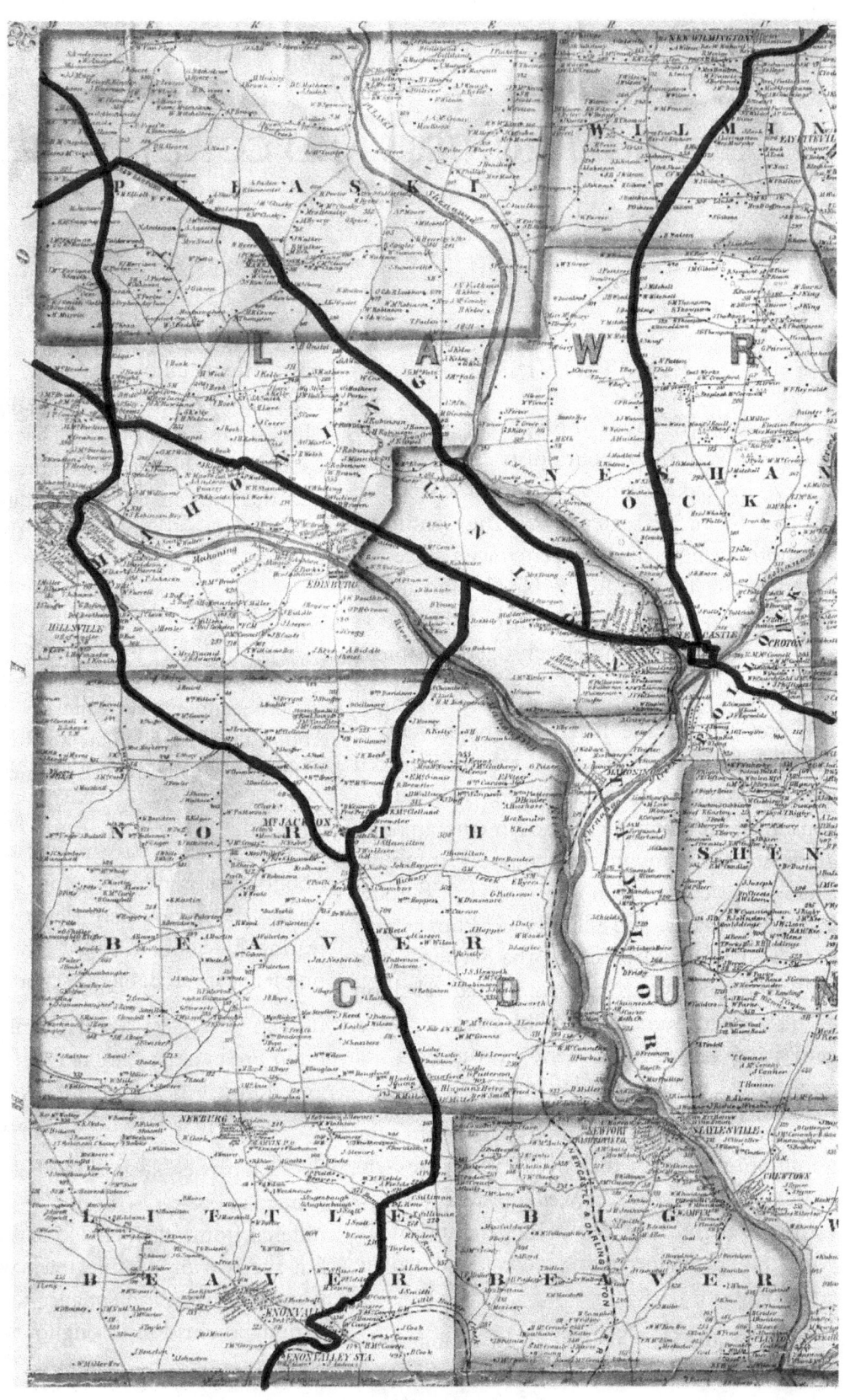

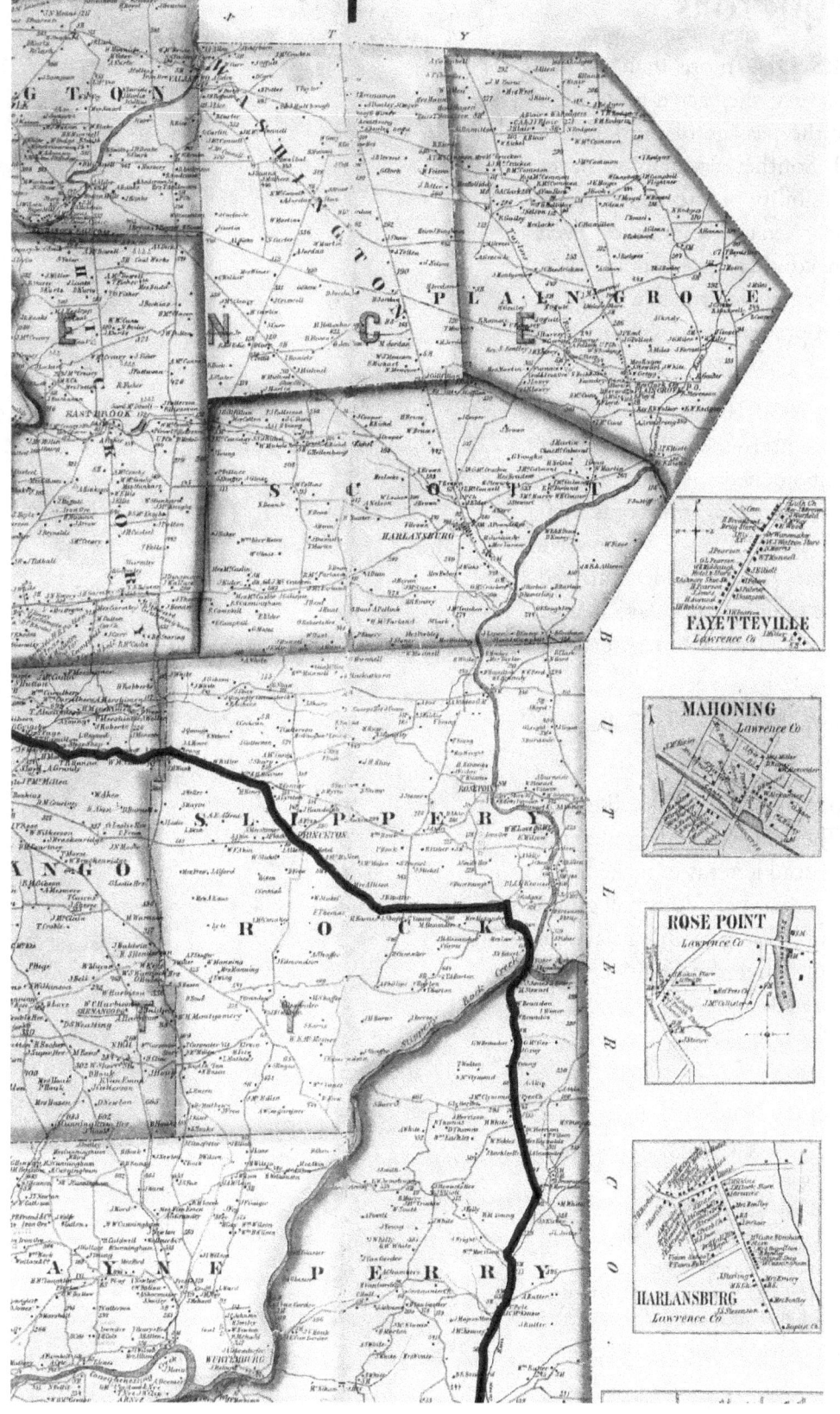

Lawrence County Pennsylvania

CONDUCTORS

CONDUCTORS DID more than mouth objections to slavery, they acted upon their convictions. Before the passage of the Fugitive Salve Law in 1850, Southerners helping slaves escape faced the possibility of late-night arrests, jail sentences, torture, and sometimes even lynching. Northern conductors faced no such threat, though slave catchers armed with guns, knives and whips did present the possibility of a violent encounter.

After passage of the 1850 law, even Northern conductors found themselves eligible for fines and jail time. Emboldened by this victory, slave hunters became more aggressive as well, increasing the potential for violence. When slave catchers Robert Stump and Peter Heck arrived in Blairsville in 1858 looking for a slave named "Newton," townspeople defended him by beating up the two men.[2]

A college student was shot at Iberia College in Ohio while trying to protect a slave.[3]

During an 1852 speech in Pittsburgh, Fredrick Douglas stated, "The only way to make the Fugitive Slave Law a dead letter is to make half a dozen or more dead kidnappers."[4] A small group would take the risk of helping escaping slaves in New Castle, especially after the Fugitive Slave Law was enacted in 1850.

Chapter Notes

1. *Abolitionist Movement*, http://www.history.com/topics/black-history/abolitionist-movement
2. http://www.undergroundrailroadblairsvillepa.com/Rescue1858.php
3. White, Joseph S., "Joseph S. White tells of Reverend George Gordon (Ohio–Morrow County)" (two page undated letter). Sierbert Collection, State Library of Ohio.
4. http://www.lib.rochester.edu/index.cfm?PAGE=4385

8

NEW CASTLE BOROUGH

"To use a slang phrase, New Castle was a red hot Abolition town."

New Castle News March 8, 1899.

EARLY IN 1798, JOHN Carlysle Stewart, with two brothers–in–law, John and Hugh Wood, and John McWhorter—all from the neighborhood of New Castle, Delaware—settled on the land where New Castle stands. John Stewart owned the land upon which the town was laid out and built a log cabin at what was known as the Falls spring.[1]

New Castle was made a borough March 25, 1825.[2] By the 1840s, the city consisted of

"one rolling mill, one nail factory that could manufacture ten tons of iron and three tons of nails per day; one flour mill with four pairs of burrs; one lumber mill with two saws; also one lumber mill, building, to go by steam; one woolen manufactory; one air foundry; one cupola foundry, driven by steam power; eight dry good stores; two groceries; one hardware store; two drug shops; four taverns; three tanneries; five cooper shops; five cabinet shops; six smith shops; one gun shop; one tin and copper shop; two wagon shops; four tailor shops; four forwarding warehouses; three hatter shops; four shoemaker shops; two saddler shops; one female seminary; three day schools; one writing school; one shovel factory; one refinery; six coal banks; an abundance of iron ore; one water power dam on Neshannock Creek."[3]

In 1858, Hon. John W. Forney published the following description of New Castle in the *Philadelphia Press*.

"We were not prepared to see a thriving island city of 7,000 inhabitants on our visit some months since to the county of Lawrence—a city of broad streets, large brick dwellings, noble schoolhouses, comfortable residences and immense manufactories. It is beautifully located, reminding one of Pittsburgh in its abundance of coal and iron and in its swarthy complexion. Yet it is fresher far than its dusky neighbor. There is an air of health in all the natural surroundings. In its romantic streams and the lovely valley in which it lies embosomed it possesses advantages of which Pittsburg cannot boast."[4]

CRAWFORD WHITE'S BRICK HOUSE

THERE ARE FEW stories about New Castle residents helping slaves in the early years of the Underground Railroad. Crawford White's home was central to one of those stories. He built the first brick house in New Castle. According to Jonathan Keller, who had hauled bricks to the Jefferson Street School construction, David Hendrickson made the brick used for this house in 1808. The house was located on the second lot north of Grant Street, today 310 North Jefferson Street.[5]

While Joseph S. White, Crawford's son, insisted that his experience with the Underground Railroad was limited, he did recall a few incidents when they lived in "the brick house near the 'big willow tree'."⁶

A colored man approached him from the sidewalk, "looking in all directions, just as a wild turkey would do scenting danger." White made it clear that he was a friend and offered the man a place to stay for the night. The man was fearful, but accepted, and the next morning resumed travelling northward.

Next came a visitor from the Georgian coast, a tall man with straight hair, "a mixture of Indian and Negro," who worked as a ship's carpenter. The fugitive said he had made two previous escape attempts, and had been captured both times in the mountains. To prevent further escapes his owners chained a ball to his leg. White wrote that the ankle had "healed but left a depression in the muscle half an inch or more in depth." White offered him a place to stay that night. In the morning, the man headed north toward the next station.⁷

By 1849, the building was vacant and in disrepair.

> "The first meeting of the Masonic brethren in the city of New Castle was held July, 1849, in the old Crawford White homestead, a brick dwelling situated in what is now the northeast corner of Jefferson and Grant Street. It is presumed that the brethren chose a place far out of the way and so undesirable as was the old deserted homestead, dilapidated and falling into ruin, because of a desire on their part to secure more secrecy and security."

When the house was torn down, some of the brick was used to build a chimney for Watson Dinsmore's house on New Castle's west side.⁸

COVENANTERS PREACHED AGAINST SLAVERY

AS EARLY AS 1825, a small group of "Society People," or "Covenanters," met in houses in the vicinity of New Castle. The Covenanters preached against slavery. In New Castle, they

---

Reverend Thomas Hannay / Hanna

Thomas Hannay was born near Kilmarnock, Ayreshire, Scotland on August 14, 1806. Raised a Covenanter, he graduated from the University of Glasgow in 1832. He studied theology in the Paisley Seminary and was licensed by the Glasgow Presbytery on March 4, 1835.

In the summer of 1841 he came to America and was received on October 6, 1841 as a Synod licentiate. He was installed as pastor of Conococheague Church in Fayetteville, Franklin County in December 1842 and served until October 1844.

On November 17, 1852 Hannay was installed as the first regular pastor of the Rose Point Reformed Presbyterian Church, Slippery Rock Congregation, and his first wife, Mrs. Elizabeth (Mowry) McCracken, was buried there two years later. He also ministered at New Castle's Reformed Presbyterian Church.

In 1860 Hannay and his second wife, Margaret Sproull, were living in the borough of New Castle. On October 29, 1861 he resigned from the New Castle Church. He later married his third wife, Catherine McGilvray of Wellsville, Ohio.

Hannay died in June 1881 after moving to Sullivan, Canada. Catherine survived him. He is buried in the Presbyterian graveyard at Chatsworth, Canada.²⁸

were led by Reverend Robert Gibson and George Scott. Reverend James Blackwood became pastor in 1834, with David Pattison as elder. In 1852, Reverend Thomas Hanna became Pastor in both New Castle and Slippery Rock until 1863. George Boggs and Robert Speer were added as elders.[9]

Joseph S. White included Hanna (Hannay) in one of his stories, relating that when a large wagonload of escaping slaves arrived from Portersville, Hanna approached Joseph with the news. Joseph conferred with this wife, and they agreed to hide half of the slaves. The rest were scattered among trusted friends.

ALVIRA FIGHTS THE SLAVE CATCHER

JOSEPH S. WHITE ENJOYED telling stories of the Underground Railroad years. In a letter to his children, he related the story of a colored woman arriving in New Castle in the 1840s to seek employment. She was hired by Andrew Lewis, who kept a tavern in a three-story building on the north side of Washington Street between the Diamond and Mercer Street, where the Saint Cloud Hotel would later stand.

After she had been employed for some time, a slaveholder recognized her. When he had finished his meal, he took hold of her, and she cried for help. Mr. Lewis was not there at the time, but his daughter, Alvira, came to the rescue, beating the man with a broom until Jackson Evans, a wagon maker passing by, heard the commotion and came to her aid. Mr. Evans punched the slave owner, knocking him down. Alvira secreted the woman away. In the end, the slave master was happy to get away with his life.

White writes:

> "The remarkable thing about this woman's deliverance is, that it was accomplished by uncompromising

Robert W. Clendenin

Robert W. Clendenin was born on the family farm in Cumberland County, Pennsylvania and moved to New Castle in 1840 at the age of 15. He worked at a dry goods store, eventually starting his own business, R.W. Clendenin & Sons, at the corner of Mercer and Washington Streets in New Castle.

In 1846, Clendenin married Belinda Pollock, and they had five children. Joseph, died in infancy and John died as a teen in 1870. William joined his father in the business.

Clendenin was elected School Director in 1853, and Councilman in 1856.[29] During the Civil War, when it was learned that Morgan's Raiders were headed toward New Castle, R. W. Clendenin rode 40 miles with great haste, scouting Morgan's location and later reporting of his capture. Clendenin was not a Conductor, but made a habit of looking the other way when escaping slaves came through town.[30]

R. W. Clendenin died at his New Castle home on February 7, 1905.[31]

Belinda (Pollock) Clendenin

Belinda Clendenin was the daughter of Joseph Pollock, and sister to Adaline Pollock, wife of Station Agent and Conductor, Joseph S. White. In 1851, R. W. and Belinda, named a son Wells Bushnell after the Conductor, Reverend Wells Bushnell. She was a member of the New Castle Free Presbyterian Church.[32]

Belinda Clendenin died on April 28, 1907 at her New Castle home.[33]

R. W. Clendenin & Sons (far right)

Democrats, who were not often found working in harmony with Underground Railroad people, but generally the slaveholder. This time their better feelings triumphed."[10]

CLENDENIN LOOKS THE OTHER WAY

R. W. CLENDENIN & SONS was established at the corner of Mercer and Washington Streets in 1848 by Robert Clendenin. The store carried dry goods, notions, carpets, draperies, oil cloth and other goods. His son, William, later joined the business. Clendenin was not a Conductor for the Underground Railroad, but had a habit of looking the other way when escaping slaves traveled through town.

A New Castle News article stated:

> "The other station, still in existence was a cellar, under the building in the rear of the store of R.W. Clendenin, who then used it as a residence. This building is located on the corner of North Mercer Street and the first alley north of Washington Street. The cellar was located under the kitchen. When Clendenin was questioned concerning this cellar, the existence of which is unknown even to the occupants of the house, he said that while he himself had nothing to do with the working of the 'railroad,' he did not doubt that some of his friends could tell of colored people they had concealed there. A twinkle in Mr. Clendenin's eyes as he said this suggested that he might not have been ignorant of what his friends were doing with his cellar. Mr. Clendenin, who although a Democrat, was an Abolitionist, entertained vivid recollections of the excitement that prevailed during the days before the war, and particularly during the time that the Kansas–Nebraska bill was before congress."[11, 12]

PRESBYTERIANS BREAK AWAY

THE FIRST PRESBYTERIAN Church was the first congregation to form in the city, being located in a lean-to next to a stream on a hill above the city, then in a log cabin. By the 1830s, the church was located in a brick building and had about 100 members who were faithful and God fearing in their attitudes. One of those members was Amzi Semple. In 1837 the First Presbyterian Church opened its Sabbath school under his able superintendency. In 1843, as a member of the church's building committee,

Amzi burnt brick for the new church on the Miller Farm two miles west of town.[13]

> "Mr. Semple seems to have been among the moving spirits of the project. It is told of him that while the fires were burning in the kiln, the wood pile ran short on Sabbath, and Amzi came to town post haste to notify the people that they must turn out at once or the brick would be ruined, and Sunday all number of teams were dispatched immediately to haul more wood."[14]

All was not at peace within the church. The question of slavery would lead to debates and then a fracture in the membership. The Free Church of the Presbytery of Mahoning was organized October 20, 1847 in response to the slavery debate.

> "As the Free-Soil Party was a political, so this organization was a religious protest against the iniquities of American Slavery."[15]

Unable to agree with the church's stance, Amzi Semple, became an active abolitionist and conductor on the Underground Railroad. Many members of Presbyterian Church broke away to form their own Free Presbyterian congregation. They began with a small group of dedicated Abolitionists in 1851.

Founding Members

Church Founders: John Emory, Catherine Emory, Alexander S. Hawthorne, White McMillen, Sarah E. McMillen, Mary McMillen, S. W. Mitchell, Mary J. Mitchell, Jane T. Pearson, Annie Semple, Martha Semple, Eliza W. Semple, Mary Semple Mitchell, James Stephenson, Margaret J. Stephenson, Jane Tidball, Joseph S. White, and Adeline White.

By 1855, the Free Presbyterian congregation boasted more than 80 members.

Record of Elders and Members 1855

Pastors: Wells Bushnell and A.B. Bradford.[16]

Alexander & Mary (McMurray) Hawthorne

Alexander Hawthorne moved from Cumberland County, Pennsylvania, and built the first hotel in New Castle about 1804. The Exchange Hotel was located at the southwest corner of North and Mercer Streets. It was later nicknamed the Pokeberry Exchange after an iron ore based paint turned it purple. He married Mary McMurray in 1807 and they had five children, James, Eliza J., Joseph, Alexander S., and Samuel Sample.

He sold the Exchange Hotel to Frederick Reinhold about 1840 and purchased a farm in southern Neshannock Township near what is now Wilmington Road. By 1850, Alexander and his wife were in their mid-seventies. Mary died in 1854, and Alexander married Cynthia Locke, who lived until 1860. Alexander Hawthorne died in 1864.[34]

Henry & Jane T. Pearson

In 1850, Henry and Jane Pearson lived in Neshannock Township with nine children. Henry was a trustee of the New Castle Female Seminary in 1839, along with Amzi Semple and Charles T. Whippo.[35]

State Commissioners appointed Pearson to survey the original Lawrence County boundaries in 1849.[36] In 1854, he purchased property from Peebles and McCormick to build a dam and gristmill to complement a saw mill he had owned since 1833. He operated these businesses through 1868, then sold the gristmill to his sons, Bevan and Warner Pearson, and son-in-law, Captain J. M. Clapp. He sold the saw mill to J. Harvey and Company.[37]

James & Margaret J. Stephenson

The Stephensons were founding members of the Buffalo Free Presbyterian Church (later Worthington Church) in Armstrong County, Pennsylvania. They lived in New Castle on North Mercer Street by 1855, but there is little documentation of their lives.[38]

Jane Tidball

In 1850, Jane Ann Tidball resided along Neshannock Creek with two sisters, Margaret and Mary, near the corner of East Street and what was then Water Street. Jane was probably David Tidball's sister.

Jane remained unmarried and died in 1858.[39]

Elders: William Bonnell, Charles Carothers, John Emery, Stephen M. Justice, White McMillen, S. W. Mitchell, James Moffatt, Thomas Morse, R. W. Stewart, John Taylor, and Joseph S. White.

Members: William Bonnell, Mrs. Emma Boyles, Mrs. Wells Bushnell, Miss Bushnell, C. Carothers, Belinda Clendenin, Joseph Clifton, Jacob Condict, Mrs. Ruth Condict, David Craig, R. W. Cunningham, Mrs. Mary J. Davis, Isaac Dickson, J. Douthett, Mrs. Catherine Emery, J. N. Euwer, Wilson Falls, M. Gentz, W. W. Gibson, James Gilleland, A. S. Hawthorne, Susan Henderson, Andrew Holtin, John Horner, Mrs. Mary L. Johnson, D. Leasure, John Mayberry, William McClymonds, John McElevy, Robert McGuffin, L. L. McGuffin, Mrs. Sarah McMillen, Mary McMillian, D. N. McNeath, Mrs. Mary Mitchell, James Moffatt, Frances I. Moffett, William J. Moffett, S. Montgomery, James Moorhead, Harriet Moorhead, Mrs. Amanda Moorhead, G. C. Morgan, Thomas Morse, D. Nelson, Henry Pearson, Mrs. Jane T. Pearson, S. Pearson, Robert Reynolds, J. R. Richardson, George P. Robinson, C. C. Sankey, Mrs. Eliza W. Semple, Martha Semple, Annie Semple, Maggie Sheal, Lydia J. Sherer, James Stephenson, Sarah E. Stephenson, Mrs. Eliza Stephenson, Anna J. Stewart, Rachel Stright, John Taylor, E. M. Thomas, David Tidball, Jane Tidball, Mrs. Sarah Wallace, David D. Waugh, W. S. Warnock, Mrs. Elizabeth Warnock, F. Weigert, James Westerman, Adaline White, Mrs. Sarah M. White, Dr. N. White, Josiah C. White, Shubael Wilder, John C. Wilson, James H. Woods, and Mrs. Mary Young.

Others with abolitionist sentiments read the publications of the time.

Supporters of the Free Presbyterian Newspaper

William Bonnell, A. B. Bradford, C. Carothers, R. W. Cunningham, John Emery, J. N. Euwer, Susan Henderson, John Horner, Reverend Josiah Hutchman, S. W. Mitchell, James Moorhead, Thomas Morse, Mrs. McCombs, D. N. McNeath, White McMillen, James Moffatt, S. Montgomery, D. Nelson, S. R. Patterson & Son, H. Pearson, E. M. Thomas, George P. Robinson, Miss Anne J. Stewart, Jane Tidball, W. S. Warnock, Joseph S. White, Josiah C. White, Dr. N. White, Mrs. Mary Young.

Supporters of the Free Presbyterian Portfolio (1860–1861) Newspaper

C. Blakely, C. Carothers, Joseph Clifton, J. Douthett, Wilson Falls, W. Gantz, W. W. Gibson, James Gilleland, John Mayberry, White McMillen, R. Reynolds, F. Veigart, E. Warnock, Joseph White, Josiah C. White, John G. Wilson, James R. Woods, Mrs. Mary Young.

Others associated with the Free Presbyterian Church

R. W. Cunningham, William McClymonds and Shubael Wilder helped with financial council early in the church's formation. They were not members at the time, but William McClymonds joined the church after the Civil War when it became Central Presbyterian Church.

JUDGE WHIPPO BRINGS SPEAKERS TO THE CITY

IN 1853, GARRISONIAN speakers Charles S. Griffing and his wife, Josephine, held two Anti–Slavery meetings in the Lawrence County courthouse to discuss moral and political action with the Free Soilers. The events were largely facilitated by prominent New Castle

Dr. Charles T. & Althea (Warner) Whippo

Charles T. Whippo was born in Washington County, New York, in 1793. He studied medicine under Dr. John Thompson, practiced in New York, and married Althea Ann Warner in 1818. Mathematics and engineering held a greater attraction for him than medicine, and he gave up his medical practice to work on the Erie Canal.

Upon moving his family to Lawrence County, he purchased two large tracts of land. Part of these holdings, some 250 acres, later became part of the city of New Castle.

In October of 1849, Whippo was elected Associate Judge for the county and served a full term of five years. In 1855, he became the first president of the Bank of New Castle, and was instrumental in organizing the New Castle Female Seminary.

It was said that he had

"...a fine library, and was an untiring student. He became interested in the study of the subject of electricity, purchased an electrical apparatus, and had a practical knowledge of the science as far as it was understood in his day."[40]

Charles and Althea were liberal when it came to religious matters, and Republican in their politics. Althea subscribed to the Garrisonian publication, *The Anti–Slavery Bugle*.

Dr. Whippo died in 1858 and Althea in 1865.

Abolitionists, Dr. Charles T. Whippo and his wife Althea (Warner) Whippo.

Griffing spoke highly of the Whippos.

"[O]ur visit to this place left a very pleasant impression on our minds, associated as it will always be with the grateful remembrance of the kindly entertainment we received at the home of Dr. Whippo and his amiable family. Here we found the most happily blended intelligence of the highest order, and a corresponding liberality and freedom of thought and investigation, peace, kindliness and spirituality, that elevates the soul, arms and strengthens it with weapons of truth and love, that only wound to heal, or kill to give a truer, better life."[17]

MERCHANTS STORE MORE THAN DRY GOODS

IN THE 1840S and 1850s, several merchants hid runaway slaves in their homes and places of business.

Euwers Dry Goods

J. N. Euwer & Sons

By 1834 JOHN N. EUWER and his brother, Daniel, had established Euwer's Dry Goods downtown to take advantage of traffic along the new Beaver & Erie Canal. Daniel left the business and another brother, Samuel, took his place. Then Samuel died, leaving John with sole ownership.[18]

In 1842, the store was located at 210 East Washington Street. It was renamed J. N. Euwer & Sons in 1867 when two of John's sons joined the firm. A fire demolished the building in 1873, but it was soon rebuilt on the same lot, now with five stories. John passed away in 1878, and the store was renamed again to J. N. Euwer's Sons' Sons.

John Euwer's obituary states:

> "He was an agent for the Underground Railroad in New Castle, and very frequently would have a number of runaway slaves secreted in his stables and cellars. He also furnished money to start the Promulgator, an Anti–Slavery newspaper established in New Castle."[19]

Henderson's Dry Goods

George Henderson, who married to John Euwer's daughter, owned a dry goods store in the 1850s at the southeast corner of Washington and Mill Streets. One of the best known and most prominent dry goods stores in the region, Henderson's store was located next to Euwer's. The proximity of the two businesses would have been ideal for sneaking slaves from one location into the next.[20]

McMillen's Hat Shop

White McMillen owned a busy New Castle hat business on Jefferson Street, south of the Diamond in 1841.

John N. & Judith K. (Henderson) Euwer

John N. Euwer was born in Allegheny County, Pennsylvania in 1812, and entered the mercantile business at a young age. By 1834 he had made his way to the New Castle area with his brother, Daniel, and they established Euwer's Dry Goods.[41]

In 1855, John was 38 years old and lived at the corner of Mill and North Streets with his wife Judith K. Henderson Euwer, children Joseph, John, Nancy, Daniel, and James, a housekeeper and two store clerks.

Judith was vice President of the Ladies of Lawrence County.[42] John participated in the creation of Lawrence County and was Clerk of the Borough Council, a member of the first Lawrence County Bible Society, original incorporator of National Bank of Lawrence County, a member of the board of directors of the Union Schoolhouse, and a deacon at the New Light Covenanter Church.[43]

By 1872, the family had moved to Croton Avenue.

George & Isabella (Euwer) Henderson

George Henderson was born in Ireland about 1815, and by 1850 was a New Castle merchant married to Isabella Euwer, a farmer's daughter from Plum Township in Allegheny County.

In 1860, George was 48 years old and lived in the city with Isabella and their seven children, Hugh, Nancy, John, Margaret, Mary, Kate and George.

John H. Magee listed George Henderson as an Underground Railroad Conductor.

Known New Castle Conductors

Reverend Wells Bushnell
Eleanor Bushnell
Thomas D. Berry
Mary Berry
George Boggs
John Euwer
Judith Euwer
Daniel Euwer
Reverend Thomas Hannay
George Henderson
Isabella Henderson
White McMillen
Sarah McMillen
Samuel W. Mitchell
Catherine Mitchell
Amzi C. Semple
Mary McMillen Semple
Eli Semple
Anna Semple
Crawford White
Dunlap White
Joseph S. White
Adaline White

White & Sarah McMillen

White McMillen was Joseph White's cousin and Amzi Semple's brother-in-law. He was also a member of the Underground Railroad.

In 1850, McMillen was 45 years old and lived with his wife, Sarah, and seven children, Mary, Joseph, Travis, Clarissa, Belinda, Anna and Ella. They shared their home with a tailor, George Enos, his wife, Ruth, and their one year old son.

In 1860, the children still lived at home. Joseph and Travis were nail cutters and Clara a teacher.

McMillen was a ruling elder for many years at the Free Presbyterian, and then the Second Presbyterian Church. In 1880, he passed away at the age of 75 in his residence on South Jefferson Street, as "one of New Castle's oldest and most highly esteemed citizens."[44]

Samuel W. & Catherine (Raney) Mitchell

Samuel W. Mitchell moved to New Castle from Neshannock, where his family were prominent farmers, and became an undertaker. The 1840 census lists S.W. Mitchell (30–40 years old) with a wife (30–40), three boys and four girls. In the 1841 business directory, S. W. Mitchell is listed as a cabinetmaker. He was also an elder with the Free Presbyterian Church.

By 1850, Samuel Mitchell owned $2400 in real–estate assets. His wife, Catherine, had died, and children residing at home included Mary, William, Martha, Joseph, Clementa, and Samuel Jr. Their house was located on the east side of Mercer Street near the intersection with North Street.

Amzi C. & Mary (McMillen) Semple

Amzi Semple, born on June 17, 1801 in New Castle, became one of the most prominent Underground Railroad personalities in the region. Joseph S. White would later recall him in this manner:

"Amzi C. Semple, I think, was the first and principal hand engaged in this [Underground Railroad] business, and he continued in it as long as he remained in New Castle."

Amzi's parents, Caldwell Sample and Martha Houston married in 1791. Their children included Samuel, Cintha, Uriah, Desmona, Amzi, Artamisa, Smiley, and Catherine. In 1808, after Martha's death, Caldwell married Ann (Nancy) McConaughy and sired five more children, Eli, Martha, Mary, John and Nancy.[45]

Amzi married Mary McMillen, Crawford White's niece, and they had five children, Scott, William, Mary, Carrie and Elizabeth. Amzi is listed in the 1829 New Castle tax roll as a carpenter. In September 1835, he served as secretary at a meeting of New Wilmington citizens convened to consider railroad matters. The group resolved that

"…this meeting believes it proper for the people of Northwestern Pennsylvania to make an effort to connect the harbor at Erie with the Beaver division of the Pennsylvania Canal at New Castle by railroad."[46]

In 1837 Semple becase superintendent of the First Presbyterian Church Sabbath school. He was also a trustee for the New Castle Female Seminary established in 1839.[47]

In 1844, Amzi served as a Congressional Elector at a convention of the Anti–Slavery party of Pennsylvania held in Pittsburgh.[48] He was also listed on an electoral ticket that recommended support of Abolitionists in Pennsylvania in the Philadelphia newspaper, *The American Intelligencer*.[49]

In the early 1850's Amzi moved to Cincinnati. He filed a patent for a windlass in 1852, and patents for vessel paddles and improved presses in 1853, listing his son, William Semple, as assignee. In 1858, he married Mary Johnson and relocated to New York City, where he would file a patent for

"…certain new and useful Improvements in the Manner of Constructing Cast–Iron Bedsteads and other Similar Furniture."

Amzi died in Manhattan at the age of 62 on April 7, 1862 and was buried in Peacham, Vermont. His son, Oliver, born a year before Amzi's death, became an attorney in New York City. Amzi's widow Mary Johnson Semple lived in Massachusetts for a while after this death, and then in New York near Oliver.[50]

Eli & Eliza (Woodard) Semple

Eli Semple, Amzi Semple's half–brother, was born to Caldwell and Ann (Nancy) Semple about 1808. In 1850, he was a 39 year old boatman living in New Castle with wife, Eliza Woodard Semple, son, Sidney, mother, Anna Semple, and sister, Martha. He was a member of the Underground Railroad and a founding member of the Free Presbyterian Church.

His wife, Eliza, was also a founding Member. After Eli's death, she married Silas Stevenson, who raised Eli's two sons, Sidney and Lewis. Eli Semple died in 1853 after a lingering illness.

"Mr. Eli Semple, of New Castle, and age about 45. The deceased was one of our most respectable citizens and much esteemed in the community."[51]

Anna Semple

In the 1850 Census, Anna (Nancy) Semple was a 73–year old widow living with her son, Eli Sample (Semple). "Annie" Semple is listed as one of 29 persons who united the Free Presbyterian Church at its formation in 1851.

When Eli died, Anna became head of a household that included her daughters Martha and Nancy Semple.[52]

She is not found in documentation after the 1860 census, and we assume she died before 1870.

"In good times Mr. McMillen employed three hands besides himself. The market was principally at home, but during the winter months they sometimes manufactured a stock of wool hats for export to Pittsburg and other large towns."[21]

Being a dealer in "hats, caps & furs," his business dealings with Pittsburgh would, have given him the ability to transport escaping slaves from one city to another.

Samuel W. Mitchell Cabinets

Samuel W. Mitchell was a cabinet maker. In 1855, his house was located on the eastside of Mercer Street, near the intersection with North Street. It would have been a convenient stopping place for slaves heading north to New Wilmington.

The Semples: A Family of Conductors

JOSEPH S. WHITE WROTE,

"Amzi Semple, I think, was the first and principle hand engaged in this business, and he continued in it as long as he remained in New Castle."[22]

As an Abolitionist, Semple attended an 1844 convention of the antislavery party.[23] Amzi wasn't the only conductor in the family. His half-brother, Eli, worked as a boatman, and participated as a conductor until his untimely death in 1853.[24] Amzi's mother, Anna, was instrumental in founding the Free Presbyterian Church and was considered part of the inner circle of conductors.

Joseph White Reminisces

ON MARCH 23, 1891, Joseph S. White wrote "Some Reminiscences of Slavery Times" for his children.[25] The article included a list of people engaged in "this business" of the Underground Railroad. He credited Amzi C. Semple as being the principle Conductor in the city. Other active participants were, Reverend Wells Bushnell, White McMillen, S. W. Mitchell, Eli Semple, Daniel Euwer, and John N. Euwer.

"[I]t is a little remarkable that all of them were Presbyterians," White wrote. He also wrote that before he "became identified with the operations of the road, a good many had passed over the New Castle branch," suggesting that he was a late arrival.

In response to the Fugitive Slave Act, White said,

"All over the Free States there were men and women who regarded the law of God above all human enactments."

He referred to slave hunters as "two–legged hounds." He also stated that, "All of this help to fugitives was in violation of the Fugitive Slave Law," indicating that he remained a conductor after 1850.

White wrote about another event that happened "one pleasant afternoon" after he was married. Reverend Thomas Hanna, the Covenanter minister, arrived at their house with news that a wagonload of fugitives had just arrived in New Castle. The group was from Virginia, and White wrote this

"was the last train on this branch road, it being abandoned because of no further need after the breaking out of the rebellion."

After speaking with his wife, White agreed to receive about half of the runaways.

"For you know [Adaline] had a particular faculty for multiplying when there was an urgent necessity."

After a good night's rest, the fugitives met at the Whites' house before dawn. White had borrowed a wagon from Mr. Magee because it was lighter than his own. Two inches of snow had fallen overnight, so the men volunteered to walk up the hill while the women and children rode in the wagon. When they reached the summit, the men climbed aboard and the group made their way to Indian Run on the road to Mercer.

THE WHITE FAMILY

Joseph S. White

Joseph White, the youngest son of Crawford and Elizabeth White, was born on December 29, 1820 into a well-respected and wealthy family. His early years might have been carefree if not for two events.

"At the age of 13, he lost his father, but as soon as he was old enough he assisted his brother James, to whom he was devotedly attached, in various enterprises in which he was engaged."[53]

When James also died, it fell upon Joseph to manage the large interests left by his father and brother. Consequently, he withdrew from his studies in literature at Jefferson College and fully engaged in running the family farming and lumbering businesses.

Joseph and Adeline White were among the founders of the Free Presbyterian Church, and Joseph was a prominent Conductor on the Underground Railroad.

"Very early in his manhood he became an active agitator for the freedom of the slave. He assisted his father in running a 'station' of the 'underground railway.' The White home was a haven of refuge for runaway slaves."

Joseph S. White died in 1913.

Crawford & Elizabeth (Dunlap) White

Crawford White, originally from Cumberland County, Pennsylvania, settled Lot 1953 of the Donation Lands in 1804. Two years later he traveled to Cumberland County to marry Elizabeth Dunlap, and returned to New Castle with his bride.[54] His brothers Josiah C. and David, and the family of their deceased sister, Mary McMillen, also settled there.[55]

Crawford built a cabin and planted young willow trees east of North Jefferson Street on the third lot up from Grant Street. The willows survived into the 1890s.

"Many children have in years past found great pleasure in playful glee on resting beneath their branches."[56]

During the War of 1812, White served at Lake Erie as a member of Captain Fisher's company. In 1818 he built a gristmill and a saw mill near the ground where Raney's grist and flourmill later stood.[57]

White was well educated, often entertained local dignitaries, and important citizens frequently visited to consult with him. White died about 1834 at the age of 60, but Elizabeth lived to the age of 97 years, leaving this world in 1875.

Crawford and Elizabeth had five children, James D., John Crawford, Joseph Semple, Amanda, wife of Dr. Miller Blatchley, and Elizabeth Ann, wife of R. W. Stewart. John Crawford died young while attending Jefferson College, and James D. died at age 45 in the West India Islands.

OF NEW CASTLE

Adaline (Pollock) White

Adaline Pollock was the daughter of Dr. Joseph Pollock and Rachel Morehead. She lived in East Moravia until 1835, when her parents moved to an old homestead on New Castle's Home Street.

On December 1, 1841, at the tender age of 17, she married Joseph White. They had nine children, Alice, wife of George Greer, Eva, wife of Eli C. McClintock, John, Carrie, wife of Eugene S. Willard, Joseph, Arthur, who died young, Frederick, Ada, who died young, and May Belle.

The family resided in several locations, leading to some confusion as to which houses they used for Underground Railroad shelters. After their marriage, they lived on the White Farm property, probably in Crawford White's house. By 1850, they were south of downtown New Castle in Shenango Township. The 1855 map shows that they owned property on County Line Street near Joseph's lumber mill, as well as two houses on East North Street.

Their son, J. Crawford White, born in 1850, remembered riding an ox from downtown past a school located south of Grant Street on the west side of Jefferson Street, up to a pasture north of Craig Street.[58]

In 1857 the Whites exchanged property with Mary Berry and moved to the Thomas Berry house on the northwest corner of Grant Street and North Jefferson. The Whites resided there in the 1860 census. By 1872, they had moved to 312 Wilmington Road.[59]

Adeline passed away in 1907 at the age of 83.[60]

J. Crawford White

J. Crawford White, son of Joseph S. White, was born on June 25, 1849. He assisted his father in his Underground Railroad work, and later corroborated some of this father's stories.

J. Crawford White died in September 1935.

They reached the James Minich farm about one in the afternoon. White described Minich as

> "...one of God's noblemen, who with his good wife received us all with warm welcome; and Mrs. Minich was soon busy getting up a good meal for all of the hungry travelers."

The story of these fugitives was highlighted in the *Pittsburgh Gazette* according to White, but he said his copy had been lost.

White also wrote of two Underground Railroad conductors who suffered because of their participation. Dr. Mitchell, a physician from Indiana, Pennsylvania, was prosecuted under the Fugitive Slave Law and stripped of all property. White couldn't remember if he had been imprisoned. Reverend George Gordon, who had twice preached at the Free Presbyterian Church and was President of Iberia College in Ohio, was cast into prison for helping escaped slaves.

White concluded his treatise with:

> "Have we ever been sorry for these acts of kindness? Never—what else could we do as followers of Him who said, 'I was a stranger and ye took me in, hungry and ye fed me, etc.'"

J. Crawford White Corroborates

J. CRAWFORD WHITE, SON of Joseph S. White, corroborated some of his father's experiences. Concerning the Thomas Berry house that his family occupied for a time, he had this to say:

> "[T]he station had been built for a special purpose, to secrete fugitive slaves hoping and trying to make the land of freedom, when pursued so closely by their masters. My father Joseph S. White was the so called station agent during the later 50s."[26]

He recalled accompanying his father on a trip to Indian Run.

> "Long before daylight, the next morning, they all assembled at the station on N. Jefferson Street. Myself, then being a small boy, accompanied my father. We started north in the dark. There were two whites and ten colored people in the covered wagon.

> "Father had a large team, and he was provided with a covered wagon into which the ten were closely packed. As the team swung into the street, I climbed in the rear end of the wagon, concealed myself among the slaves. They kept my adventure from father, and I was mum untill (sic) we had gone too far for him to send me back home. When my presence had been discovered he said, 'you are the first stow–away with the slaves. I shall not forget this incident.'"

He also described the hidden place in the cellar.

> "There was no ingress or egress to or from this dungeon, except through a secret trap door, hidden beneath a rug in the pantry of the home."[27]

Chapter Notes

1. Hazen, 51.
2. Hazen, 63.
3. Hazen, 70-73.
4. Hazen, 81.
5. *New Castle News*, July 28, 1922.
6. White, Joseph S., "Some reminiscences of slavery times", March 23, 1891 Letter. Wilbur H. Siebert Underground Railroad Collection, State Library of Ohio.
7. Ibid.
8. "The First Brick House". *New Castle News*. November 2, 1887
9. "Looking Back In New Castle," *New Castle News*, March 29, 1932, 6.
10. White, Joseph S., "Some reminiscences of slavery times."
11. "New Castle Pioneer Dies; Had Store There 57 Years," *Pittsburgh Weekly Gazette*, February 8, 1905, 7
12. "R. W. Clendenin Has Passed Away," *New Castle News*, February 8, 1905, 2.
13. *New Castle News*, June 6, 1922.
14. *New Castle News*, June 21, 1893.
15. "Church Histories—Interesting Stories of the Early Religious Work of New Castle," *Daily Courant* (New Castle), March 15, 1890.
16. WOO Spec Coll. BX8947.03F74, Wooster College, Free Presbyterian Church of Ohio papers, 1818-1884, 1824-1868.

17 Letter from Crawford County, *Anti-Slavery Bugle*, April 2, 1953, 3.
18 Hazen, 75.
19 John N. Euwer Obituary. *Lawrence Guardian*, November 18, 1878.
20 United States Census: Pennsylvania, Lawrence County 1860.
21 Durant, 46.
22 White, Joseph S., "Some reminiscences of slavery times."
23 New York Daily Tribune, February 28, 1844.
24 Eli Semple Obituary, *Lawrence Journal*, November 5, 1853.
25 White, Joseph S., "Some reminiscences of slavery times."
26 "J. Crawford White Relates Early Days at Martin Gantz," *New Castle News*, May 28, 1928, 6.
27 J. O. Rodgers letter, Lawrence County Historical Society.
28 1881 Census of Canada, Ontario Grey North, Sullivan; Glasgow, W. Melancthon (1888) History of the Reformed Presbyterian Church in America at 534-535.
29 "Forty-four Years Ago Tomorrow Morgan Made New Castle Tremble," *New Castle Daily Herald*, July 25, 1907, 4.
30 Ibid.
31 "New Castle Pioneer Dies; Had Store There 57 Years," *Pittsburgh Weekly Gazette*, February 8, 1905, 7; "R. W. Clendenin Has Passed Away," *New Castle News*, February 8, 1905, 2.
32 Wells Bushnell Clendenin Obituary, *New Castle Herald*, February 27, 1919, 2.
33 "Mrs. Belinda Clendenin Dead," *New Castle Herald*, April 29, 1907, 1, 5.
34 Hazen, 879.
35 Laws of the General Assembly of the Commonwealth of Pennsylvania No. 135, "An Act To incorporate the New Castle Female Seminary, in the county of Mercer."
36 Hazen, 41.
37 Hazen, 115.
38 Johnston, Nathan Robinson, *Looking Back from the Sunset Land: Or People Worth Knowing*, The University of California, 1898, 33.
39 United States Census:Pennsulvania, Lawrence County, 1850.
40 Hazen, 530-531.
41 Hazen, 750.
42 Judith K. Henderson Euwer Obituary, *Lawrence Guardian*, September 27, 1878.
43 New Castle News, November 25, 1896.
44 White McMillen Obituary, *Lawrence Guardian*, October 22, 1888.
45 Booklet by Mary Anderson Sample referenced at http://archiver.rootsweb.ancestry.com/th/read/SAMPLES/2002-07/1026171315

46 *History of Mercer County, Pennsylvania: its past and present*, Brown, Runk & Co. Chicago, Illinois, 1888, 175.
47 *New Castle News*, June 6, 1922.
48 *New York Daily Tribune*, February 28, 1844.
49 *Tioga Eagle*, July 10, 1844.
50 New York municipal deaths.
51 Eli Semple Obituary, *Lawrence Journal*, November 5, 1853.
52 United States Census: Pennsylvania, Lawrence County, 1860.
53 "Nearly Half a Century," *New Castle News*, March 8, 1899.
54 Hazen, 54.
55 Early Days in New Castle, *New Castle News*, August 6, 1907, 4.
56 A Bit of History. *New Castle News*, February 22, 1896.
57 Hazen, 54.
58 "J. Crawford White Relates Early Days at Martin Gantz," *New Castle News*, May 28, 1928, 6.
59 J. O. Rodgers letter, Lawrence County Historical Society.
60 "Death Claims last survivor of pioneer family," *New Castle News*, July 15, 1907, 1.

9

HICKORY TOWNSHIP

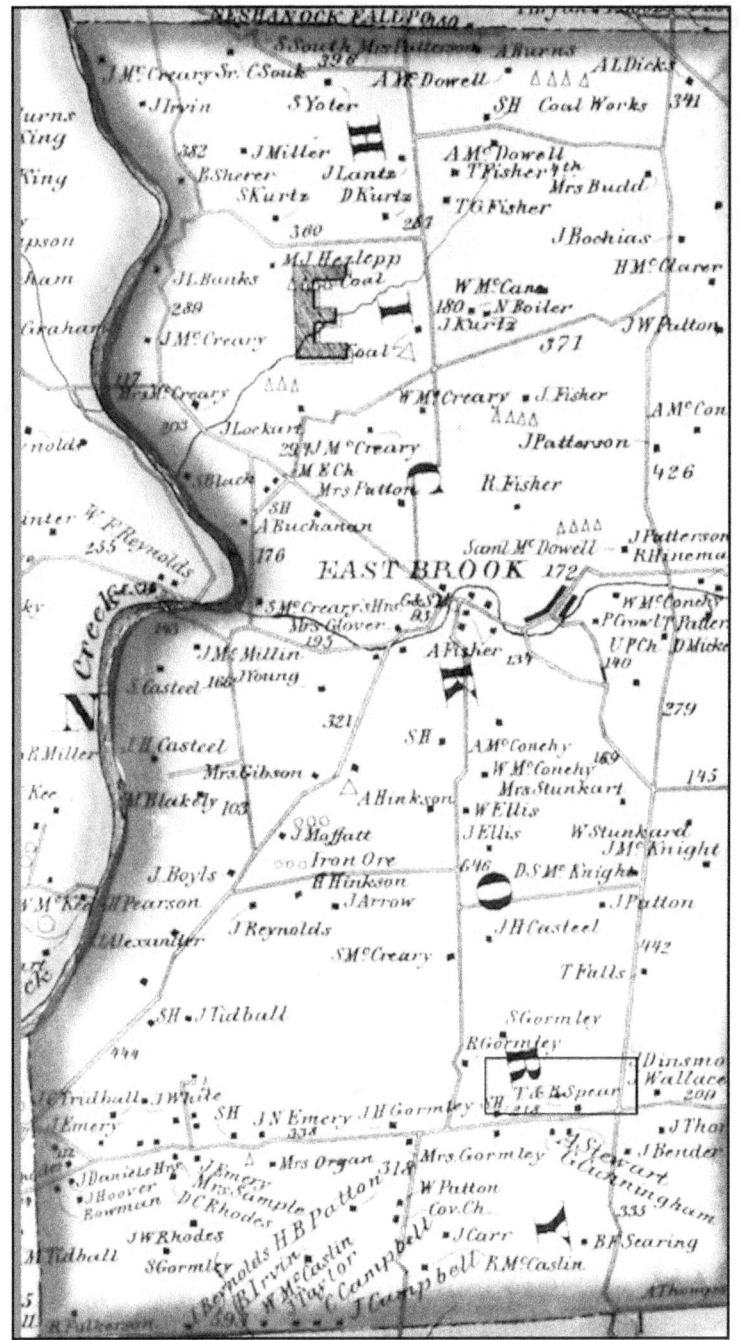

HICKORY TOWNSHIP was created from the eastern part of Neshannock Township about 1859. It was rich in both agricultural and mineral resources and traversed by Big Neshannock Creek and its tributaries that offered a power source. On this stream were, in the distance of about three and a–half miles, no less than seven dams at one point. Early settlers in 1798 included, John H. and Robert Gormley, who purchased 500 acres when he moved to the area in the late 1790s. Robert Gromley divided his property and sold parcels to John H. Robert and Samuel Gormley, Robert (probably Thomas) Speer, John Green, Alexander Stewart, John Carr and Hugh B. Patton. The first road through the area was the Harlansburg Road.[1]

The first schoolhouse was built out of round logs about 1815–16. A hewed–log schoolhouse was put up in the corner of the graveyard, near the old Neshannock Church, about 1828–29. The first teacher was John Tidball. The Covenanters or Reformed Presbyterians organized about 1818, and held their first meeting in William Patton's barn. Reverend William Gibson led the organization, and became its first pastor. The original congregation was small, and included the Patton, Speer, and Wilson families. Their first church was a log building, but a frame church was constructed later.[2]

EASTBROOK

THE VILLAGE AND post office were named after the stream that flows through the place. The first store was opened by John Fisher, about 1835–6. Another store followed in 1838, operated by T. H. Harrah. It changed ownership several times until John Waddington was sole proprietor in 1864. There was also a shoe–shop opened by Oliver Bascom, about 1840; a blacksmith–shop maintained by Philip Crowl, in 1832; Benjamin and Wilkes Waddington's machine–shop; Philip Crowl's small foundry; and John McNickel's wagon–shop, which opened in 1840.[3]

CONDUCTORS

KNOWN CONDUCTORS IN THE AREA included Thomas Speer and Mary (Shields) Speer.

Thomas & Mary (Shields) Speer

Thomas Speer moved from South Carolina to Hickory Township in 1805–6 and purchased farmland from Robert Gormley. His farm was located off of Harlansburg Road on the east side of the township. He and his wife, Mary Shields, lived on the farm with their children through the 1860s.[4]

Their son, Robert, born in 1827, took ownership after his parents' passing. He married Rachel Wilson, daughter of Thomas and Margaret Wilson of Slippery Rock Township, in 1852. It was noted in the New Castle News that,[5]

"Mr. Coon (colored), of New Castle, is working for Robert Speer. He is a 'Brick.'"[6]

Robert was a member of the Reformed Presbyterian Church.

Chapter Notes

1. Durant, 73.
2. Durant, 73.
3. Durant, 76.
4. Hazen, 224,
5. Hazen, 889.
6. *New Castle News*, July 13, 1891.

10

LITTLE BEAVER TOWNSHIP

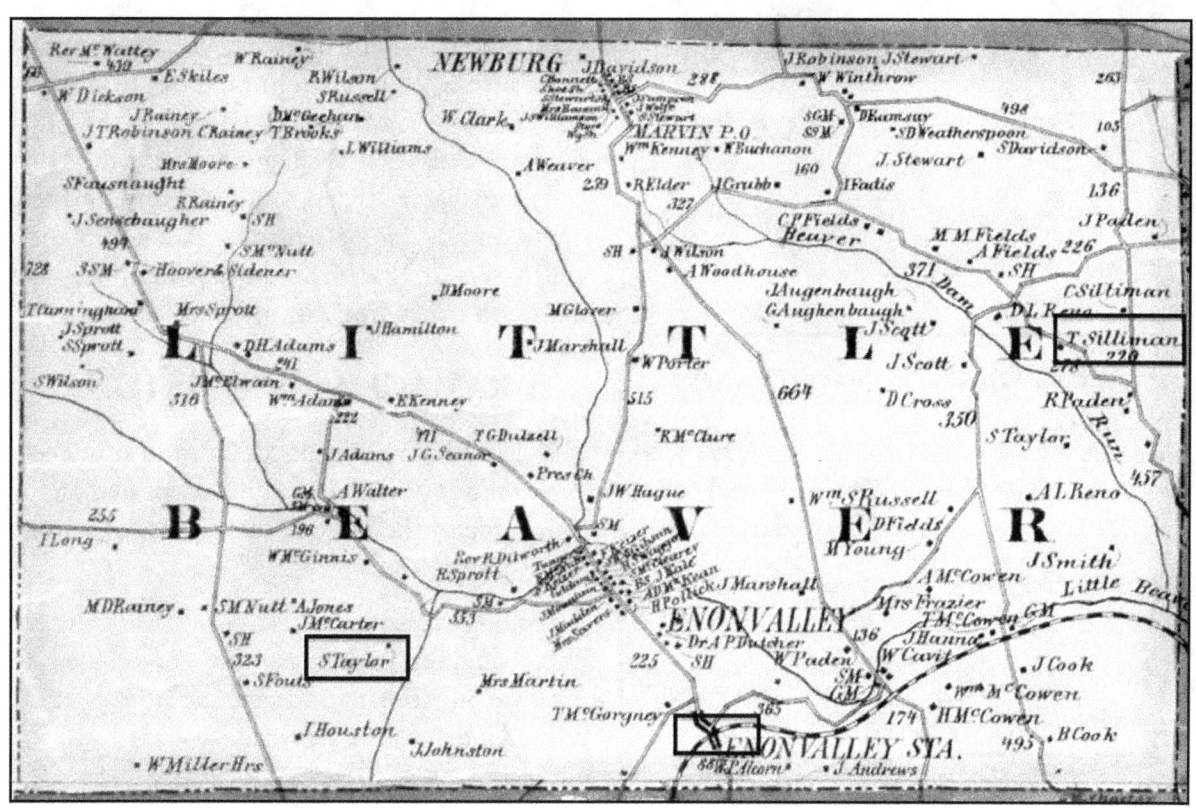

ONE OF THE ORIGINAL 13 townships of Lawrence County, Little Beaver Township contains an area of about a 1,400 acres. Its southern border is also the southern border of Lawrence County which abuts Beaver County's Northern border. Initially, the land was the property of the Pennsylvania Population Company, and each settler was entitled to part of the tract.

The first actual settlement by whites occurred in early 1796 by a company of twelve to fifteen men who had come the previous year to make improvements to the land, building cabins, and clearing forest, which none of them could have done alone. They chose the finest sites in the township, generally in the valley along Little Beaver creek, and called themselves the "Settlers of '96."

Among the men forming this company were John and Samuel Sprott, John Beer, James McCowin and William Robison, and possibly Philip Aughenbaugh, Andrew Moore and others.[1]

The township includes the villages of Enon Valley (Old and New) and Newburg. Old Enon and

Newburg were thriving villages in the stagecoach days.

The Ohio & Pennsylvania Railroad reached Enon Valley in the fall of 1850, and the next six months saw a construction boom as the station building, Saint Lawrence Hotel, and Enon Valley's first retail store, Ramage & McQuiston's, were built.

While there is no incontrovertible evidence that slaves arrived on trains at Enon to venture north, the *Pittsburgh Gazette* reported in July 1855 that six fugitive slaves had taken a train on the Ohio & Pennsylvania RR en route to Canada. These slaves would have passed through Enon Station which was at that time the northernmost rail station in the county east of Ohio.

RAMAGE & McQUISTON

IN 1850 RAMAGE & McQuiston opened in New Enon Valley. The store was located on the south side of the railroad tracks, east of present day Route 551.[2]

According to a note left by the owners' granddaughter in a glass mug once used to measure out cinnamon drops, the store was part of the Underground Railroad.

> "Farmers brought wagonloads of raw wool to the store that they bartered for merchandise. Runaway slaves were sometimes hidden in the wool, and the Ramages then shielded them at the store. Their daughter Martha, who was too young to be suspected of abetting fugitives, brought food to the slaves."[3]

SAMUEL TAYLOR STATION

JUDGE SAMUEL TAYLOR, an Irishman, was said to have helped mold local public sentiment and to have opened his home to slaves on their way to freedom in the North.[4] The 108 acre tract of land he owned remains intact at 1165 Old Enon Unity Road, Enon Valley.

Benjamin & Almira (Seavey) Ramage

Benjamin Ramage was born on April 28, 1817 in Washington, Pennsylvania, and his wife, Almira Seavey, on October 2, 1824 in Allegheny, Pennsylvania.

In 1850 the couple moved to New Enon Valley and opened the area's first store, Ramage & McQuiston. By 1860 they had seven children, named James, Emma, Martha, Samuel, Anna, Mary, and Charles. In 1861 Benjamin was appointed U.S. Postmaster.

Benjamin died in October 1866 at Enon Valley, and Almira died December 15, 1881 in Allegheny.

Silliman House

THE SILLIMAN HOMESTEAD

WHEN THE CURRENT OWNERS of the Thomas Silliman homestead renovated the old house, they discovered a false foundation wall in the basement that concealed a strange hidden room. An attached crawlspace littered with antique cans and bottles seems a probable hiding spot for fugitive slaves.[5]

OLD COVENANTER CHURCH

"When the Old Covenanter Church in the Valley split in the 1830's over the issue of suffrage the Sillimans and the Davidsons, and especially politically–minded Thomas, joined with other progressives in the building of a new church which they called The Reformed Presbyterian Church." [6]

Samuel & Charity Taylor

Samuel Taylor was born April 9, 1806 in Northumberland County, Pennsylvania. As a young man he learned the potter's trade, but left this vocation to engage in farming in Little Beaver Township.

Originally a Whig and subsequently a Republican, he was a loyal and active partisan, serving two five-year terms as Associate Judge of Lawrence County in 1866 and 1871. At that time, non-lawyers were eligible for election to the post.

Samuel and his wife, Charity, were members of the Disciple Church and had 15 children, named William M., Ann, who died soon after her marriage, John P., Thomas C., Harriet J., Samuel S., Daniel W., Martha E., Joseph I., Enos M., Lee, Lucretia, Matilda, Addie, and an infant, deceased.

Samuel Taylor died in 1888.

HOME GUARDS

ON APRIL 26, 1861, the Home Guards organized at Enon Valley to protect

"…our homes and our neighbors' homes from any invasion or attempt to do so by any enemy who has threatened, or may hereafter threaten to do so; that we shall watch and carefully guard against such and by these presents pledge ourselves, our homes and our means for the faithful performance of the same."

Benjamin Ramage, Samuel Taylor, and Thomas Silliman are known to have joined the Home Guards.[7]

CONDUCTORS

KNOWN CONDUCTORS in the area include Benjamin Ramage, Almira (Seavey) Ramage, Samuel Taylor, and Thomas Silliman.

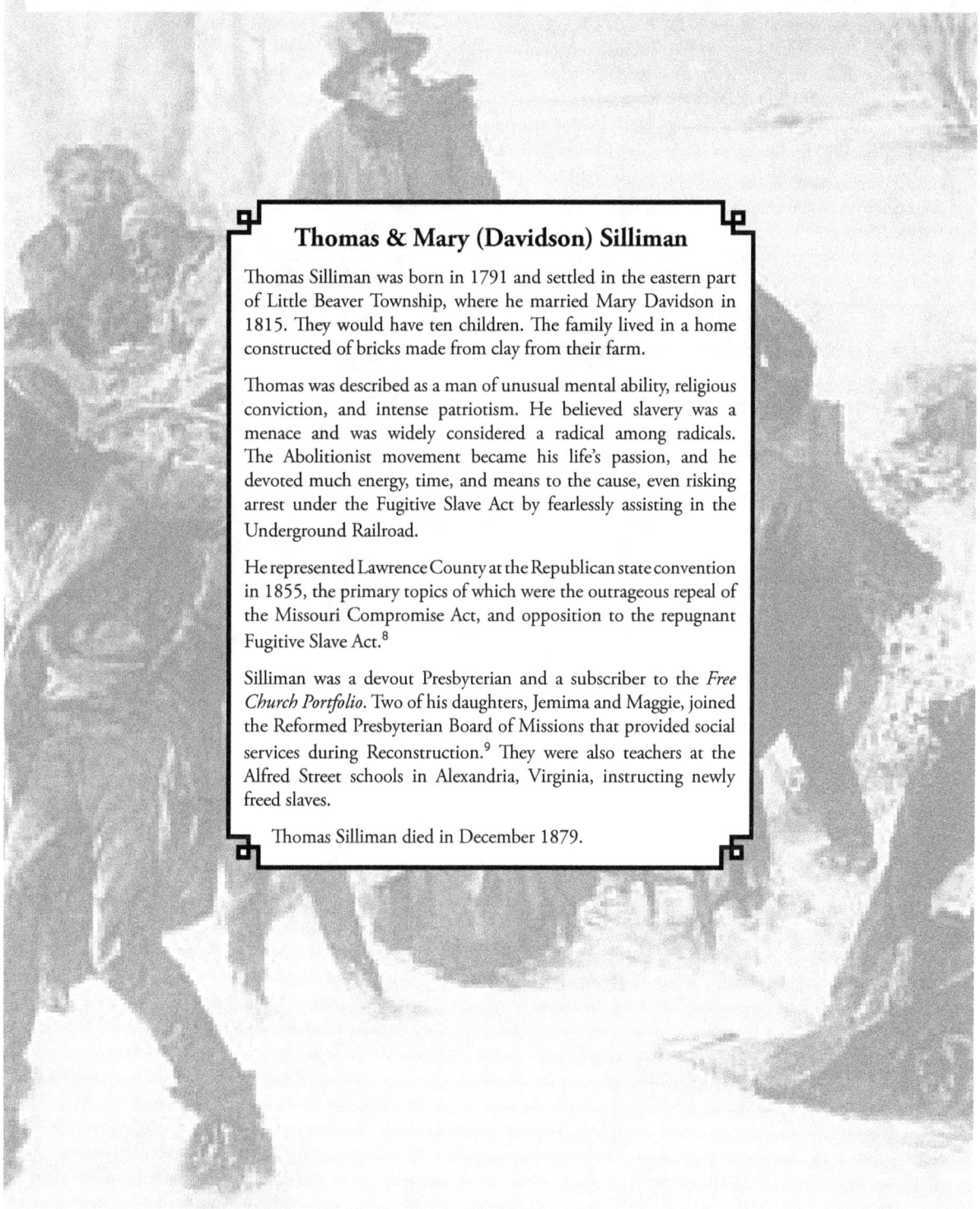

Thomas & Mary (Davidson) Silliman

Thomas Silliman was born in 1791 and settled in the eastern part of Little Beaver Township, where he married Mary Davidson in 1815. They would have ten children. The family lived in a home constructed of bricks made from clay from their farm.

Thomas was described as a man of unusual mental ability, religious conviction, and intense patriotism. He believed slavery was a menace and was widely considered a radical among radicals. The Abolitionist movement became his life's passion, and he devoted much energy, time, and means to the cause, even risking arrest under the Fugitive Slave Act by fearlessly assisting in the Underground Railroad.

He represented Lawrence County at the Republican state convention in 1855, the primary topics of which were the outrageous repeal of the Missouri Compromise Act, and opposition to the repugnant Fugitive Slave Act.[8]

Silliman was a devout Presbyterian and a subscriber to the *Free Church Portfolio*. Two of his daughters, Jemima and Maggie, joined the Reformed Presbyterian Board of Missions that provided social services during Reconstruction.[9] They were also teachers at the Alfred Street schools in Alexandria, Virginia, instructing newly freed slaves.

Thomas Silliman died in December 1879.

Chapter Notes

1. Hazen, 235-238.
2. The former site is currently the parking lot of the Enon Valley Inn.
3. Letter to the Editor from Jean Martin, Pittsburgh, Pennsylvania, *Smithsonian Magazine* December 1996, at 20-21. Martin a descendant, states she learned this from a note that Martha's daughter left in a tiny glass mug that had been used to measure cinnamon drops in the store.
4. Bausman, Joseph Henderson, *History of Beaver County, Vol. 2.* Knickerbocker Press. 1904, 1144.
5. Personal communications between Yoders and Judith M. Foster, Silliman descendant and President, Enon Valley Historical Society.
6. Silliman, Robert B., *The Silliman Family History.* 1966, 126-128.
7. *New Castle News*, January 22, 1895.
8. *The Jeffersonian* (Stroudsburg, Pennsylvania), September 19, 1855, 2.
9. Silliman, Robert B. *The Silliman Family History*, 126-128.

11
MAHONING TOWNSHIP

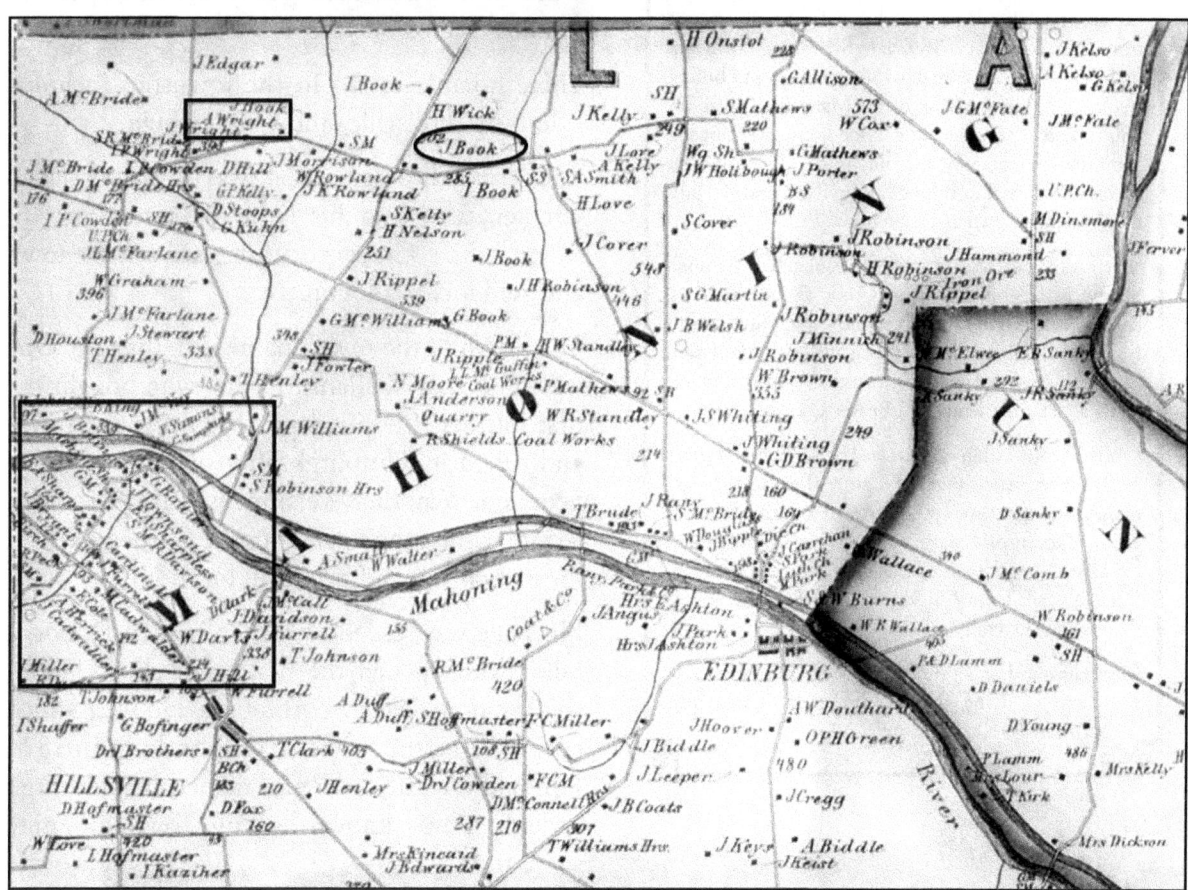

IN JUNE, 1793 A GROUP of about 45 persons left Allegheny City, now northwest Pittsburgh, headed for the Mahoning Valley intending to settle on the north side of the river. They forded the Shenango River where New Castle now stands and traveled west to the Youngstown region.

Unhappy with the land there, they went back to Allegheny City. About a dozen of the original group subsequently returned to settle both sides of Mahoning River, building cabins and planting apple and peach orchards. By 1794 most had moved families to the new settlement. Mahoning Township formed sometime between November 1805 and February 1806.[1]

Gristmills appeared throughout the region. John Angel built a gristmill about 1825 on a small run one–and–a–half miles above Edinburg that empties into the Mahoning River. The McWilliams family built a mill that remained in operation until 1837 near the mouth of Coffee Run. In 1844 James and John Raney constructed

> ### Septimus & Sarah (Dallas) Cadwallader
>
> Septimus Cadwallader and his wife, Sarah, moved from Redstone, Pennsylvania, to Mahoning Township in 1803, where he settled a 400 acre tract and built a frame house on the bank of the Mahoning River. By 1805, he had constructed a stone house and opened a milling business by his old home. The mill was eventually moved to Falling Spring Run, near the falls that became known as Quakertown Falls.
>
> Septimus and Sarah's children included Samuel, Septimus, Joseph, Eli, Lydia, Amy, Elizabeth, Mary and Sarah. Amy married Benjamin Sharpless, son of Isaac and Elizabeth Sharpless. Cadwallader's daughter, Elizabeth, married Talbot Townsend, son of Francis and Rachel Townsend from Beaver County.
>
> Elisha M. Stevenson of New Bedford stated in a letter to Professor Siebert that the fugitives he received were mainly brought from Quakertown by Cadwallader. From Stevenson's farm, they were transported to Liberty or Brookfield, Ohio. Edward and Eli "Kidwalader" from Quakertown were also listed as Conductors arriving in Poland, Ohio.
>
> It is believed that Septimus died by 1820, as his wife was listed as living alone in the 1820 census near Septimus, Jr.

> ### Eli & Elizabeth (Hawley) Cadwallader
>
> Born to Septimus and Sarah Cadwallader, Eli appears in 1820 Mahoning Township census with his wife and two sons. He was nominated and appointed as an elder at the Quaker Monthly Meeting in Stark, Ohio in 1835. Eli married Elizabeth Hawley after receiving approval at the Quaker Meeting in March 1841.

a large mill on the canal three–fourths of a mile north of Edinburg.

Coal was mined in many locations, including the old Hillsville station. Iron ore was present, but never extensively excavated. Limestone was quarried and shipped to furnaces in Youngstown, Ohio, or manufactured locally into lime, perhaps in kilns erected on Joseph Wright's farm.[2]

Three notable towns in the township included Edinburg, Hillsville, and Quakertown.

The first Edinburg settler was probably Jacob Cremer, who sold his land to James Park. In August 1824, Crawford White laid out the town and sold lots at auction.[3]

The origin of the town's name is in dispute. One version is that William McFate, who bought the first lot, had the privilege of naming the town, and called it Edinburgh after his native city in Scotland. Another version is that Crawford White named the town after the Garden of Eden for its rich soil and beautiful location.

Hillsville was settled by a man named Donot, a tailor who opened the first tailor shop. Donot sold land to Peter or Abraham Hoover, which later became the property of John Hill. In 1824 Hill laid out the town and named it Hillsburgh though it was known as Hill Town for quite some time.[4]

Quakertown's pioneer was probably Septimus Cadwallader, who arrived about 1804. He settled on a 400 acre tract, built a frame house, and a gristmill on the Mahoning River. Around 1808, Benjamin Sharpless and Talbot Townsend joined him. As all three men were Quakers, the area became known as Quakertown. Quakertown no longer exists.[5]

The first school was probably near Quakertown on the north side of the Mahoning. In 1806 or 07, a second schoolhouse was built near the

Mahoning United Presbyterian Church. Other schoolhouses were probably built in the villages, but there is no documentation.

The Mahoning United Presbyterian Church formed about 1799 two miles northeast of Lowellville, Ohio. For a number of years, prayer meetings were held from house to house throughout the community. The first sermon was delivered on Captain Thompson's farm.

The Methodist Episcopal Church started about 1822, and their first chapel built in 1826. The Harbor United Presbyterian Church was organized about 1852 by Reverend R. A. Browne, and the Christian Church by Reverend Abraham Sanders about 1830.[6]

WRIGHT FARM

ALEXANDER WRIGHT JR.'S son, Joseph, wrote to Professor Siebert about the family's participation in the Underground Railroad. Since Quakertown was a flourishing manufacturing town, and fugitives might be easily discovered there, Wright Jr. began concealing them on his farm about 1835.

The first slaves came from Benjamin Sharpless of Quakertown.[7] Wright would keep them until the excitement died down and then send them north to the next station ten or fifteen miles away. Joseph recalled one family of eight, a mother and seven children, who were being hotly pursued. Wright hid them for two to three weeks before sending them on. Unfortunately, it was later learned that the family was captured at Lake Erie.[8]

Because of mounting delays, Wright Jr. and Joseph's brother, Alexander III, began transporting slaves overnight to the home of Wright Jr.'s brother–in–law, Charles Stewart, in Liberty, Ohio.

Alexander Wright, Sr.

Alexander Wright Sr., came from Ireland and settled originally in Washington County, Pennsylvania. About 1795, he moved to Mahoning Township with his wife and five children and a few years later purchased 100 acres of Population Company land south of the Somerville or Andrew Davidson farm. When he died in 1838 at 92, his property passed to his children.[11]

Alexander, Wright, Jr.

Alexander Wright Jr., was born on April 15, 1782. In the War of 1812 he served as a Sergeant in Pennsylvania Militia's 135th Regiment, commanded by Lieutenant Andrew Christy. The troops were on duty from September 1812 until May 1813 and were called upon to protect the fleet during construction at Presque Isle.

In 1842 Alexander Wright, Jr. ran for County Commissioner on the Abolitionist Ticket. By the 1850s he maintained the family farm with his wife and two adult sons, Joseph and Isaac.

Alexander Wright, Jr. died on July 30, 1853.[12][13][14][15]

Alexander Wright III

Alexander Wright, III was born September 25, 1817 to Alexander Wright, Jr. and his second wife, Margaret Bevington. He participated with his father in the Underground Railroad, sheltering escaped slaves on the elder's farm, and helping to transport many of them to stations in Ohio. In the 1850 census Alexander Wright III, lived near his father's farm with his wife, Rachel, and two small children John and Elizabeth.

Alexander III served as County Commissioner in 1887. He died on June 3, 1894, a highly respected member of Mahoning Township.

CONDUCTORS

KNOWN CONDUCTORS IN THE AREA included Alexander Wright, Jr., Elizabeth Wright, Septimus Cadwallader, Eli Cadwallader, Talbot Townsend, Elizabeth Townsend, Benjamin Sharpless, and Amy Sharpless.

Benjamin & Amy (Cadwallader) Sharpless

Benjamin Sharpless, born in 1777, came to Quakertown in 1808.[16] He had married Amy Cadwallader in 1801, and now joined his father-in-law, Septimus Cadwallader, in a milling enterprise along the Mahoning River. Records state that he was one of the leading members of the local Underground Railroad, transporting slaves to the Wright farm.

Benjamin and Amy had at least four children, named Septimus C., Ellen T., Edwin A. and Albert F. Sharpless.

He likely died in September, 1845.[17]

Talbot & Edith (Ware) Townsend

Sometime before 1808 Talbot Townsend arrived in Quakertown, having married Septimus Cadwallader's daughter, Elizabeth, in 1806. He joined his father-in-law's milling business, and also assisted in the Underground Railroad, along with his brother-in-law, Benjamin Sharpless, who would join them within a year.[18]

Joseph Wright stated in a letter to Professor Siebert that Townsend and Sharpless were "Friends from Quakertown" who began aiding and harboring fugitives about 1835.

In 1815 Talbot married Edith Ware. It is likely that Elizabeth died, possibly in 1812.

Their son, Milo A. Townsend, was an Abolitionist, Quaker Schoolmaster, and editor of New Brighton Times in Beaver County. Milo and Talbot were "untiring in their assistance to the poor fugitives."[19] [20] [21]

In 1847 "Milo, his wife and parents" welcomed into their home William Lloyd Garrison and Frederick Douglass. Garrison wrote of Townsend:

"Milo is one of the truest reformers in the land, and wields a potent reformatory pen, but his organ of hope is not quite large enough. There seems to be no branch of reform to which he has not given some attention."[22]

ABOLITIONISTS

KNOWN ABOLITIONISTS INCLUDED Edwin A. Sharpless, Eliza Sharpless, John P. Calvin, Horace Greely Reed, and John C. Book.

Horace Greely Reed

Horace Greeley Reed was the son of a noted Abolitionist and worked as a driver on the Erie & Pittsburgh Canal after his father's early death. He grew up in North Beaver and then Mahoning Township before moving to McKeesport in 1872. In 1894, he became a citizen's candidate for McKeesport Mayor.[23, 24, 25]

John C. & Mary Book

John C. Book lived with his wife, Mary, and four children on a Mahoning township farm. He ran for Prothonotary on the Abolitionist Ticket in 1842.[26, 27]

Edwin A. & Eliza (Williams) Sharpless

Edwin A. Sharpless was born in 1809 to Benjamin and Amy (Cadwallader) Sharpless. Quaker church records listed Edwin A. as a "dis joining Separatist," who had left the church. A notation for his mother indicated, "dis disunity."[28] He contributed and subscribed to the *Anti–Slavery Bugle* as did his mother.[29, 30]

Edwin married Eliza Williams and lived in Hillsville, Mahoning Township. They had several children, including Elma Sharpless Kincaid, born in October 1843. The 1860 Census shows Franklin, Laura, Mifflin, Ellonor and Abbe, ages 9 to 21, living with them.

On one occasion, Wright, Jr. and his fourth wife, Elizabeth, drove to Liberty in their Dearborn wagon with a fugitive following on their old gray horse, Ned. They spent the day with Charles Stewart and then returned home.⁹

Joseph estimated that 40 or 50 slaves were transported between 1835 and 1845. After the Fugitive Slave Act passed in 1850, not more than three or four passed through their station.

S. P. Stuart of Clark Township, Mercer County, confirmed that Alexander Wright, Jr. was a Conductor on the Underground Railroad. Slaves were transported from the Wright farm to his Stuart's home, and then on to Charles Stewart in Hubbard, Ohio, Ambrose Hart in Brookfield, Ohio, and Captain Bushnell in Hartford, Ohio.¹⁰

Chapter Notes

1. Durant, 77-82.
2. Ibid.
3. Ibid.
4. Ibid.
5. Ibid.
6. Ibid.
7. "Joseph Wright of Villa Maria, Pennsylvania. Route from Quakertown, Lawrence County, Pa. to Liberty, Trumbull County," March 15, 1897. Wilbur H. Siebert Collection, State Library of Ohio.
8. Ibid.
9. Ibid.
10. "S. P. Stuart of Clark, Mercer County, Pennsylvania. Route from Lawrence Co., Pa to Hubbard, Brookfield and Harford," December 26, 1895. Wilbur H. Siebert Collection, State Library of Ohio.
11. Hazen, 228, 249, 255.
12. White, John G. *A Twentieth Century History of Mercer County Pennsylvania*, Lewis, 1909 Vol 1, 178.
13. *New Castle Gazette*, September 14, 1842.
14. United States Census: Pennsylvania, Lawrence County, 1850.
15. Alexander Wright Obituary, *Guardian*, June 6, 1894, 5.
16. *U.S.Encyclopedia of American Quaker Genealogy, Vol. IV.* Ohio Monthly Meetings, 77.
17. Durant, 82.
18. Ibid.
19. *U.S.Encyclopedia of American Quaker Genealogy, Vol. IV.* Ohio Monthly Meetings, 661.
20. Douglas, Frederick, "The Frederick Douglass Papers 1842-1852." John R. McKivigan, ed. Yale University Press. 2009, 12.
21. Bausman, Joseph Henderson, *History of Beaver County, Vol. 2*, 1142.
22. Garrison, Wendell Phillips & Francis Jackson Garrison, *William Lloyd Garrison 1805-1879: The Story of His Life Told by His Children, Vol. III*. Century Company. 1885, 193-194.
23. *Anti-Slavery Bugle*, November 7, 1857, 1.
24. United States Census: Pennsylvania, Lawrence County 1850.
25. "A Lawrence County Boy," *New Castle News*, January 25, 1894, 1.
26. *New Castle Gazette*, September 14, 1842.
27. United States Census: Pennsylvania, Lawrence County 1850, 1860.
28. *U.S.Encyclopedia of American Quaker Genealogy*, Ancestry.com.
29. *Anti-Slavery Bugle*, September 20, 1856, 3.
30. *Anti-Slavery Bugle*, March 23, 1850, 3.

12
NORTH BEAVER

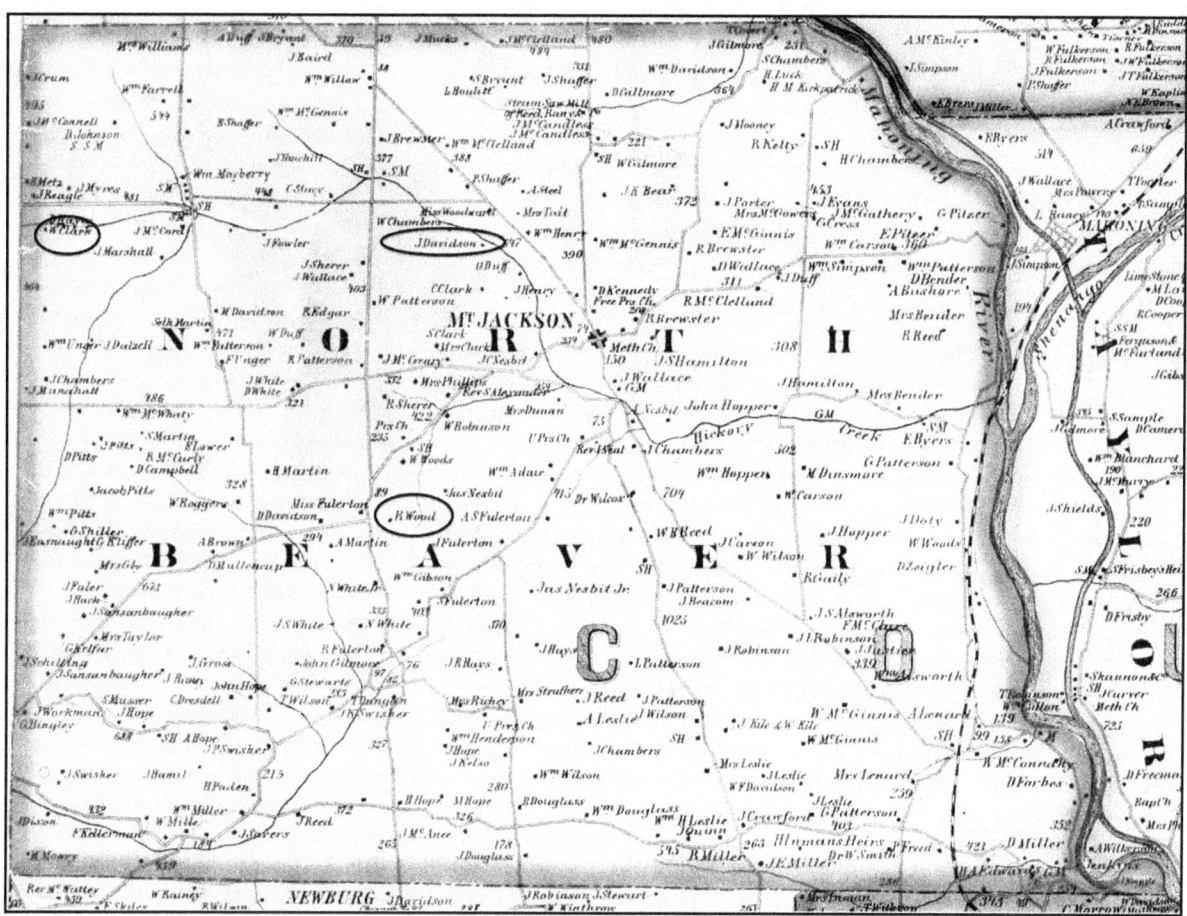

North Beaver was one of the original 13 Lawrence County townships and its largest subdivision, having an area of about 26,800 acres, including the villages of Mount Jackson and Moravia. The terrain is varied, broken by hills and ravines. Principal streams are the Mahoning and Beaver rivers and the Hickory Creek.

> "The appearance of the country was truly beautiful. The rich, loamy appearance of the soil, the density of the forest and thickets, the wonderful multiplicity, variety and gorgeousness of the blossoms and flowers, the exhilarating perfume they sent forth, the continual singing of the birds, the chattering of the many squirrels, the beautiful plumage of the vast flocks, of turkeys, and the nimble skipping of the deer and fox, produced a sublimity and grandeur far beyond anything we have in the cleared fields and meadows into which these forests have been transformed."[3]

Major Edward Wright was one of the first settlers, arriving from Allegheny County in the spring of 1797. He built the fourth house in the township and planted the first apple trees in

1799, hauling 45 trees from Washington County. Other settlers included William Wood in Mount Jackson, Francis Nesbit, Thomas Cloud and Walter Clarke.

Clark bought 450 acres and divided it among his children and grandchildren. His son, John, was married and had two children, and one daughter was married and had two children. Records also list two orphaned grandchildren and a "colored girl".

Some of the township's early businesses include a distillery built by Lawrence Dobbins in 1801, and a gristmill constructed by William Espy and Francis Nesbit in 1802. By 1817 upwards of a dozen distilleries graced the area.

The Westfield Presbyterian Church was established as early as 1802. Elder John Edgar started a distillery near it, operating a still in conjunction with a gristmill.

The old Indian trail from Moravia to Edinburg ran along the top of the ridge or "backbone" for some distance between Hickory Creek and the Big Run. The earliest road was the New Castle and Beaver Road opened as early as 1800 and known as the "Beaver Road."

Asa Adams came from Washington County, Pennsylvania, before the War of 1812 and settled a mile from the state line in the western portion of the township.[4]

ABOLITIONISTS

SUBSCRIBERS TO THE FREE CHURCH PORTFOLIO, 1860–1861, included William Alsworth, Wells Bushnell, John Carson, S. D. Clark, Clement Clark, John Davidson, C. Elliott, Esther Justice, Joseph McClelland, William Mintz, Margaret Robinson, and Robert Woods.

William Alsworth

William Alsworth was the youngest of three siblings who came to Moravia with their parents from Franklin County, Pennsylvania, in November 1804. Three more children were born into the family after their arrival. William's father James Alsworth settled a 200 acre tract and made the first improvements upon it.[1]

Esther (Hopper) & James Justice

Esther Hopper, daughter of Robert Hopper, who came to North Beaver Township from Ireland in 1797, married James Justice. James died in 1815, leaving his wife and three daughters, Margaret, Elizabeth, and Esther. His wife, only 28 years old at the time, remained faithful to his memory until her demise in 1870, having been a widow for 55 years.[2]

Chapter Notes

1. Hazen, 286.
2. Hazen, 277.
3. Durant, 66-67, citing *New Castle Gazette and Democrat,* February 21, 1868 article written by Dr. Allen Nesbit.
4. Hazen, 286.

13

PERRY TOWNSHIP

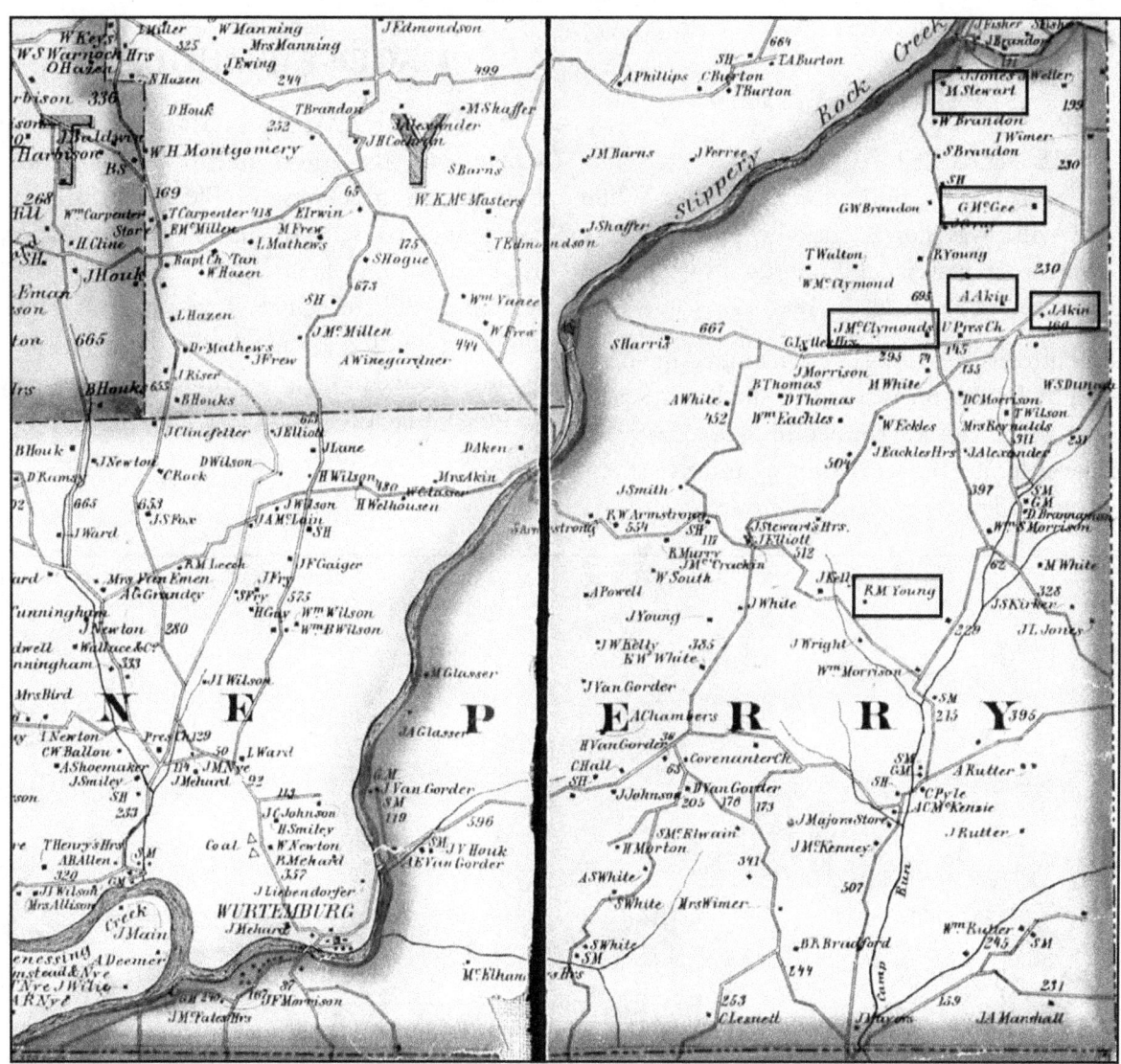

PERRY TOWNSHIP WAS ONE of the original thirteen townships in Lawrence County, positioned on the southeast corner of the county and comprised of parts of Beaver and Butler Counties. The land is generally fertile but uneven, with hills rising hundreds of feet above Slippery Rock Creek. The area was also rich in coal, iron ore and limestone.

A large portion of the township was known as the Chew District, named after Benjamin Chew of Philadelphia, who purchased the area and divided it into 400–acre tracts. Matthew Murray was first to settle the area in 1796. Even so, the township remained rural, boasting a population of only 847 by 1907.

Being rural, Perry Township offered many roadways for transporting escaping slaves from Pittsburgh and Beaver County. Many farmers participated as conductors.[1]

PORTERSVILLE

THE NEAREST TOWN was Portersville, located on the Butler County border. While Portersville was not technically part of Perry Township it played an important role in the Underground Railroad.

The Portersville area was first inhabited in about 1796 by Robert Stewart, and a small settlement sprouted up. Roads connected New Castle to Zelienople in Beaver County, and Matthew Stewart built a gristmill on his property. The first school was built in 1805, and another in 1812. About 1820, a local militia was organized, called the Hornet Rifles.

Churches included Mountville United Presbyterian Church organized as a Seceder Church by 1810 and Covenanter Presbyterian about 1840.[2]

MAGEE FARMHOUSE

GEORGE HAMILTON Magee's farmhouse was on the south side of Magee Road, about a half–mile west of Pfeiffer Road. The basement contained a small room with one door, one window, and a dirt floor. Escaping slaves were housed here. Once it was safe to move them, Magee used a wagon with a false bottom, making the five to six hour trip to New Castle or the much longer journey to the station in Indian Run, Mercer County.

Magee Farm House

In a letter to a local paper George's son, John, wrote that Joseph White of New Castle used Magee's wagon at one point. He remembered one time when seven slaves were hidden in the load.

A CLOSE CALL

AMONG THE reminiscences provided by John Magee was a story of a close call having occurred at the Magee Farmhouse when he was young.

> "I remember two men, supposed to be slave hunters, being entertained in my father's house overnight, when in the basement there were six slaves being hidden. The wood–burning fireplace was plentifully supplied with fuel, and my mother was carrying provision and bedding the back way for these people. Two small children were in the group but not a sound came from them.
>
> "These men and women, whom I have mentioned, knew they were breaking federal law, but were like the Apostles, where they were commanded not to speak in the name of Jesus, and answered, "Whether it is right, to obey God or men?"[3]

AFRICAN PERRY

> "Perry Township in Lawrence County was called African Perry because of the many friends of the oppressed residing there. These, Dr. John Cowden, John Oliver and Mr. Hall, in Portersville, considered it unsafe to secrete any runaway slaves about their homes, but aided them in finding refuge."[4]

THREE RUNAWAY SLAVES

JOHN MAGEE RELATED a story of three runaway slaves caught by slave hunters near Portersville. The captives were taken to the Oliver Hotel and held overnight.

People of the community gathered to liberate them, but the hunters had charged the slaves with horse stealing, complicating matters greatly. When the Portersville justice refused to try the case, the captives were transferred to Prospect, tried, and acquitted. Their captors were ordered to return them to Portersville, restore any property confiscated, and liberate them.

After this story got out, slaves knew Portersville was safe.[5]

CONDUCTORS

KNOWN CONDUCTORS IN THE AREA included George Hamilton Magee, Sarah Magee, James Aiken, Margaret Aiken, Andrew Aiken, Rachel Aiken, Robert Young, Mary Young, John McClymonds, Mary McClymonds, Matthew Stewart, Sarah Stewart, and Reverend Thomas Hannay.

George Hamilton & Sarah Magee

Around 1837, George Hamilton Magee moved to Perry Township from Connoquenessing Creek in Butler County, and purchased 200 acres from Robert Aiken. In the 1850 census, he was 45 years old and living with his wife, Sarah, and children, Thomas and Nancy. An African American boy, Samuel Wright, age 14, was also listed in his home.[6]

James & Margaret Aiken

James Aiken was a Conductor based in Perry Township. His father, Robert, moved there in 1804 from Youghiogheny Valley, south of Pittsburgh, and purchased land from Edward White. He was one of the founding members of the Associate or Seceder church.[7] Robert's wife died in 1835, aged 66 years, and Robert in 1850, at the age of 80.[8]

In 1850 James was 50 years old and living with his wife, Margaret, and children, James, Mary, Susannah, Alexander, Margaret, Trisha, and Emmaline.[9]

Robert & Mary Young

Even with so much land available, disputes occasionally arose, such as when Robert Young and William Scott settled the same tract of land. For years there was considerable strife between the two men, but they finally settled the dispute by dividing the tract, and afterwards lived amicably as neighbors. Young had made improvements near the tract's center and when the division was made, Scott took a strip from either side in order for Young to keep his improvements.

In the 1850 census, Robert was 50 years old and living with his wife Mary and children, Margaret, Mary, Matilda, and Elizabeth. He was among the founders of the Associate or Seceder Church and donated the land upon which the church was built.[10]

Andrew & Rachel (Adams) Aiken

Andrew Aiken, James Aiken's brother, was born in 1802 in Westmoreland County, Pennsylvania, and brought to Perry Township in 1804. Andrew inherited the property when his parents died, and carried on their agricultural pursuits until his death.

He married Rachel Adams, whose father owned land along Muddy Creek. They raised a large family. In 1850, Andrew was 47, and resided with Rachel Aiken and children, James, Glenn, Martha, Erskine, Isaiah, and David. They would eventually have ten children in total.

Isaiah Henderson Aiken entered the Federal Army in 1861 as became a member of Company F, 137th Regiment, Pennsylvania Volunteer Infantry. He served for nine months and was honorably discharged. Two other sons, Erskine E. and David were members of the famous Roundhead regiment. All escaped serious injury.[11]

Matthew & Sarah Stewart

In 1798, James Stewart moved from Adams County, Pennsylvania to Perry Township. He had served in the Revolutionary War, and is said to have jumped over a covered wagon while in the army. His son, Matthew Stewart, followed in his footsteps. A tall, athletic man, Matthew could stand and jump over "anything he could lay his chin over."

In the 1850 census, Matthew, 54, lived with his wife, Sarah and children, Sarah, Calvin, Nathan, and Matilda. Matthew Stewart was one of the organizers of the Reformed Presbyterian Church in Rose Point with Thomas Speer, Thomas Wilson and John Love.[12]

John & Mary McClymonds

In the 1850 census John McClymonds was 50 years old and listed as a farmer. He lived with his wife, Mary, adult son, William, a carpenter, and four other children, John, Elizabeth, Mary and Margaret.

John McClymonds died of consumption in 1860.[13]

Chapter Notes

1. Hazen, 286-288.
2. Hazen, 292.
3. "Looking Back In New Castle," *New Castle News,* March 29, 1932, 6.
4. Ibid.
5. Ibid.
6. Hazen, 290.
7. Durant, 91.
8. Durant 92.
9. United States Census: Pennsylvania, Lawrence County, 1850.
10. Durant, 92.
11. Hazen, 951.
12. Hazen, 337.
13. U.S. Federal Census Mortality Schedules 1850-1885.

14

PLAIN GROVE TOWNSHIP

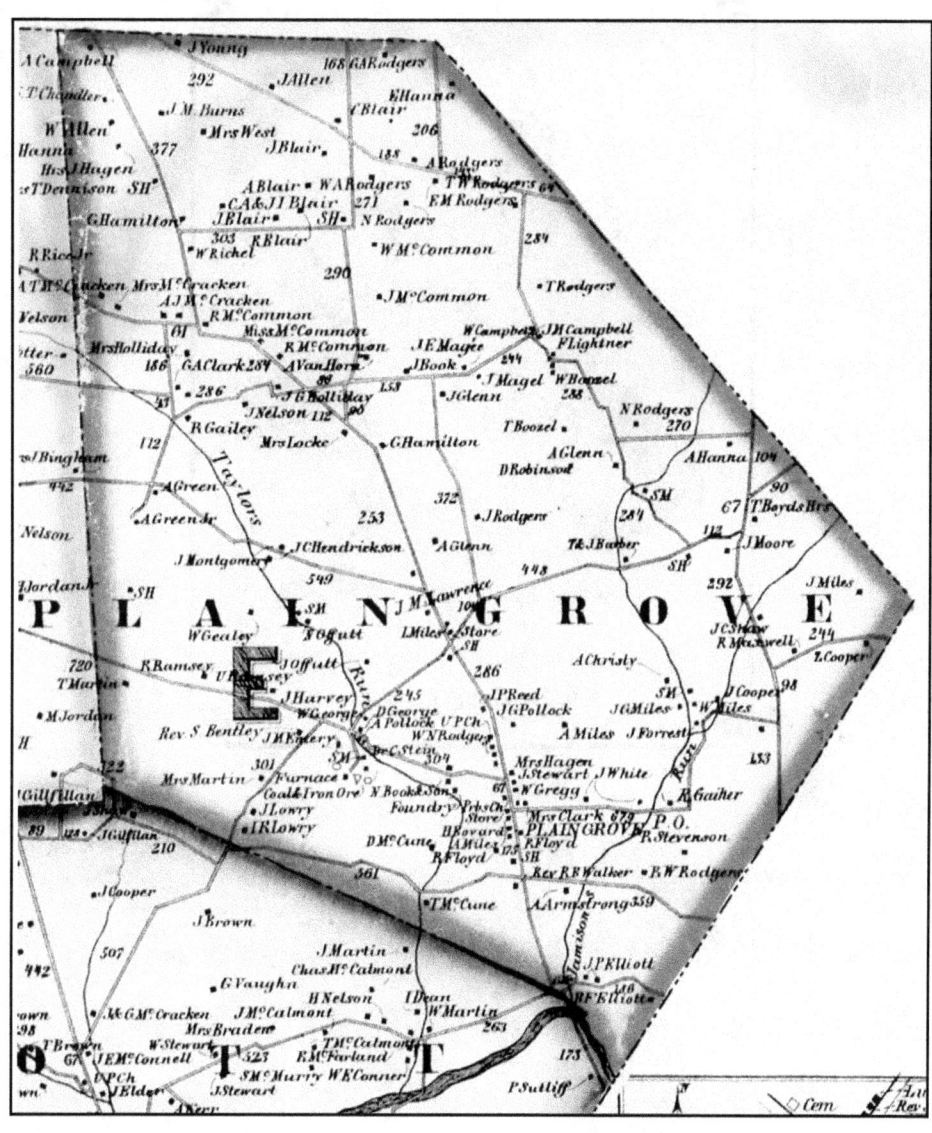

PLAIN GROVE TOWNSHIP was formed in 1855 from parts of Scott and Washington Townships. A post office was established there about 1835. In 1877 the town of Plain Grove was scattered along a public road for a distance of a mile and a half, and contained two stores, a blacksmith shop and churches. The Blairs, Gealeys, McCunes, McKees, Offutts, Ramseys, Taylors, and Wallaces were among the early settlers.[1]

CONDUCTORS

KNOWN CONDUCTORS in the area included Reverend J. C. Bigham.

Reverend J C Bigham

ABOLITIONISTS

KNOWN ABOLITIONISTS in the area included John Offutt.

John Offutt

John Offutt was born in Washington County, Pennsylvania, and became one of the early settlers in Plain Grove where he engaged in farming throughout his life. He was a prominent and aggressive Abolitionist.[2]

Chapter Notes

1. Durant, 118.
2. Hazen, 450.

15

PULASKI TOWNSHIP

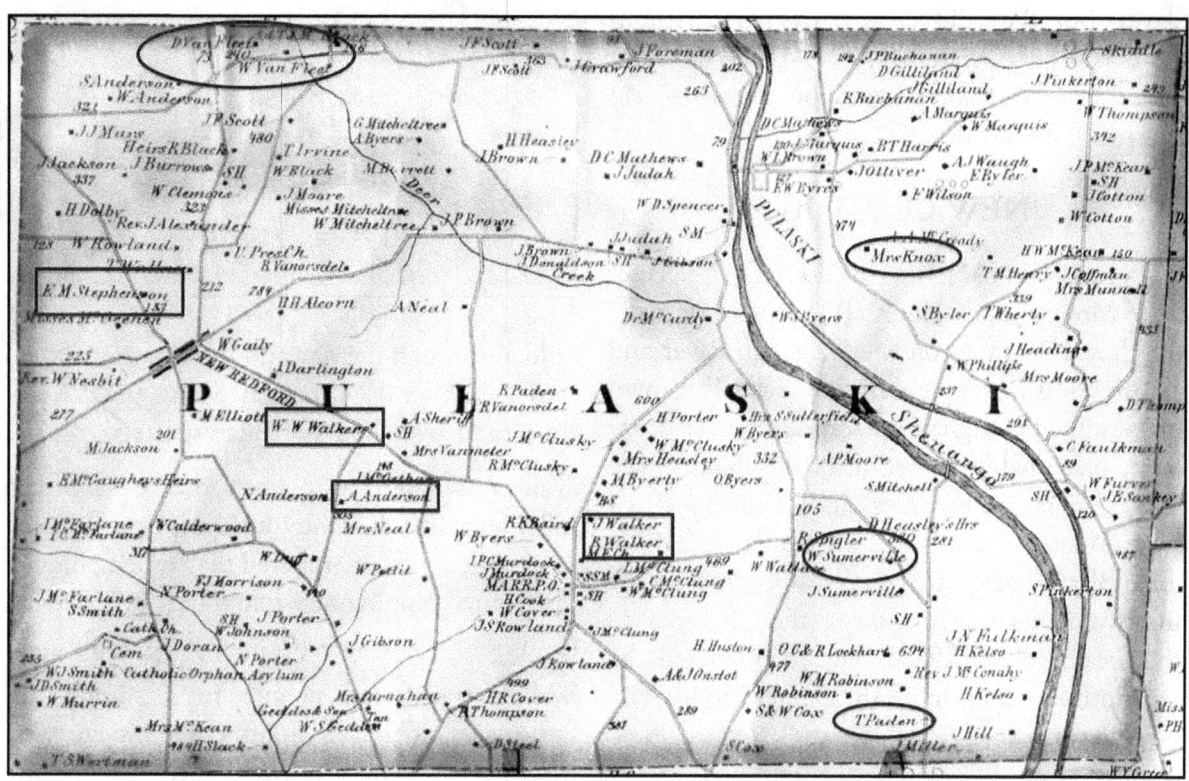

PULASKI TOWNSHIP WAS PART of Mahoning Township until its creation in 1849. Its terrain is more level than much of the county, the soil rich and productive. The township is crossed by several waterways, the largest being Shenango River. Smaller streams include Deer Creek and Coffee Run. Mercer and Youngstown Road was laid out about 1802 and passed through New Bedford. It became a postal route in 1827. Another road, running north to south, opened about 1808.[1]

The first schoolhouse was a log cabin built before the War of 1812 near the residences of James Judy and James Donaldson. James Neal taught classical languages and continued the school until joining the army in 1813. James Walker taught school as early as 1802–3 in other parts of the township, including New Bedford.[2]

Several churches were located within the township. The Associate Presbyterian Church, later the United Presbyterian at Deer Creek, was organized about 1800, two miles northeast of Lowellville, Ohio. The Hopewell Church (Presbyterian) was organized in New Bedford some years before Deer Creek Church.[3] The Sisters–of–Mary Orphan farm was founded as a boarding school in 1856 by the Franciscan Brothers of Pittsburgh. When that did not succeed, the Sisters of Charity took charge and established an orphan school for girls.[4]

The most active period for the Underground Railroad in the township was from 1839 to 1846. Prior to that, kindhearted citizens assisted slaves, but they did it as individuals without systematic cooperation. After 1846 constant agitation of the slavery question, the road was not much operated.

NEW BEDFORD

DR. NATHANIEL BEDFORD, Dr. Peter Mowry and James Patterson originally purchased 26 tracts on the Shenango River and 13 on the Connoquenessing Creek. The town of New Bedford grew on some of the Bedford land, presumably named after the doctor. The first settlers were James and Thomas Black from Adams County, Pennsylvania, in 1796. The Blacks built the first cabin and made improvements before moving their families to the area.[5] Robert McCullough constructed the second house and, in 1818, Daniel Inbody laid out the town.[6]

Escaping slaves were transferred to the New Bedford route only when danger threatened them on the New Castle to Mercer road. Then they would go to William W. Walker or E. M. Stevenson.

A TEN-SIDED HOUSE

IN THE MID-1800'S, William Walker erected a ten-sided two-story brick home on his property that still stands today.

It is likely this house was used to harbor runaway slaves, as Walker was an avid Abolitionist and Conductor. On Walker's route, the fugitives usually traveled by horseback. He kept slaves

William W. Walker House

hidden through the day and took to the road no earlier than ten P.M. nor later than three A.M., since these were hours of greatest safety.

Walker's stations were from twelve to fifteen miles apart, so that the round trip was from 24 to 30 miles. He remembered that at one point he made three trips in one week, traveling "72 miles, in the dark hours on each side of midnight."

Walker transferred people to a number of safe places, including John Gilbert near West Middlesex, Pennsylvania, Sampson Moore and Walker's brother–in–law, David Bailey in Coitsville, Ohio, James Adair in Poland, Ohio, Charles Stewart in Vienna, Ohio, a tailor in Brookfield, Ohio, and Alexander Wright and David Young in Lawrence County.[7]

Walker also recalled a story of two slaves travelling on the route from New Castle to Mercer, and in danger of being overtaken by their masters. Mrs. David Young, "a brave and good woman," brought them from New Castle to Walker's station, and their master was directed on to Mercer.

When the master discovered he had been misled, he was told by local Abolitionists, "with great plainness of speech," what they thought of him and slavery.

> "In great anger he gave up the chase and returned home, breathing curses loud and deep against the Abolitionist."[8]

Reverend William Nesbit

On another occasion, the Walkers took in six fugitives, three men and three women, who were being pursued closely and in danger of being caught.

> "I never lost a passenger. The business was managed with such uniform care and caution that it ran smoothly and successfully, without any remarkable incident."

Even though their Presbyterian minister at New Bedford, Reverend William Nesbit, denounced the Abolitionists from the pulpit and said they were "far more vile in the sight of Gawd (with a drawl) than horse thieves," Walker cheerfully participated. He was doing it for the "sake of humanity," not for the honor.[9]

PULASKI

THE FIRST SETTLER on the land where Pulaski now stands was probably Daniel Ault from Deer Creek. Ault built his first gristmill about 1800 on Shenango River's west bank. A sawmill at the east end of the dam was possibly built by John Piper.

In 1832, William Byers and John Piper laid out the town with Byers owning everything south of Union Street, and Piper the north side. The Pennsylvania Canal Erie Extension was completed to Pulaski about 1836.[10]

In 1837, the Presbyterians of Pulaski appointed a committee to apply to the Presbytery for a church. The request was granted, and Reverend William Nesbit was appointed to organize the church. That fall, the church had a membership of 37 from congregations in Neshannock (New Wilmington) and Hopewell (New Bedford). The first elders were Patrick Wilson, Alexander Cotton and John P. Wright.[11]

The Methodist Episcopal Church was organized in 1854 or 1855. Their first meetings were led in the schoolhouse by Reverend Robert Caruthers.[12]

THE ALMA ACADEMY

Celebrated as one of the apostles of the Anti–Slavery movement in the Associate Church, Reverend John Walker of Pulaski platted the town of New Athens, Ohio on February 1817, and in 1818, founded Alma Academy.[23]

Located about 25 miles from what was then the Virginia border at Wheeling, the academy became a bastion of Anti–Slavery advocacy, the fountainhead of the abolition sentiment of eastern Ohio, and the school credited with graduating the first Black student in Ohio.[13]

Administration, faculty and students all demanded immediate and uncompromising abolition of slavery. The campus would later become Franklin College.[14]

WANTED: DEAD OR ALIVE

John Walker was a known conductor of the Underground Railroad. From 1840–1855 either Walker or one of his sons, Beveridge, John G., or Hughston (Houston) Walker, brought slaves to J. B. Lee's home in Mount Pleasant, Ohio.

In a letter to Wilbur Siebert, dated October 25, 1895, Mr. Lee estimated that the Walkers handled hundreds of fugitives. In one instance,

CONDUCTORS

KNOWN CONDUCTORS IN THE AREA included William W. Walker, Anna Jane Walker,

William W. & Anna Jane (Bailey) Walker

William Walker was born on his father's farm in 1819. He erected a ten–sided two–story brick home on his property that still stands today.

Walker was a Republican, and in religious views, an independent thinker.

"Faculties for education very moderate, but by his own application and reading he acquired an unusually large fund of information, on general topics and especially in the departments of history, science and theology."[16]

According to letters written to Professor Siebert by William Walker Jr., William Walker became an Abolitionist in 1833 and Conductor on the Underground Railroad in 1838 or 1839.

Walker was also active in the Western Anti–Slavery Society. At a Convention of the Anti–Slavery Young Men and Women of Ohio held in Mahoning County, Ohio, he was elected to serve on its Business committee.[17] Financially he supported the efforts of the Western Anti–Slavery Society through donations to the *Anti–Slavery Bugle* and subscriptions thereto.[18]

In 1851 he was involved in obtaining support for a Coitsville petition requiring peaceful dissolution of the Union between the free and slave states.[19] Considered an infidel by the church, he was engaged to debate the reliance on the Bible in support of slavery.[20]

In 1848, Walker married Anna Jane Bailey of Coitsville, Ohio, and they raised six children. Anna Jane's father was an early Abolitionist and frequently acted as a station keeper.

Reverend John Walker

Reverend John Walker was born in Washington County, Pennsylvania in 1786, and settled in New Bedford sometime after 1797 near his brother James Walker.[21] John was educated in Theology at Jefferson College and was ordained by the Presbytery of Ohio on July 11, 1811.

He was the first to enter the ministry from his family's congregation at the Deer Creek Church in New Bedford, where his father, Robert, had been a member of the first session. John served as "pastor of Mercer and connections" in Pennsylvania until 1814, and then left New Bedford for Harrison County, Ohio to assume the pastorate of Associate Churches in that area.[22]

Reverend Walker died on March 8, 1845 at New Athens.[27]

CONDUCTORS (CONTINUED)

John Walker, Alexander Anderson, Lavina Anderson, Elisha M. Stevenson, and Nancy Stevenson.

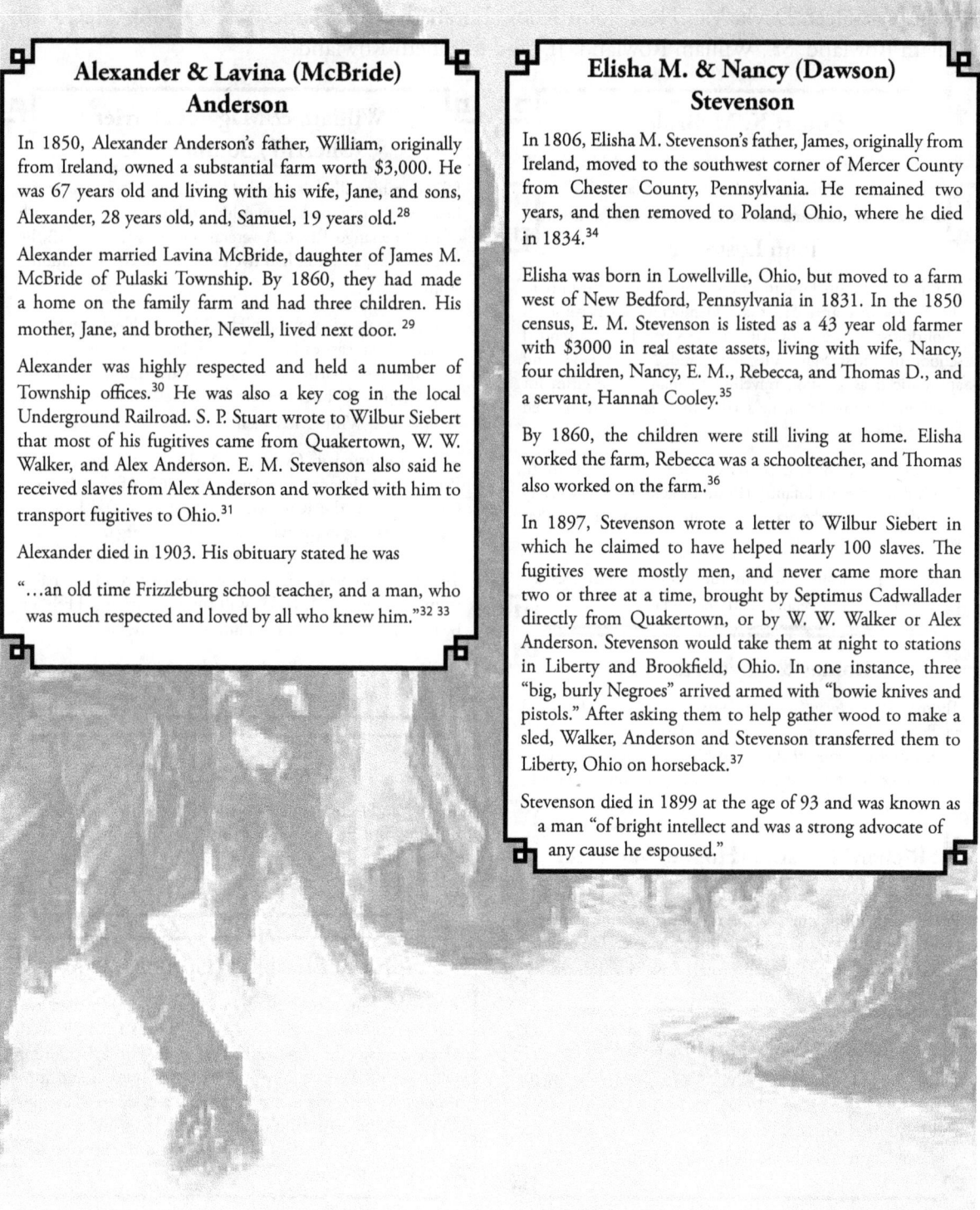

Alexander & Lavina (McBride) Anderson

In 1850, Alexander Anderson's father, William, originally from Ireland, owned a substantial farm worth $3,000. He was 67 years old and living with his wife, Jane, and sons, Alexander, 28 years old, and, Samuel, 19 years old.[28]

Alexander married Lavina McBride, daughter of James M. McBride of Pulaski Township. By 1860, they had made a home on the family farm and had three children. His mother, Jane, and brother, Newell, lived next door. [29]

Alexander was highly respected and held a number of Township offices.[30] He was also a key cog in the local Underground Railroad. S. P. Stuart wrote to Wilbur Siebert that most of his fugitives came from Quakertown, W. W. Walker, and Alex Anderson. E. M. Stevenson also said he received slaves from Alex Anderson and worked with him to transport fugitives to Ohio.[31]

Alexander died in 1903. His obituary stated he was

"...an old time Frizzleburg school teacher, and a man, who was much respected and loved by all who knew him."[32][33]

Elisha M. & Nancy (Dawson) Stevenson

In 1806, Elisha M. Stevenson's father, James, originally from Ireland, moved to the southwest corner of Mercer County from Chester County, Pennsylvania. He remained two years, and then removed to Poland, Ohio, where he died in 1834.[34]

Elisha was born in Lowellville, Ohio, but moved to a farm west of New Bedford, Pennsylvania in 1831. In the 1850 census, E. M. Stevenson is listed as a 43 year old farmer with $3000 in real estate assets, living with wife, Nancy, four children, Nancy, E. M., Rebecca, and Thomas D., and a servant, Hannah Cooley.[35]

By 1860, the children were still living at home. Elisha worked the farm, Rebecca was a schoolteacher, and Thomas also worked on the farm.[36]

In 1897, Stevenson wrote a letter to Wilbur Siebert in which he claimed to have helped nearly 100 slaves. The fugitives were mostly men, and never came more than two or three at a time, brought by Septimus Cadwallader directly from Quakertown, or by W. W. Walker or Alex Anderson. Stevenson would take them at night to stations in Liberty and Brookfield, Ohio. In one instance, three "big, burly Negroes" arrived armed with "bowie knives and pistols." After asking them to help gather wood to make a sled, Walker, Anderson and Stevenson transferred them to Liberty, Ohio on horseback.[37]

Stevenson died in 1899 at the age of 93 and was known as a man "of bright intellect and was a strong advocate of any cause he espoused."

ABOLITIONISTS

KNOWN ABOLITIONISTS IN THE AREA included Robert K. McBride, John Lostetter, Thomas Paden, William Sommerville, Richard Van Fleet, Sarah Van Fleet, Phoebe Van Fleet, George Van Fleet, David Van Fleet, John Knox, Elizabeth Knox, James Walker, John McConahy, William Rowland, Sr., William Rowland, Jr., and Elizabeth Rowland.

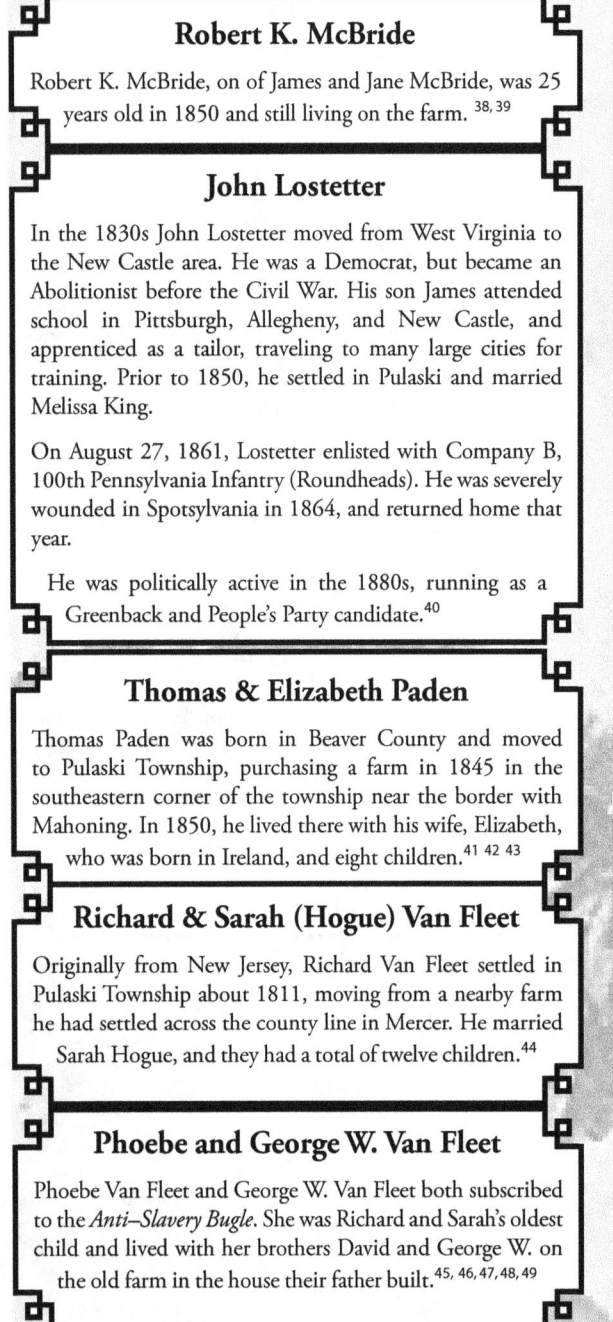

Robert K. McBride

Robert K. McBride, on of James and Jane McBride, was 25 years old in 1850 and still living on the farm. [38, 39]

John Lostetter

In the 1830s John Lostetter moved from West Virginia to the New Castle area. He was a Democrat, but became an Abolitionist before the Civil War. His son James attended school in Pittsburgh, Allegheny, and New Castle, and apprenticed as a tailor, traveling to many large cities for training. Prior to 1850, he settled in Pulaski and married Melissa King.

On August 27, 1861, Lostetter enlisted with Company B, 100th Pennsylvania Infantry (Roundheads). He was severely wounded in Spotsylvania in 1864, and returned home that year.

He was politically active in the 1880s, running as a Greenback and People's Party candidate. [40]

Thomas & Elizabeth Paden

Thomas Paden was born in Beaver County and moved to Pulaski Township, purchasing a farm in 1845 in the southeastern corner of the township near the border with Mahoning. In 1850, he lived there with his wife, Elizabeth, who was born in Ireland, and eight children. [41 42 43]

Richard & Sarah (Hogue) Van Fleet

Originally from New Jersey, Richard Van Fleet settled in Pulaski Township about 1811, moving from a nearby farm he had settled across the county line in Mercer. He married Sarah Hogue, and they had a total of twelve children. [44]

Phoebe and George W. Van Fleet

Phoebe Van Fleet and George W. Van Fleet both subscribed to the *Anti–Slavery Bugle*. She was Richard and Sarah's oldest child and lived with her brothers David and George W. on the old farm in the house their father built. [45, 46, 47, 48, 49]

William & Magaret Harriet (Sherriff) Sommerville

John Sommerville (also spelled Summerville) was one of the first settlers in Pulaski Township and owned a farm south of the Shenango River. A veteran of the War of 1812, he and his wife, Eleanor, had five children by 1850, including William. [50]

William married Margaret Harriet Sherriff whose family owned a farm east of New Bedford. He was an Abolitionist and may have participated in the Underground Railroad with Joseph S. White, Reverend Bushnell, Amzi Semple, Eli Sample, and White McMillen. [51]

William enlisted in Company A, 134th Regiment of the Pennsylvania Infantry, on August 9, 1862. After training at Camp Curtin, the Regiment marched to several locations before engaging in the Battle of Fredericksburg in December 1862. Fourteen were killed, 106 wounded, and 19 missing. The Regiment also engaged in Burnside's second campaign from January 20–24, 1863. William was discharged Feb 6th by the surgeon and returned home as an invalid. [52]

His wife, Margaret, lived more than 80 years as a proud patriot and active American Red Cross member. [53]

David Van Fleet

David Van Fleet attended a National Disunion Convention in 1857 and was appointed to a committee to nominate permanent officers and committees to serve the Convention. [54]

John & Elizabeth (Gordon) Knox

Reverend John Knox, born in Ireland, accompanied two brothers to America when he was 17. He married Elizabeth Gordon, sister of Reverends George and Joseph Gordon (all born in Washington County, Pennsylvania), and for a number of years she and her husband resided in Mahoning County, Ohio before moving to Pulaski Township, Lawrence County, Pennsylvania, where he would die on July 6, 1857 at his farm.

ABOLITIONISTS (CONTINUED)

Pulaski Townshop Subscribers to the *Anti-Slaver Bugle* included L. M. Bootman, Joseph S. Boynton, A. M. Hart, George McNabb (New Bedford), and John. A. Walker (Pulaski).

James & Agnes (McFadden) Walker

James Walker was born in Ireland in 1774 and traveled to Washington County, Pennsylvania, with his father, Robert Walker. James was a self–educated scholar and schoolteacher. He married Agnes McFadden in 1794 and had one son, Robert. His second marriage, Mary Anderson, produced seven children. The family settled in Pulaski Township about 1814.

Walker served in the War of 1812 under Commodore Perry and was politically active, elected to various county offices, including four terms as Auditor.

"He was an Abolitionist from 1833, and was one of the first movers in the Temperance cause, and took an active leading part in all the moral reforms of his day."[55]

He was a ruling elder in the Hopewell Presbyterian Church for 44 years, but when Reverend John Knox organized the Free Presbyterian Church, Walker joined the new congregation, remaining with it for two years.

"He was a most liberal–minded man in all matters of religious opinion, and was fully pledged to the investigation of truth in all things and earnestly impressed these principles upon his family."[56]

John & Martha (Smith) McConahy

Reverend John McConahy was one of the best known and highly respected men of Pulaski. He was born in a little log cabin and grew up in the rural countryside. He spend his life visiting widely separated communities traveling on horseback and performing the duties of a pastor of the Baptist Church.

He served Hillsvale, Sharon, and nearby places, but never disregarded calls to isolated farms. He was a strong Abolitionist in his early years and later a staunch supporter of the Republican Party.

He married Martha C. Smith of Columbus, Ohio. Two of their children were Mary V., wife of John F. Mitchell of Pulaski and Zenas W. McConahy, also of Pulaski.[57]

William, Jr. & Elizabeth (Allison) Rowland

William Rowland, Jr. was born in Beaver County and accompanied his parents to Mahoning Township as a boy. He later farmed in Pulaski Township, then moved to another farm near New Bedford about 1857.

Rowland, Jr. was active as an Abolitionist and a Republican prior to the Civil War. His wife was the former Elizabeth Allison.[58]

William Rowland, Sr.

William Rowland, Sr. was an Abolitionist and worked with the promoters of the Underground Railroad.

Walker, with ten well-armed men on horseback, guided and guarded fugitive slaves to a safer station.[24]

Walker also helped found a free labor store that refused to sell anything produced by slave labor. He convinced neighbors not to cooperate with slave hunters.

One slave hunter demanded "...the nigger-loving preacher must be horsewhipped." A a $1,000 reward was reportedly offered for delivering Reverend John Walker dead or alive[25] to New Orleans during the height of the Anti-Slavery controversy.[26]

FREE PRESBYTERY OF MAHONING

IN 1847, REVERENDS A. B. Bradford, Samuel A. McLean, and Joseph Gordon of the Free Presbyterian Church, formed the Free Presbytery of Mahoning at New Athens.

> "[T]he Seceders, led by Reverend John Walker, were prominent in aiding slaves to gain liberty and in working for abolition."[15]

Chapter Notes

1. Durant, 98.
2. Durant, 99.
3. Ibid.
4. Durant, 100.
5. Durant, 101.
6. Durant, 102.
7. Walker, W. W. "Passengers to Ohio, Mahoning and Trumbull Counties," October 15, 1898, Wilbur H. Siebert Collection, State Library of Ohio.
8. Walker, W. W. "Routes through and Activity in Lawrence County, Pennsylvania," March 14, 1896, Wilbur H. Siebert Collection, State Library of Ohio.
9. Walker, W. W. Letter to McMillan Co. Publishers, September 21, 1898, Wilbur H. Siebert Collection, State Library of Ohio.
10. Durant, 103.
11. Durant, 104.
12. Durant, 105.
13. Erving E. Beauregard, Ohio's First Black College Graduate, Spring 1987 harrisonhistory.org
14. Hanna, Charles Augustus, *Historical Collections of Harrison County, In the State of Ohio*. 1900, 134.
15. Minutes of the Free Presbytery of Mahoning, p.3, Dr. Isaac Ketler Collection, Grove City College.
16. Durant, 194.
17. *Anti-Slavery Bugle*, Lisbon, Ohio, October 6, 1849, 1.
18. *Anti-Slavery Bugle*, Lisbon, Ohio, May 12, 1848, 3; August 21, 1858, 3; January 15, 1859, 3; May 4, 1850, 3; August 21, 1858, 3; April 30, 1859, 3.
19. *Anti-Slavery Bugle*, Lisbon, Ohio, March 29, 1851, 3.
20. *Anti-Slavery Bugle*, Lisbon, Ohio, March 8, 1856, 4.
21. Sommerville, Charles W. *History of the Hopewell Presbyterian Church, New Bedford, Lawrence County, Pennsylvania The One Hundred and Fiftieth Anniversary, October 12-15, 1950.*
22. Hanna, Charles Augustus, *Unity Church, Historical Collections of Harrison County*, 133-138.
23. Franklin College Register: Biographical and Historical By Franklin College, New Athens, Ohio. Board of Trustees. Wheeling: West Virginia Printing Co. 1908.
24. Lee, J. B. (Letter). Wilbur H. Siebert Collection, State Library of Ohio.
25. Beauregard, Erving, *Reverend John Walker, Renaissance Man*. P. Lang. 1990, 97.
26. *History of the United Presbyterian Church, New Bedford, Lawrence County, Pennsylvania, Centennial Celebration October 15, 1908*. Lawrence Printing House. Grove City, Pennsylvania.

27 *New-York Daily Tribune*, April 4, 1845, 3.

28 United States Census: Pennsyvlania, Lawrence County, 1850.

29 United States Census: Pennsyvlania, Lawrence County, 1860.

30 *Biographical Sketches of Leading Citizens, Lawrence County Pennssylvania*, 349.

31 Stuart, S. P. "Route from Quakertown, Lawrence County, Pennsylvania to Hubbard, Brookfield, Liberty, and Hartford, Trumbull County, Ohio," December, 26, 1895. Wilbur H. Siebert Collection, State Library of Ohio.

32 Stevenson, E. M. "Route from Quakerstown, Lawrence County to Liberty Township or Brookfield," February 24, 1897. Wilbur H. Siebert Collection, State Library of Ohio.

33 Alexander Anderson Obituary, *New Castle News*, January 28, 1903.

34 Durant, 98.

35 United States Census: Pennsyvlania, Lawrence County, 1850.

36 United States Census: Pennsyvlania, Lawrence County, 1860.

37 Stevenson, E. M. "Route from Quakerstown, Lawrence County to Liberty Township or Brookfield," February 24, 1897. Wilbur H. Siebert Collection, State Library of Ohio.

38 United States Census: Pennsylvania, Lawrence County 1850.

39 *Anti-Slavery Bugle*, September 1, 1848, 3.

40 *New Castle News*, January 25, 1899.

41 Hazen, 513.

42 United States Census: Pennsyvlania, Lawrence County, 1850.

43 *Anti-Slavery Bugle*, January 19, 1861, 3.

44 Upton, Harriet Taylor, *History of Western Reserve, Vol. 3*, New York, 1910, 1573.

45 Ibid.

46 *Anti-Slavery Bugle,* March 3, 1848, 3.

47 Anti-Slavery Bugle, March 2, 1849, 3.

48 Anti-Slavery Bugle, July 30, 1859, 3.

49 Anti-Slavery Bugle, January 1, 1861, 3.

50 Hazen, 305.

51 "Nearly Half a Century," *New Castle News*, March 8, 1899.

52 http://www.pacivilwar.com/regiment/134th.html

53 "New Bedford Woman Aids," *New Castle News*, September 18, 1918.

54 Upton, Harriet Taylor, *History of Western Reserve, Vol. 3*, 1573.

55 Durant, 195.

56 Durant, 194.

57 Hazen, 467.

58 Hazen, 674.

16

SHENANGO TOWNSHIP

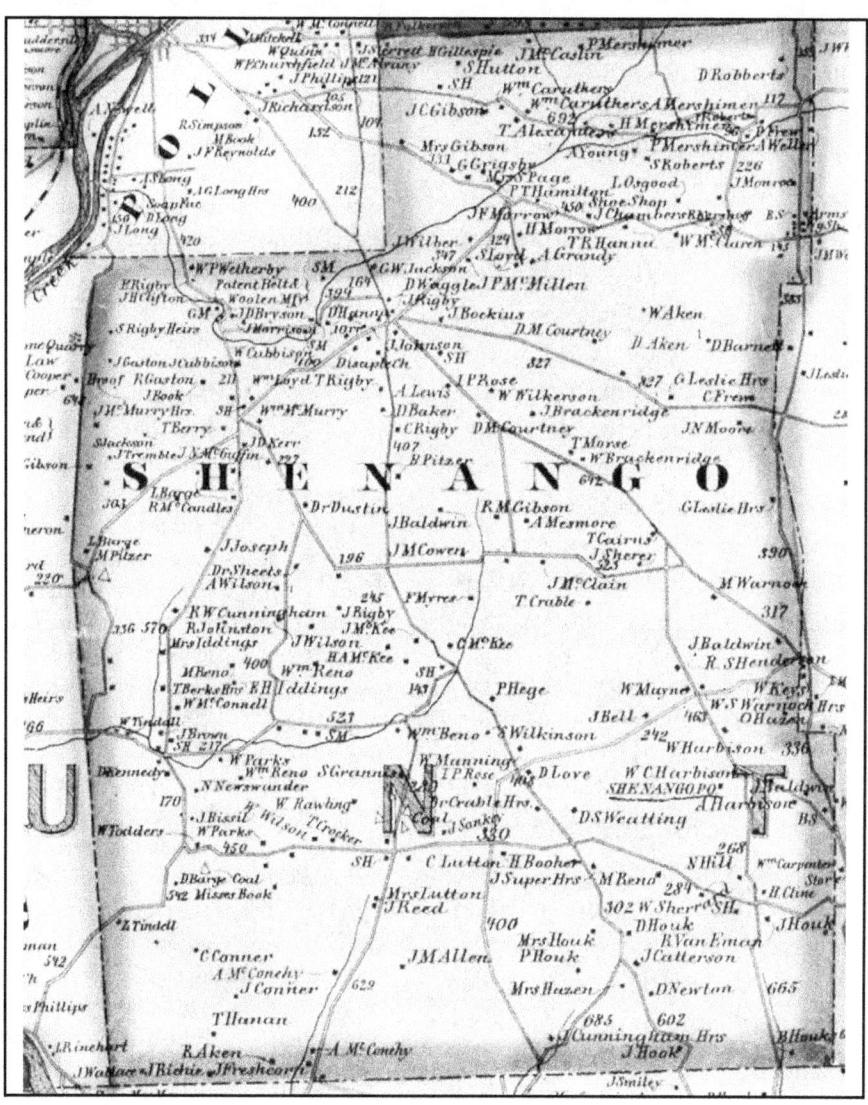

SHENANGO TOWNSHIP was one of the original 13 townships of Lawrence County, and comprised a large part of Beaver County before 1849. The northern and eastern terrain is rolling and well adapted to agriculture. In the south, ridges rise 300 or 400 feet above the Beaver River, and an abundance of coal was found halfway up the hillsides.[1]

Settlement began as early as 1796 in the northern and northeastern portions of the township. With access to the newly completed Pennsylvania canal and its branches, Shenango developed more rapidly than other townships. Its coal, iron and limestone deposits contributed wealth to the landowners.

One of the first settlers, William Cairns arrived with his family, made a clearing, built a cabin, and began farming. Other early settlers included Robert McWilliams who, in about 1816, built a gristmill and sawmill on Big Run. In 1841–42 John Armstrong, Esq., erected another gristmill in the township's northeast corner, an area so prosperous that Zachariah Tindall opened a bank in 1850.[2]

In 1805, children in the north and western portions of the township traveled to Moravia to attend school. In 1810 or 1811, a log cabin was converted into a school by James Leslie, and education became more convenient. The first log schoolhouse was built before 1812 and an Englishman named Cornelius Stafford, who taught in nearly every township in the southeast part of the county, was its first teacher. Another school began in 1813 on a farm owned by Robert Irwin. Its first teacher was John Gibson.[3]

Shenango Township had several churches. The Center United Presbyterian Church held tent–meetings in the early 1820s. Reverend David Norwood was ordained and installed as their first pastor April 5, 1826. The Savannah Methodist Episcopal Church was organized about 1820, and their first church building constructed in 1851. The Congregation of Disciples at Normal Glen was organized about 1833, with Elder Sanders and Elder William Hayden of Ohio delivering the sermons, but they had no building until 1847.[4]

A REMINISCENCE

NOT LONG AFTER Henry Williams moved his family to Kansas the following story was published in the *Free Presbyterian* and reprinted in the *Anti–Slavery Bugle*.[5] The "Mr. W__" referred to below appears to match his identity.

Mr. Dear Brother:—Among the emigrants who lately left this place to well the number of Free State settlers in Kansas was ___W___, a highly respected member of the Reformed Presbyterian Church. That you may know the kind of stuff he is made of, and whether he is the man for the times, I send you the following incident in his history which now for the first time is made public.

In the year 1826 Mr. W___ was returning to his home from a trip down the Ohio River in company with two other persons. On the National Road between Claysville [Pennsylvania] and Wheeling [West Virginia] they met a man driving a coffle of slaves, all marching two abreast, their wrists tied together with strips of raw–hide. The man rode a fine looking horse and was armed with whip and pistols and other implements of his trade. Two of the slave women had children in their arms and as they lagged behind a little, the driver would give them a cut with his long whip to hurry them on, much after the fashion of a Western drover when the cows and calves don't keep up with the rest of the herd. Mr. ___ had often heard of human beings treated as slaves and driven to market in gangs like horses, but he had never till then witnessed such a scene. His whole soul was therefore roused into indignation at the sight and without a moment's hesitation he proposed to his fellow travelers that if they would stand beside him he would release the poor heart–broken wretches, and give them their liberty. The slaves had been bought up for a plantation in Louisiana dragged away from their friends and relatives were overwhelmed with distress. Mr. W___ companions affected like himself with the heart rendering sight, instantly complied with his proposal and promised to see him through. W___ then hailed the driver of the gang and asked him where he was bound for. "To Wheeling," was the reply– "what are you going to do with all these colored people that you have tied together?" "They are slaves," said the driver; "I am going to take them to Wheeling to ship them there for Louisiana." "But what right have you to do this? These people have as good a claim to their liberty as you have." By this time the gang had stopped and was listening with deep emotion to the colloquy between their master and the travelers. "I bought these niggers in the neighborhood and paid my money for them," said the driver, "and I reckon I have the best right to them." "But, replied W__, "you might as well buy me and take me away as these people. I say again they have as good a right to their liberty as you have to yours—and they shall have it, too." With this he stepped forward and took the bridle reins of his horse and ordered the slave–driver to dismount. Instead of doing so, however, he drew from his holsters a large horse pistol and swore he would blow the brains out of any many who stopped him. "You need not shoot," said one of the other men as he saw the slave driver aimed his pistol at W___'s head, "for you can only kill one man, and if you do, you had better say your last prayers for you are a dead man." "Get off your horse," thundered W___ in a tone which taught the slave driver that he had met with ugly customers. "If you do, not a hair on your head shall be hurt, and be quick about it, for these poor creatures shall go free." Being rather slow in the motion the travelers helped him off. One of the party took the horse and hitched him to a tree near by and the other two removed the kidnapper to a sapling on the other side of the road. Here they removed his neck–handkerchief, and having made a rope of it tied his hands behind him and around the sapling. W___ then took out his knife and having cut the rawhide thongs which bound the slaves together, said to them, "Now put to your scrapers my good fellows, and no more than two go together. And you," addressing him to a couple of stout active men, "take care of these women and children." The slaves with a look of gratitude never to be forgotten and with "alacrity" truly Websterian, obey the orders and dash off into the woods like a flock of sheep.

Mr. W___ then went to the driver with a sapling at his back and after a brief abolition lecture, told him to halloo to the first descent looking traveler that came along who would untie him and let him go on his way rejoicing. Bidding him farewell the travelers pursued their journey towards Pittsburgh, where in due time they arrived. They then separated and Mr. ___ went to his home some miles from that city.

In a few weeks after, having business in Pittsburgh, Mr. W___ stopped at a hotel and while waiting for dinner, took up one of the newspapers and in it read a prominent advertisement, offering a large reward for the apprehension of the twenty–two Negroes, and especially the three "ruffians" who liberated them. An accurate description was given of the "ring leader" his looks and particularly his dress. Mr. ___ read the advertisement with considerable interest, but of course said nothing. He listened to the remarks made by different persons in regard to the matter, some few approving and others not, but never breathed a word of it to a human being, not even to his own wife, far many years after. I almost forgot to say that the advertisement stated the fact that all the slaves made good their escape but two, probably the poor women with their children. Could the fact of the rescue have been proven, it might have cost the parties their property and their liberty, for at that time Abolitionists were rather scarce in the country. They therefore wisely heard what people had to say of the act but kept the secret to themselves.

Last winter, Mr. W___ being confined to his room by sickness, sent me word that he would like me to go over and sit a few hours with him. I did so and during the interview he gave me the substance of what I have written. As it was a "Jerry rescue" which antedates the one of Syracuse by more than a score of years, I, in admiration of the heroic act, done at such a time and such a place and under such circumstances, have rescued it from oblivion and given it to your readers. Mr. W___ wrote to a friend in New Castle, two days before the sacking of Lawrence and in his letter published in the Freeman, agrees exactly with you that the leaders in Kansas are deficient in courage—that if the people and especially the women, had leaders worthy of them, they could chase the Amalekites beyond the border and have peace founded on righteousness.

This is the second day of the Republican Convention in Philadelphia. Fremont, it seems from today's dispatch has the best prospect of the nomination. He may be the man for the time, but we know a little of him that is difficult to estimate him. If he be nominated for the Presidency on the score of availability, sure the convention ought to put the name of Charles Sumner on the ticket for Vice Presidency. It would sugarcoat the pill if it must be swallowed.

New Castle, Pennsylvania June 1856.

CONDUCTORS

KNOWN CONDUCTORS IN THE AREA included Henry Williams and Mary Williams.

Henry & Mary Williams

Henry Williams, initially from Pittsburgh, became the superintendent for J. D. White's New Castle shovel factory in 1838. When the property sold, Williams, Benjamin White, and William Clark, erected a building to house a gristmill, carding mill, and wood working lathes. Fire destroyed the building in 1844, and he went to work as an engineer for Crawford & Co. in their nail factory. In the 1850 census Henry was living in Shenango Township with his wife, Mary, and six children, Charles, Albert, Mary, William Margaret, James and Robert.

Williams was an Elder in the early Covenanters Church in New Castle. His congregation would later join the Free Presbyterian Church founded shortly after the Fugitive Slave Bill was signed. Fellow elders included Robert Davis, J. N. Euwer, and Daniel Minnick. Meetings of the congregation were held at White Hall in the Free Presbyterian Church, with Reverend A. B. Bradford and Reverend G. Riley McMillan preaching.[6]

Henry and his family moved to Kansas in 1854.

ABOLITIONISTS

KNOWN ABOLITIONISTS IN THE AREA included William Cairns and Reverend Robert Sample.

Reverend Robert Sample

Chapter Notes

1. Durant, 109.
2. Durant, 113.
3. Durant, 113.
4. Durant, 114.
5. *Anti-Slavery Bugle*, July 19, 1856, 2.
6. "History of Local Covenanters," *New Castle News, Weekly Edition*, February 28, 1901, 6.

17

SLIPPERY ROCK TOWNSHIP

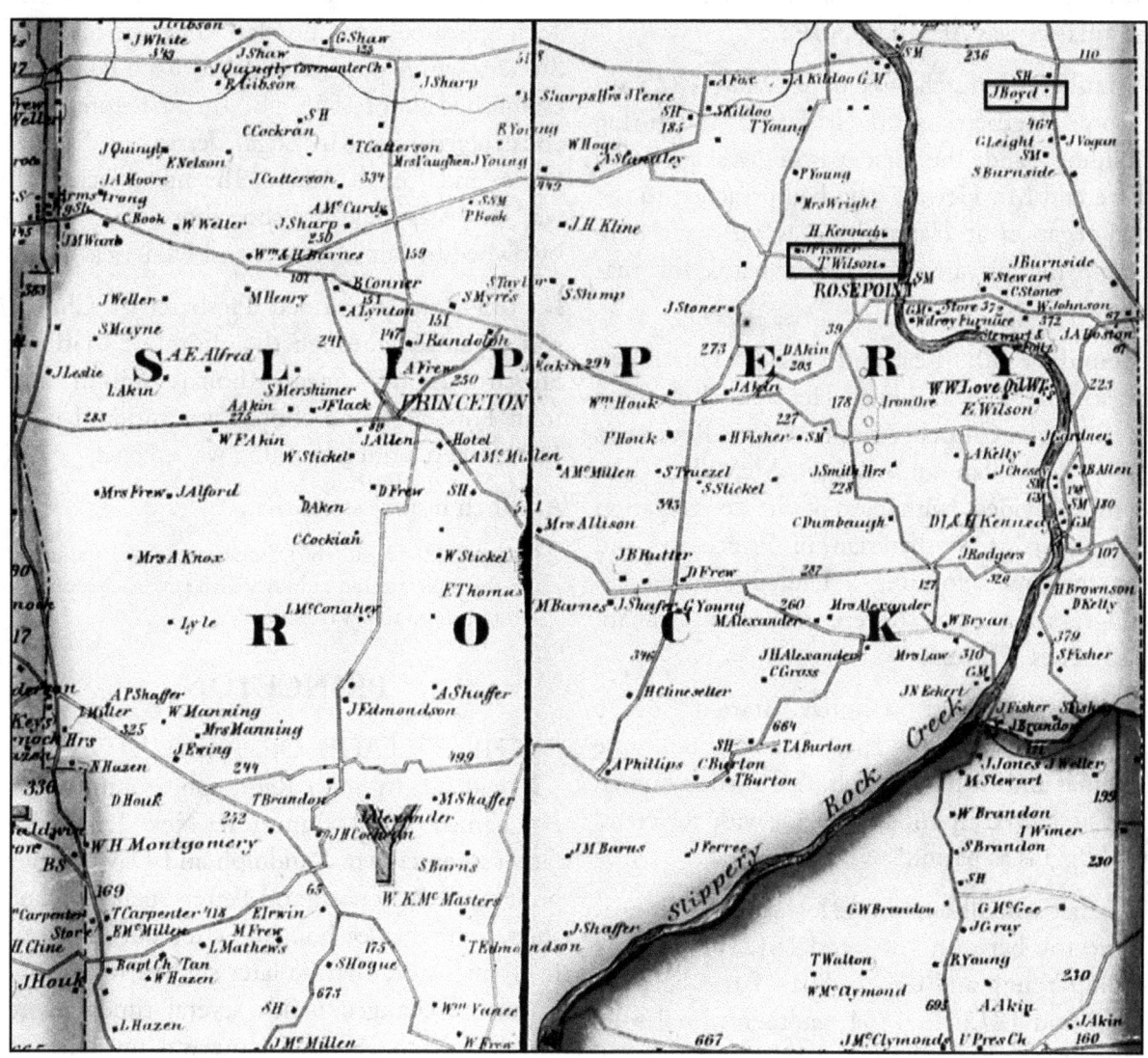

SLIPPERY ROCK WAS one of Lawrence County's original townships, being part of Beaver County before 1849. Its landscape is hilly, with rocky gorges found along the Slippery Rock and Muddy Creeks.[1]

In 1809, Peter Fox came from Westmoreland County and settled on the east side of Slippery Rock Creek. He built the first gristmill some distance below the present McConnell's Mill. Matthew Young arrived in the spring of 1813, and established the farm later owned by Robert

Young. Robert and John Burnside and Andrew Stanley followed in 1817.[2]

As the settlements grew, a postal route was established in the early 1840s between New Castle and Butler, through Princeton, and afterwards through Rose Point. A post office was approved at Princeton a year later. The first postmaster was Alexander Aiken.[3]

A Lutheran church was built about 1825 on George Herbert's farm. It was a rough log building, and the first pastor was probably Reverend Mr. Hewitt, who had preached to the congregation at Harlansburg as early as 1800, employing private houses and barns for that purpose.

Around 1840, Reverend Josiah Hutchman organized The Mount Hermon Reformed Presbyterian Church. After him came Reverends Riley McMillan and Robert McMillan. The church divided, with part of the congregation organizing as Presbyterian in Princeton, and the remainder forming a United Presbyterian congregation under Reverends Robert Graham and James Whitten.

Harmony Baptist Church started in a schoolhouse in 1849. Their first ministers were Thomas and Daniel Daniels. A Christian church was organized in 1864 or 1865, with Reverend O. Higgins as pastor.[4]

The first schoolhouses were log cabins built near Princeton between 1808 and 1812, and on the Phillip Young and George Shaw farms between 1810 and 1812. In 1834, another school took form in Shady Dell and by 1875, schools had appeared in Slippery Rock Township.[5]

ROSE POINT

ROSE POINT'S FIRST settlers in 1803 were Abraham Wigle from Westmoreland County, and Samuel Stickle. About 1825, Wigle built a gristmill and sawmill where the road crosses the stream southwest of the village. High water later washed the mills away. McMaster built a carding machine and gristmill on the creek in the late 1840s.[6]

Around 1850, John Stoner purchased land where the village now stands. A small cluster of houses soon appeared, and the place took the name of Stonertown. A post office called Rose Point was established about 1855–58. The first stores were constructed by a Mr. Edgar, Jessie and Samuel Jones, and Joseph Aiken. The first blacksmith was John Chesney, and shoe shops were owned by owned by James Adams and Frederick Weir.[7]

In 1834, the Reformed Presbyterian Church was organized through the efforts of Matthew Stewart, Thomas Speer, Thomas Wilson, and John Love. A frame church was uitilized until 1871, when a brick building was erected.

A church history states that,

> "Between 1852 and 1861 Stonertown was a station on the underground railway which gave shelter and protection to runaway slaves."[8]

PRINCETON

THE VILLAGE OF PRINCETON was laid out by John Randolph around 1841. He named it for Princeton, New Jersey, his father's hometown. Randolph and David Fetter built the first houses, and Fetter opened a shoe shop. John Eckles bought Fetter out, and put in a small store that he later sold to Randolph. The store changed hands several times before burning down. Another store was owned by a Mr. Henderson, and subsequently by several people in the village's early history.[9]

CONDUCTORS

KNOWN CONDUCTORS IN THE AREA included Thomas Wilson and George Magee of Perry Township, Dr. Cowden of New Castle, Thomas Speer from Hickory Township, Matthew Young, Joanna Young, and John Boyd (listed as William).

Thomas & Margaret Wilson

Before the 1820s, Thomas Wilson owned land on both sides of Slippery Rock Creek, north of Rose Point. In 1850, the census showed him farming the west side where he and his wife, Margaret, lived with four children, Jacob, Rachel, Jemima and Henna.[10]

Wilson was a founding member of the Reformed Presbyterian Church.[11] Johnson Knight purchased a mill site from him in 1824–5 and built a gristmill, sawmill, carding mill, oil mill, and the first dam at that location.[12]

Matthew & Joanna (Coovertt) Young

Matthew Young was born about 1804 on his father's homestead in Slippery Rock Township. He learned the harness maker, shoemaker, and the tanner trades, and bought a farm on which he built a log cabin. As soon as he was able, he erected a fine set of frame buildings and a tannery, and carried on a tanning, harness, saddle and shoe making business.[14]

Matthew was Presbyterian and a Whig with strong Anti–Slavery sympathies, who actively identified with Abolitionists. As an agent of the Underground Railroad he rescued many slaves "from bondage and from the lash."[15]

His wife was Joanna Coovertt, daughter of Colonel John Coovertt, veteran of the War of 1812. The couple had eight children, Sylvester M., Caroline, Matilda, Amanda, Sarah Jane, Samantha, Marcus, and William H.

Young died in Mercer County when he was about 44 years old, having removed to Wolf Creek Township.

John & Dorcas (McWilliams) Boyd

John Boyd owned a farm in the northeastern corner of Slippery Rock Township, on the east side of Slippery Rock Creek. In 1850, he was 50 years old and lived in Princeton with his wife, Dorcas, and children, Elizabeth, John, William, Nancy and Wilson.

William Boyd is listed as a member of the Underground Railroad in the Churches of Lawrence County, but this is probably an error, as he was only 11 years old in 1850. It's more likely that his father, John, was the Conductor.[13]

Chapter Notes

1. Hazen, 330.
2. Hazen, 331.
3. Hazen, 338.
4. Hazen, 339-340.
5. Hazen, 339.
6. Durant, 117.
7. Durant, 118.
8. Richards, Bart, *Churches of Lawrence County*. Universal Printing Co. 1964, 37.
9. Durant, 118.
10. United States Census: Pennsylvania, Lawrence County, 1850.
11. Richards, Bart, *Churches of Lawrence County*, 37.
12. Durant, 117.
13. United States Census: Pennsylvania, Lawrence County, 1850.
14. U.S. Federal Census Mortality Schedules, 1850-1885.
15. *Biographical Sketches of Leading Citizens, Lawrence County Pennsylvania*, 399.

18

UNION TOWNSHIP

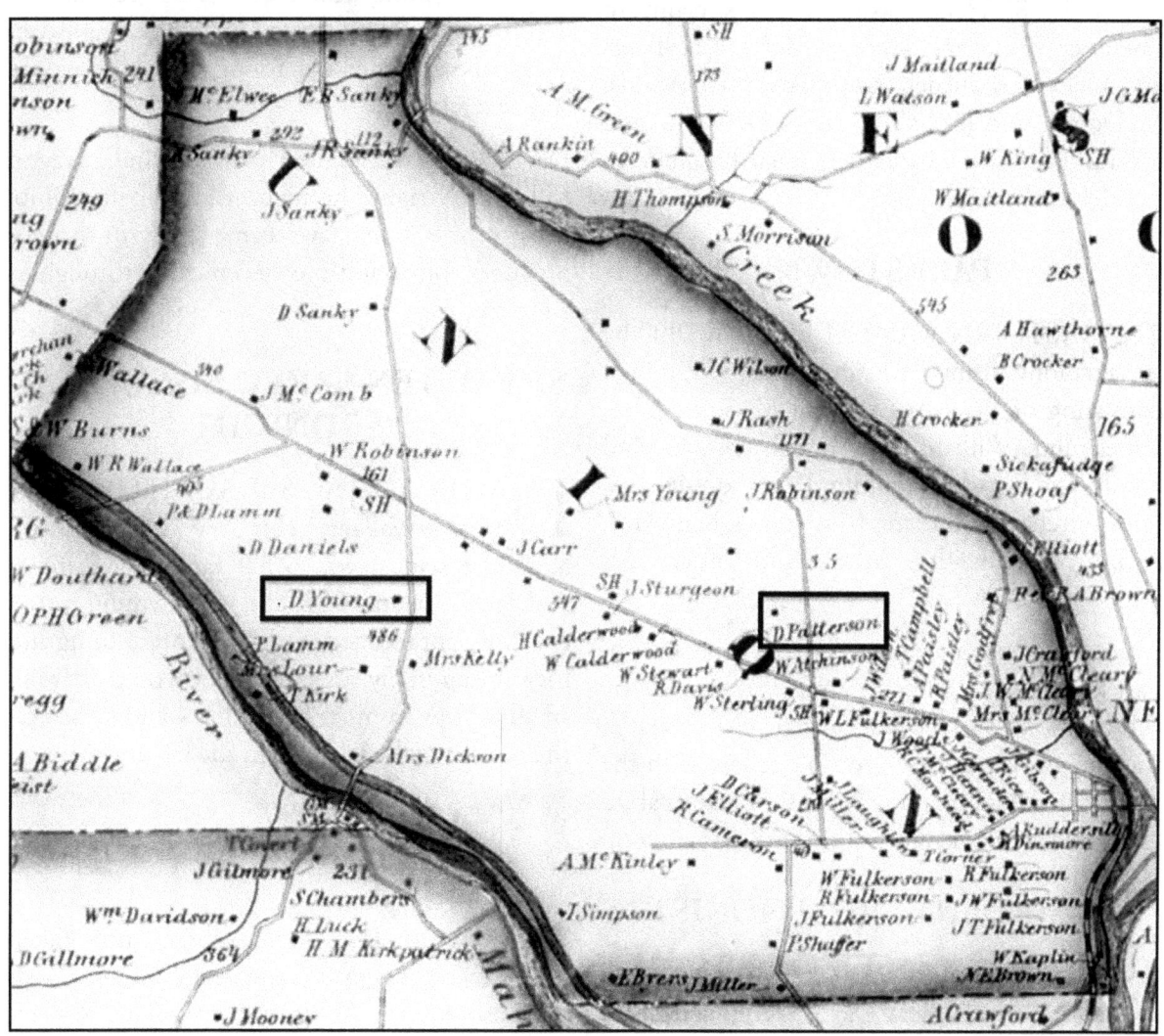

UNION TOWNSHIP WAS CREATED in 1859 from portions of Mahoning, Neshannock and Taylor Townships. It is bounded on the north by the Shenango River, and on the south by the Mahoning River. The land features superior soil quality for producing grain crops and fruit. There was also an abundance of limestone, particularly along the Mahoning River bluffs. Coal was found in several locations and mined extensively on Robert Wallace's farm in the southwestern part of the township.[1]

First settlers were Cornelius Hendrickson and his son Daniel, arriving about 1798. They built cabins along the Shenango River, west of New

Castle and established a canoe ferry. Daniel ran the ferry and frequently accommodated parties, traveling as far as Beaver Falls.

Around 1810, William Young, from Cumberland County, Pennsylvania, settled a farm located along the New Castle and Youngstown road.

About 1818, Hendrickson sold his claim to Ebenezer Byers and George McDowell. Byers and McDowell divided the property. Afterwards, McDowell sold his half to James D. White and his administrators. Byers bargained his share to Ezekiel Sankey.[2]

PARKSTOWN

PARKSTOWN WAS SETTLED in 1800 by a colony from Berkeley County, Virginia, consisting of William Park and his sons, John, James and William, Jr., Joseph Brown and family, and Thomas Franklin, Park's son–in–law. They purchased 300 acres from John Chenowith, Arthur Chenowith's father, who afterwards settled in New Castle.

Union Township's first school opened in Parkstown in 1806. It was supported by subscriptions, and the first teacher, a Mr. Shearer, was "an Irishman, and a terrible fellow with the rod." The school building was a simple log cabin, and some students walked three miles to attend.[3]

AN ARDENT ABOLITIONIST

MRS. W. A. OFFUTT of Volant described her grandfather, David Young, and his participation in the Underground Railroad to the *New Castle News*. He was, she said, an "ardent Abolitionist" who owned a farm in Union Township, about three miles west of the city.[4]

In a letter from W. W. Walker to Wilbur Siebert, Walker recalls an eveing when Mrs. David Young, "a brave and good woman," transported fugitives from New Castle to his father's station. Their master was diverted to Mercer.[5] In another letter he mentioned that they received slaves from David Young in the early forties.[6]

Slaves were brought at night from Arthur B. Bradford's home near New Galilee to Covert's Station, where they crossed the Mahoning River. When they reached the Young farm, they would stay several days.

David Young would then haul them in his wagon to Joseph Wright's home near Lowellville, Ohio. Most of the time, slaves came singly or in twos or threes, but one time eleven came through as a group.[7]

SHE OFTEN BAKED BISCUITS AT MIDNIGHT

DAVID YOUNG'S DAUGHTER, Mrs. Sarah Wallace, confirmed that Joseph S. White sent slaves to her father's Parkstown Station. Born in 1837, she was a young girl at the time, but recalled the family entertaining and forwarding many fugitives. They would arrive in small groups from A. B. Bradford and knock on the door, usually at night in the fall and winter.

As White relayed the story,

> "...her mother often baked biscuits for them at midnight."

The escaping slaves were subsequently taken to the Wrights' farm, and then on to E. M. Stevenson's farm. White reported Mrs. Wallace recollecting,

> "one fugitive who was in danger of being captured and a number of neighbors guarded the place on the Sabbath with guns and clubs..."[8]

William W. McCombs, Mrs. Wallace's grandson, said that his grandmother washed the travelers' clothing and gave each woman a bonnet. The family would then rub their guests' feet with onions to throw bloodhounds off the trail. The slaves would wash in a spring along Covert Road and be placed in a horse–drawn wagon, covered with hay and transported at night to New Bedford or another station.[8]

CONDUCTORS

KNOWN CONDUCTORS IN THE AREA included David Young, Jane Young, David Pattison, and Jane Pattison.

David & Jane (McGuffey) Young

David Young haled from Cumberland County, the son of William Young, who was one of Union Township's early settlers. David was born about 1791 and married Jane McGuffey, born in Ohio about 1799.[10]

By 1850, Young was a 59 year-old farmer with $5,400 in real estate assets. He resided with wife, Jane, and children, Hannah, Amanda and Sarah.

David & Jane (Stewart) Pattison

David and Jane Pattison lived in Union Township as early as 1832 when their son, David, was born. A daughter, Mary, followed a year later.[11][12]

In the 1860 census David is listed as a 50 year old Scottish-born farmer with $4,000 in real estate assets and $600 in personal possessions. He lived with Jane and four younger children, William, a carpenter, Ginett, Robert, a farm laborer, and Alex, a shoemaker.

Mrs. Robert Wallace recalled David Pattison as "a Scotchman living about two miles west of New Castle" who once brought a group of eleven fugitives to her father's house.[13]

ABOLITIONISTS

KNOWN ABOLITIONISTS IN THE AREA included Mary Jane Davies.

Mary Jane (Mitchell) & William Davies

Mary Jane Davies was listed as one of the founding members of the Free Presbyterian Church in New Castle. Her father, Samuel W. Mitchell, was the first undertaker in the city, conducting his business on Mercer Street.

Mary Jane married to William Davies, a general laborer in Union Township. They had at least eight children, Mary, Robert, Anna, Agnes, William, Charles, Alex and Harry. William died in March 1891.

In 1900, Mary Jane resided in Union Township with the family of her daughter, Mary C. Leslie. By 1911, she was living with another daughter, Mrs. James Hasley.[14]

Mary Jane Davies died on September 11, 1911.[15]

Chapter Notes

1. Durant, 123.
2. Ibid.
3. Ibid.
4. "Recalls Another Station on Underground Railway," *New Castle News,* May 13, 1925.
5. Walker, W. W. "Routes through and Activity in Lawrence County, Pennsylvania," March 14, 1896. Wilbur H. Siebert Collection, State Library of Ohio.
6. Walker, W. W. "Passengers to Ohio, Mahoning and Trumbull Counties," October 15, 1898. Wilbur H. Siebert Collection, State Library of Ohio.
7. "Recalls Another Station on Underground Railway," *New Castle News,* May 13, 1925.
8. White, Joseph S. "Recollections of Mrs. Robert Wallace's Account of her Father David Young's Underground Railroad Activity," February 19, 1897. Wilbur H. Siebert Collection, State Library of Ohio.
9. Bodnar, Don, "Eyes on the road," *New Castle News*, October 13, 1972, 15.
10. *20th Century History of New Castle and Lawrence County Pennsylvania and Representative Citizens*, 461.
11. David C. Pattison Obituary, *New Castle Weekly Herald*, October 4, 1905, 2.
12. "Aged Resident of County Dies, Mrs. Mary B. Boggs, 88, Life-long Resident Here Passes Away This Morning," *New Castle Herald*, December 27, 1921, 2.
13. White, Joseph S. "Recollections of Mrs. Robert Wallace's Account of her Father David Young's Underground Railroad Activity," February 19, 1897. Wilbur H. Siebert Collection, State Library of Ohio.
14. "Sudden Death of Aged Resident," *New Castle News*, September 21, 1911, 1.
15. *New Castle News*, March 15, 1891.

19

WILMINGTON TOWNSHIP

WILMINGTON TOWNSHIP was created in 1846 from portions of Neshannock and Lackawannock Townships. The area is diverse, with hills, valleys, woods and streams, including Big Neshannock Creek.

The first settler was likely William Hodge in 1797, who canoed up the Beaver and Shenango Rivers. Hodge built a cabin, made a clearing, and later sold it to William Porter and his wife, arriving on foot from Westmoreland County. Porter was followed by James Hazlep, John McCrum, and James Waugh, who purchased land where New Wilmington now stands. Waugh and his sons laid out the town about 1863.[1]

NEW WILMINGTON

AROUND 1814, THE Beaver and Mercer State Road was cut through the area, and the settlement that would become New Wilmington began to take form. Revolutionary War veterans James and John Waugh were the first settlers in the area, claiming more than 400 acres of land apiece.

In the early days, the village consisted of two parallel north–south streets.[2] The first log house was built by Dr. Hindman. The first schoolhouse was erected around 1810, a log building a quarter mile west of New Wilmington.[3] In 1824 or 1825, Rich Hill schoolhouse was constructed from round logs and a cabin roof, but the two–

story brick school wouldn't take form until 1868.[4]

By the 1820s businesses included David Carnahan's wagon shop, John Galloway's tannery, Thomas Wilson's harness and saddle shop, a shoe store operated by Robert Hamilton, and a general store run by Phillip Crowl.

New Wilmington's oldest church was Neshannock Presbyterian Congregation, organized about 1800. Reverend William Wick, ordained in connection with Hopewell in the village of New Bedford, was its first pastor. Fourteen of the area's 20 families were Neshannock Presbyterian Church members, and most of the others belonged to the Seceder Congregation. Rich Hill Presbyterian Church began in 1840 with a congregation of about 30 members, mostly from the Neshannock Congregation.[5]

Around 1845-46, Theodore Powers and A. L. Crawford built an iron–furnace built south of New Wilmington. It was called the Fremont Furnace, and operated for about seven years.[6]

A LITTLE BAND OF NOBLE MEN

ROBERT RAMSEY, one of New Wilmington's most interesting inhabitants, was more than just an inventor, furniture maker, and hearse builder, it turns out.

> "Early in life he took sides with the abolition movement in this section and the colored man fleeing to freedom found in Mr. Ramsey a kind host ever ready to help him with purse and hand. The Erie Dispatch in making mention of his death says he was the last survivor of the little band of noble men composed of Dr. James Smedly, Ephraim Smedly, Philetus Glass, Sr., Deacon Kingsbury, Gilbert Belnap and William Durand, (all from North East Borough, Erie County) all Underground Railroad directors."[7]

CONDUCTORS

KNOWN CONDUCTORS IN THE AREA included Irwin Sampson, Sarah Sampson, Robert Ramsey, and Prudence Ramsey.

Irwin & Sarah Sampson

Squire Irwin Sampson was born and raised on a farm southeast of New Wilmington and

"...possessed an excellent memory, which made him an interesting companion."

He knew President William McKinley as a boy, and called him "Little Bill" to distinguish him from his father, who operated an iron furnace outside the village.

"Squire Sampson was a strong Abolitionist in slavery days, and not only argued in behalf of his belief, but acted. He was one of the operators of the 'Underground Railroad,' and helped many a Black man to liberty across the Canadian line." [8]

Robert & Prudence Ramsey

Robert Ramsey was born in the Borough of North East, Erie County. He was still living there in 1840, but moved to New Wilmington by 1843 and opened a furniture store where he built cabinets and caskets. As the local undertaker, he built his own hearse, which continued to be used by his son, John, after his death. [9]

Robert and his wife, Prudence, had eight children, six girls and two boys. They were members of the Methodist Episcopal Church where, in 1843, Robert was superintendent of the Sunday school. [10]

Robert was an inventor and held at least two patents, one in 1865 for a bag holding bracket, and another in 1868 for a fence post improvement.

Robert died in 1885 at the age of 78 at his home in New Wilmington. [11]

ABOLITIONISTS

KNOWN ABOLITIONISTS IN THE AREA included Dr. Seth Poppino, and Sarah Poppino.

Dr. Seth & Mary E. (Junkin) Poppino

Seth Poppino was born in New York on January 27, 1815 to Seth L. and Sarah (Underwood) Poppino. Seth was one of the founders of the Methodist Episcopal Church in New Wilmington in 1839 or 1840. By July 1845 he was practicing medicine in New Wilmington.

From 1845 through 1846 he attended medical school at the Western Reserve Medical College in Hudson, Ohio with Dr. Isaac Cowden as his preceptor.[12] Cowden was also a practicing physician in New Wilmington and many students learned medicine by his instruction.[13]

Poppino was described as a man of honor, and his word was known to be as good as his bond. He was always found at his post, rarely taking even a single day off from the duties of his profession. His home and office still stand in New Wilmington, and the home has for many years now been known as The Tavern, a quaint restaurant.

The construction of that house began in 1849. Seth wrote on October 17, 1849 to his brother:

"I am putting up a building where my old one stood 40 by 40 feet two stories high fronting on two streets which I find is rather an expensive undertaking…"[14]

The structure had not been completed when the 1850 census was taken, which revealed Seth to be living with George Clark and his family.[15]

Dr. Seth Poppino married Mary Elizabeth Junkin about 1856, and they had six children, Sarah L., Anna Mary, Hatti, who married Alex McClelland, Martha P., who married Reverend J. H. Spencer, Charles W., and James J.[16]

Dr. Poppino died December 3rd, 1875 in New Wilmington.

Mary died January 20, 1917 at the home in New Wilmington.[17]

Chapter Notes

1. Durant, 133-134.
2. *The History of New Wilmington, Pennsylvania 1797-2003*, H. Dewey De Witt, Paul Gamble, Delber L. McKee, Eugene G. Sharkey, G. Alan Sternbergh, eds. New Horizons Publishing Co. New Wilmington, Pennsylvania. 2004, 5-13.
3. Hazen, 370-371.
4. Durant, 136-137.
5. Ibid.
6. Durant, 133-136.
7. Robert Ramsey Obituary, *New Castle Guardian*, March 27, 1885.
8. Irwin Sampson Obituary, *New Castle News Weekly Edition*. July 19, 1899, 1.
9. *The History of New Wilmington, Pennsylvania 1797-2003*, 21.
10. Durant, 56.
11. Robert Ramsey Obituary. *New Castle Guardian*, March 27, 1885.
12. Catalog of the Officers and Students of Western Reserve College 1845-1846, *Ohio Observer* (Hudson, Ohio).
13. Durant, 162.
14. Seth Poppino letter to unnamed Brother, New Wilmington Oct. 17, 1849. Displayed at The Tavern, New Wilmington, Pennsylvania.
15. United States Census: Pennsylvania, Lawrence County, 1850.
16. Seth Poppino Obituary, *Guardian*, January 15, 1875; Seth Poppino Obituary, *Guardian*, January 8, 1876.
17. Mary Poppino Obituary, *New Castle News*, January 20, 1917, 2.

20
SLAVES WHO TRAVELED THROUGH LAWRENCE COUNTY

LEWIS' TAVERN RESCUE

JOSEPH WHITE RELATES the story of an unnamed colored woman who arrived in New Castle seeking employment in the 1840s. She was hired by Andrew Lewis, who kept a tavern in a three–story building on the north side of Washington Street, between the Diamond and Mercer Street (119–123 E. Washington today).

After she had been employed for some time, a slaveholder entered the tavern and recognized her. When he finished his meal, he took hold of her, and she cried for help.

Mr. Lewis was not there at the time, but his daughter, Alvira, came to the rescue. She beat the man with a broom until Jackson Evans, a wagon maker who happened to be passing by, heard the commotion.

Mr. Evans entered the establishment and punched the slave owner, knocking him down. Alvira led the woman away and secreted her. In the end, the slave master was happy to get away with his life.

Joseph White wrote:

> "The remarkable thing about this woman's deliverance is, that it was accomplished by uncompromising Democrats, who were not often found working in harmony with Underground Railroad people, but generally the slaveholder. This time their better feelings triumphed."[1]

SLAVES RIOT & ESCAPE TO NEW CASTLE

IN A LETTER to his children, "Some reminiscences of slavery times," Joseph White states that this event occurred right before the "breaking out of the rebellion." The *Pittsburgh Gazette* devoted nearly an entire column to the story. White had lost his copy, but related as much as he remembered.[2]

A group of five men, three women and two children, arrived in Uniontown, Fayette County, Pennsylvania. The Virginian owners were in hot pursuit, and when they arrived in Uniontown the slave owners were guided to the fugitives' hiding place by "some low specimens of humanity."

The runaways were not caught totally off guard and armed themselves with corn–cutters and other weapons to make a furious resistance.

> "The battle waxed hot, but the slaves were victorious and drove back their assailants."

Women and children fled during the altercation and did not meet up with the men again until Portersville. The slave owners followed their trail as far as Pittsburgh, and there "it ran into the ground."

The fugitives had been delivered to Conductors in what was then Butler County (Perry Township, Lawrence County today).

"[Mr. Magee], a good man of that neighborhood, brought them to New Castle in a two–horse covered wagon, and arrived with his valuable cargo about four o'clock in the afternoon."

One day, many years later there came a knock at the door. Standing in front of Mr. White was a former slave, his hair white with age. He had come to personally express his gratitude to the man who had befriended him in his dire distress. The former slave was returning to the South in search of relatives, but he had not forgotten White's kindnesses. J. Crawford White believed this man was one of the ten slaves discussed above.[3]

A SHIP'S CARPENTER

J. CRAWFORD WHITE RELAYED the story of another slave who was assisted by Joseph White. He came from the coastal town of Savannah, Georgia, and was a very valuable slave, being trained as a ship carpenter.

The man had attempted to escape at various times, but using bloodhounds the slave catchers had always caught him. After each instance, his master would put a ball and chain on his legs.

In a final attempt, he again made his escape on the crest of the mountains extending into Pennsylvania. One evening at dusk, the poor man went up Jefferson Street, casting furtive glances to the right and left, like a hunted bird. When he was opposite Joseph White's home, he thought he had found the place he had been directed to.

White received him with kindness and he was kept in the old brick house until he passed on to Indian Run. The case of this slave so moved the citizens at Indian Run that a public meeting was called in the local schoolhouse for the citizens to view the curse of slavery. At the meeting, the man turned up his pant legs and showed where those cruel iron bands had cut into his muscles, two fingers deep.[4]

AN IDENTIFIED ESCAPED SLAVE

CHARLES A. GARLICK WAS BORN Abel Bogguess in 1827, near Shinnston, Virginia (now West Virginia) on the plantation of bachelor, Richard Bogguess. Garlick's parents were slave laborers on the farm, and he was one of eleven children. Richard Bogguess died some four months prior to Mr. Garlick's escape, leaving a will that, it was understood, made his colored people free, but the will was contested.

Charles Garlick

Wanting freedom, his mother left with Garlick and five of the smaller children. They traveled north 15 miles to the home of William Hefflin, an aged, hospitable neighbor. Hefflin took them in and fed them.

Afterward, they hid in the dense woods and remained until the following morning. Uncle Elijah Bogguess and Tom McIntyre found their retreat and advised his mother to return with the children. They told Garlick, aged 16, that he could go, and he took advantage of the opportunity.

"I started on the long and dangerous trip for that haven where slavery was unknown."

Garlick made use of the Underground Railroad wherever possible, there being occasional stations where his safety was assured. In a week he reached Uniontown, Pennsylvania, where his safety came into question once again.

"[A]gents of the Underground Railroad at the ferry in Greensburg instructed me to go. There I lay concealed in the haymow of a zealous friend of my race, who provided me with food until an opportunity offered three days later for me to continue my journey."

He fled under cover of darkness on a horse his host provided, accompanied by a mounted guard. They neared Pittsburgh the following night, and his guard left him to return with the horses. Garlick made his way on foot some seven miles "to the smoky city."

J. B. Vashong and Thomas McKeever gave him refuge for three days, and sent him on to Samuel Marshall some 15 miles away at the next station. In 1849 Marshall held an associate judgeship, and would continue to hold it until his death in 1880.

Garlick rested at Marshall's home for a week before accompanying John Rainbow, a Patent Right Agent in New Brighton, to Neshannock Township (now west New Castle). There where he found refuge at Reverend Bushnell's home.⁵

From Bushnell's, Garlick traveled to Amos Chew's in Brookfield, and left for Hartford, Trumbull County the following morning, where he

"found kind friends in the persons of Ralph Plumb and Seth Hayes, merchants, in whose cheese warehouse I worked for two weeks."

When Garlick heard that slavers were in the vicinity, he made a hasty journey to West Andover, and Anson Kirby Garlick's hospitable home. He had plans to continue to Canada, but remained with Garlick from 1843 to 1846, attending district school a portion of the time during the winter, working on the place the rest of the time.

"On accepting Garlick's hospitality and home, he addressed me as 'Charley' and becoming known as Charley Garlick, I, at my benefactors suggestion, adopted this the name I have ever since borne."⁶

In 1846 Garlick returned to Butler County in search of his brothers. To his delight, he found them living at or near Marshall's home. Garlick remained there for a year. At the time there were a dozen or more colored men who had escaped their masters about Mr. Marshall's farm.

One day Garlic was hitching up the horses after dinner when he saw 13 horsemen wearing the broad–brim hats of slavers. Garlick informed Marshall, turned over the horse team, and he started at a run to warn the escaped slaves.

The cavalcade spurred after him, but he was able to elude them through a ravine and sound the alarm that brought together a squad of eight men, two of them white. Some had shotguns and others clubs, while the salve holders held Colt revolvers.

Hot talk ensued, and the men were ordered to leave or take the contents of the guns sighted upon them. As they finally left, someone in Marshall's party shot into the air, which quickly hastened the retreat.

The slavers were not heard from again. Squire Marshall was said to have inserted a notice in the papers warning that if they came again, they would be given a warm reception and hospitable graves.

"This ended the last raid of the slave holding, slave–catching cohorts to that station of the Underground Railroad."⁷

MILLIE DAVIS ESCAPES IN PITTSBURGH

MILLIE WAS A SERVANT of a Captain Davis, an officer of the regular Army in Kentucky. One day Davis' four year old son pestered Millie for plum pudding she was preparing for dinner. She sent him on his way.

The boy complained to his mother that Millie had scolded him. Mrs. Davis was quick to put Millie in her place, informing her that she was not to scold the young master. Millie replied that she had not scolded him, but merely told him he must not bother her about dinner. This brought a severe blow to the face from Mrs. Davis.

Millie was so incensed that she returned the blow. Mrs. Davis called in Captain Davis and Millie was told she must be whipped for her actions. She fought off the beating, requiring the Captain to obtain assistance. Millie was bound and lashed so severely that blood streamed down her lacerated back.

Millie had served this family from the time they were married and this was the first instance of mistreatment. She had accompanied them up and down the Ohio and into the Free States without even the thought of attempting an escape.

Now the thought of freedom burned in her soul, and she bided her time for the right opportunity. When Captain Davis was eventually called to Pittsburgh and took his family and Millie with him, Millie was ready. She made contact with friends in the city.

Davis grew suspicious and decided to leave sooner than planned. Their belongings were stowed on an evening boat and the family went down into the cabin. When the Captain left to see to some matter of business, he instructed his wife not to allow Millie out of her sight.

He had been gone but a moment when Millie seized her opportunity. She was standing beside her mistress' chair holding the purse for the family supplies.

"What, sir?" she said.

"What do you mean, Millie?" said the mistress.

"Why, master called me. I'll run and see what he wants. Here, you keep the money."

It happened so suddenly, and her handing over the purse completely deceived Mrs. Davis. Millie ran over the gangplank as it was about to be hauled in and the boat swung into the river.

A friend met her. When she stepped ashore, a cloak was thrown over her shoulders and a hat placed on her head. Disguised, she followed her guide through the crowd to a carriage outside the city limits.

They departed as rapidly as possible, knowing that Captain Davis would put the boat ashore to search for his property, which was exactly what he did. He enlisted the assistance of local authorities, and they searched in vain for several days.

Millie was hauled by way of New Castle and [New] Bedford, Pennsylvania, to the home of Deacon Stewart, a veteran agent in Hubbard, Ohio. There she remained a week, telling her story and showing the scars on her back.

The Deacon reportedly took her to James Lane in Warren, who passed her on to Bloomfield where she was taken to the home of William Howe and, in a closed carriage, transported to Fairport for passage across the lake to Canada.[8]

FREDERICK DOUGLASS

IN 1847 NEW ENGLAND Abolitionist William Lloyd Garrison, and former slave Frederick Douglass, began a speaking tour of the West. At their first stop in Harrisburg,

Pennsylvania a mob ensued when Douglass rose to speak.

It was the first time a "nigger" had dared to publicly address the people of Harrisburg, and the mob regarded it as an act of unparalleled audacity. Rioters equipped with rotten eggs and brickbats (a piece of brick used as a weapon), firecrackers, and other missiles, yelled "out with the damned nigger." Rocks were thrown and pane glass broken.[9]

The two made their way to Pittsburgh, where meetings were well attended. Douglass wrote,

> "What a commentary on the religion of Pittsburgh it is, that every church in the place was closed against us. All were too holy to plead the cause of our common humanity."

From Pittsburgh they took the steamboat, Beaver, to New Brighton, home of their friend Milo A. Townsend. Milo, his wife, and parents welcomed them into their home.[10]

While it was customary to serve dinner on the Beaver, no dinner was served on this trip. If Douglass and the other Blacks that accompanied him were to be served, it might offend white travelers.

Arriving in New Brighton, Garrison and Douglass held two meetings.

> "[H]ere too, the churches were closed against us, and we were compelled to take an upper room in a flour store. Thus making good the proposition, that humanity is received more cordially in the street than in the church."[11]

William Lloyd Garrison noted:

Frederick Douglass

> "New Brighton is a small village of 800 inhabitants, but there are several other villages in its immediate neighborhood. There have been a good many lectures on slavery given in it by our leading Anti-Slavery lecturers such as Stephen and Abby Kelley Foster, Burleigh, Pillsbury, Douglass, etc.; but the people generally remain incorrigible."

Douglass and Garrison took a canal boat from New Brighton, travelling 40 miles along the Beaver River and the canal through Lawrence County, on into Youngstown.[12]

In his 1868 return to Lawrence County, Frederick Douglass addressed a large audience in New Castle. The lecture was most likely held at the newly constructed Shenango Hall at 19–21 Mercer Street. What follows is a firsthand account of his visit:

> In New Castle there was a lecture lyceum that brought some able and popular lecturers...Frederick Douglass gave his lecture on "The One Man Power," or against the veto power. His greatness as an orator did not appear so manifest as in former years when he pleaded for his people in bonds. But the meanness of the caste feeling or of prejudice against color was shown by the shameful neglect shown to Douglass by the lyceum in which were Democrats and former Pro-Slavery professional men. It was the rule and had been the practise of the lyceum to make provision for the entertainment of all the lecturers, and a committee or an officer of the lyceum was expected to meet the coming speaker at the railroad station and escort him to the appointed place of lodging. But the eloquent orator was a Negro. When his train from Pittsburg arrived no representative of the lyceum was there. I was not a member, but as a personal friend I went to meet him and welcome him to our city. After salutations he said to me, "Where is the committee?" "I do not know." I was

much ashamed of my neighbors but I could only try to apologize for them supposing that there might be some mistake somewhere. He said nothing more, but Frederick Douglass had sharpness sufficient to see it all. Taking his gripsack in my hand I conducted him all the way up Main Street to our little cottage to the wonderment of many beholders who had never before seen Frederick Douglass. And so we had the pleasure of entertaining the popular colored orator, and we were glad if for no other reason than that we had the opportunity of silently testifying against caste prejudice. But though he said nothing Mr. Douglass was mad. We walked with him to the hall where we were met by the president of the lyceum, a United Presbyterian and a city teacher, to whom I introduced Mr. Douglass. They went upon the platform together. Professor Aiken rose and said: "Ladies and Gentlemen, I have the pleasure of introducing Fred Douglass who will speak to you on 'The One Man Power.' " Mr. Douglass arose and said: "Ladies and gentlemen, Negro slaves were presumed to have only one name. My master called me Frederick. My name is Frederick Douglass." As soon as the applause ceased he proceeded to give his lecture; and it was an unanswerable argument against the veto power whether presidential or gubernatorial. We had the pleasure of entertaining Mr. Douglass and we enjoyed his company, yet there was one thing wanting. The great orator lacked the one thing needful. He was not a foe to religion but he was destitute of that piety that so generally characterized the slaves and the freedmen. If he had had the religious element as highly cultured as was desirable he would have been a far greater power for the elevation of his race.[13]

FRANK JACKSON BORN A FREEMAN—EIGHT YEARS A SLAVE

FRANK JACKSON WAS THE OLDER brother of Civil War veteran Elijah Jackson, Jr.. (See "African Americans in the Civil War") Several versions of the Frank Jackson story have been published over the years. Here we try to separate truth from fiction.

The Facts

Frank Jackson was born a Black freeman to Elijah and Sarah Jackson of New Castle, formerly of Mercer County. He was raised by John Young, Jr., a stalwart Abolitionist and the son of slaveholder.[14]

Jackson was described as "rather deficient in natural talents and therefore might easily be made the dupe of a scoundrel"… and so it appears that he was.

There was a noted horse market in Mercer County's early days, and every year horses were gathered there and herded over the mountains for sale at Baltimore.

Charles May, a horse drover from West Greenville, Mercer County, hired Jackson to assist him as a hostler and saddle fitter. In early 1851 May enticed Jackson to accompany him to Virginia. In Richmond, May sold Jackson on the auction block to a slaveholder by the name of Jones (some accounts say the name was Scott).

Frank soon escaped, only to be captured and confined in Fincastle Jail, Botetourt County, Virginia, about 150 miles west of Richmond. An attorney named W. A. Glass wrote to Mercer and New Castle for certificates evidencing his free status. Certificates were sent.

Everyone in Mercer knew Frank was born free. Still, Frank was not released. A number of newspapers carried the facts of his kidnapping and subsequent enslavement, including the Boston Liberator, and in the Free Presbyterian.[15]

In the spring of 1852, William F. Clark, editor of the *Free Presbyterian* and former New Castle newsman, traveled to Virginia to make a special inquiry about Frank Jackson's status. He learned that, while certificates of Jackson's freedom were indeed delivered to Fincastle, the person receiving them had acted "treacherously."

Frank's whereabouts were unknown until his friends were informed by letter that a man by that name had been taken to Richmond, and was lodged in Jones' slave pen. Certificates were again sent and steps taken to gain his release, but when the group went to gather him, he was gone. It is believed he was secreted away to avoid rescue.[16]

By June 1852, the *Free Presbyterian* wrote that Jackson was being held in Campbell County, Virginia, about 120 miles west of Richmond. Judge Reynolds of New Castle and the Honorable William Stewart of Mercer made every effort to liberate him. Suits for release were again filed against former and present claimants. [17]

Reynolds and Stewart were told that Jackson would be returned if his identity as a freeman could be firmly established. George C. Morgan, a tailor from New Castle, was sent to Virginia to identify Jackson, but upon his arrival at the Campbell Court House, Jackson was no longer there. He had been taken farther South.[18]

It was probably about this time that Jackson was sold to a North Carolina trader. Jackson made another escape attempt, but was once again captured and jailed, this time in Moore County, North Carolina. In chains, he was transported to Cameron, North Carolina, but not before an attorney, George C. Mendenhall of Jamestown, North Carolina, himself a slaveholder, had learned of his dilemma.

Mendenhall requested the names of people Jackson knew in Mercer and New Castle, and Jackson identified the Honorable William Stewart, attorney, and John Young among others. Jackson did not wait for Mendenhall to ascertain his claims, but ran away again, was caught and placed in the Randolph jail.

Mendenhall paid Jackson's bail, bought him clothes and brought him to his own plantation.

He stayed there a few weeks until his owner, Frederick W. Swan, arrived to retrieve him. Mendenhall secured Jackson's power of attorney and brought suit against Swan for Jackson's release and $1500 in damages.

John Reynolds

The trial, postponed several times, was finally scheduled for August 23, 1858 at Moore County, North Carolina. George C. Morgan, by then an elected justice of New Castle, traveled once more to testify on Jackson's behalf. He proceeded to Colonel Mendenhall's home and made his introduction. The trial was to take place the following day.

At the courthouse, Colonel Mendenhall introduced Morgan, who possessed a dignified and commanding presence, to his fellow planters as Colonel Morgan of Pennsylvania. After waiting at the courthouse for some time, Jackson was brought to the proceeding. Mendenhall exclaimed, "there comes the nigger with his owner."

At first Jackson did not recognize Morgan. Morgan supposedly addressed Jackson, saying, "See here you Black rascal, don't you know me?"

Jackson jumped excitedly and yelled, "Blessed if youse aint Mr. Morgan from New Castle. Is it you in de tailoring business yet Mistah Morgan?" Morgan joined in the uproar of laughter at his own expense.[19]

George C. Morgan

The trial began with depositions from Mercer County citizens. Morgan identified Frank Jackson as a free man of color. It was further proven that Jackson had been sold to a South Carolina trader on the block in Richmond by his horse drover, then by the trader to McInnis and Murchison of Wilmington, North Carolina, and by them to Frederick W. Swan.

The jury found in favor of Jackson, and he was released. There is no report of monetary damages awarded to Jackson.

Morgan and Jackson left for Pennsylvania, but experienced delays in the slave states. In Baltimore Morgan was precluded from putting Jackson on a train until he was "vouched for." Morgan remembered that a Presbyterian minister near Mercer had a charge in Baltimore. He applied for and received a favorable recommendation and was allowed to leave.

The pair arrived in New Castle on September 6, 1858. Frank Jackson was again a freeman after eight years a slave.[20, 21]

A North Carolina newspaper carried news of Jackson's release.

> "It is a fact honorable to the South that no party is surer of ready justice in the Courts of the Southern States than a Negro, bond or free."[22]

Frank Jackson was said to have enlisted in, and survived, the Civil War. In 1877 he had a large and respectable family. By 1897, he and his entire family were deceased.[23]

The Folklore

There is no doubt that Frank Jackson lost years of his life to slavery. There is a question however as to the circumstances that perhaps brought him to the auction block.

Captain C. W. Whistler was the editor of the *Mercer Press*. What follows is derived from an article written by Whistler.[24]

Mercer had its own "General Jackson." He "was neither warrior nor statesman, nor was he altogether fool." On numerous occasions he had assisted and accompanied an unnamed horse dealer, a "worthy citizen" of the town, in delivering herds to the Baltimore market.

While Jackson always accompanied the drover, he was never known to return with him. Sometimes he would follow in a few days, other times many weeks, and another time perhaps months intervened.

Then, from one trip he did not return. His absence was noted, and the drover was suspected of having done something illicit.

A year passed and Jackson's disappearance remained a main theme of discussion. A letter was finally received by the drover from a town in Southwest Indiana, written by a lawyer for General Jackson, who was being held as a runaway from a Tennessee planter. The lawyer asked that witnesses of character, who could certify Jackson as being a native of Mercer and a freeman, come to his relief.

The drover hastened to William Stewart and William Stephenson, supplied them with cash, and sent them to Indiana, where they had little difficulty in releasing "our colored hero." Whistler indicates that this story was "never made public for obvious reasons."

> "One thing is certain… that the 'general' was cured of his propensity to travel in that direction. The risk of getting away from the slavery, which he had for the while adopted, was too great. Up to this time, it had been simply fun, to be sold and resold; to escape after a few days or weeks; and return to Mercer, where his share of his chattel value was turned over to him by our Mercer drover…"

> "We would not have ventured upon the tale of Jackson's entering into collusion with another to sell himself into slavery had Squire Robert Stewart been other than the truthful man he was; he revealed it from his brother, the Hon. William, who with William Stephenson released Jackson in Indiana from the slaveholder's clutches, as related. It was a close squeak for the 'general.' And a close one for the Mercer horse dealer too. Never mind about the blame of the Mercer drover who made merchandise of the 'coon.' He is dead and turned to clay long ago.

> "We are glad to be corroborated in the main facts of this recital by H. Magaffin, Esq. of this town, who tells us since the foregoing was written, of having heard the same tale while yet a lad from his father the much respected Dr. James Magaffin."

It appears that many of the above recollections are a muddling of information handed down through the generations, as nothing has been found that would substantiate the claim that Jackson was taken to Tennessee, or rescued in Indiana. While possible, it seems doubtful that a man who had been held in slavery for more than a year would again cast the die with his freedom and end up once again enslaved.

It is obvious that Jackson was determined to escape, but was unsuccessful in those attempts from 1851–1858. This leaves one to wonder whether he possessed the ability to actually escape slavery and make it back to New Castle as many times as Whistler's account claims. Whistler's story most probably had at its roots the factual accounting of Jackson being sold at the block in Richmond.

The question remains as to whether the "General" acquiesced to his being sold into slavery for financial gain, whether it was one time, or on numerous occasions.

PASSMORE WILLIAMSON

PASSMORE WILLIAMSON assisted George C. Morgan in his efforts to rescue freeman Frank Jackson from slavery.[25] Williamson, a member of the Pennsylvania Anti–Slavery Society and Chairman of the Vigilance Committee in Philadelphia, and was described as one of the "most fiery zealots" of the cause.[26]

A well–known Abolitionist, he made national news for whisking away Jane Johnson and her two sons, slaves owned by the newly appointed American Minister to Nicaragua. Williamson was imprisoned in Philadelphia for 100 days for failure to divulge their whereabouts.

PORTERSVILLE POSSE

IN OCTOBER 1841, the *Mercer Luminary* reported that six or eight Negro hunters from Virginia came upon four Negroes at a house in Portersville and claimed them as runaway slaves. They bound them for removal to Virginia the next morning. It was reported that one of the Blacks had a knife and cut the cords from his hand and feet, fleeing through Mercer County, (and current day Lawrence County) for Canada.

Some of the friends of law and justice in Portersville thought it was proper to inquire into the legality of the claims of the Virginians to the remaining Blacks. After an examination before a magistrate, it was determined that the slavers had no authority to arrest them. The Blacks were set free and their captors arrested for kidnapping.

A somewhat different and more detailed account was found in the Pittsburgh Daily American, republished in the *New York Tribune*, and reproduced here in its entirety.

> Failure of a Speculation—We have just been informed of a circumstance which occurred a few days since, in Butler county, in this State. A reward of $300 had been offered, in Virginia for the apprehension of four Negroes, who, it was ascertained had found their way to Butler county, and two men from Virginia had started, handbills in hand, to apprehend them and pocket the reward. They came upon the objects of their pursuit near Portersville while the Negroes were at supper, and arrested them; tied them and had proceeded about seven miles on the back track with the fugitives, when they were overtaken by a constable and posse, who arrested the white men as kidnappers and brought them back to answer for the offence. The Negroes were released and started on their way to Canada—the kidnappers getting off as well as they could, and glad of whole skins.—Though the arrest of the Negroes happened after night, the constable who retook them is said to have been attended by more than 50 men, whom the circumstances had induced to volunteer in the service. They have very abstract notions in Butler on the subject of slavery.[27]

Chapter Notes

1. White, Joseph S. "Some Reminiscences of Slavery Times," March 23, 1891. Wilbur H. Siebert Collection, State Library of Ohio.
2. White, Joseph S., "Some Reminiscences of Slavery Times," 5-7.
3. J. O. Rodgers letter, Lawrence County Historical Society.
4. "J. Crawford White Tells Dramatic Tale of Father's Underground Railroad Station," *New Castle News*, March 17, 1930,12.
5. Garlick, Charles A. *Life, Including His Escape and Struggle for Liberty of Charles A. Garlick, Born a Slave in Old Virginia Who Secured His Freedom by Running Away From His Master's Farm in 1843*. 1902, 7. http://docsouth.unc.edu/neh/garlick/garlick.html
6. Garlick, 7-8.
7. Garlick, 8-9.
8. *Johnson's Lake Shore Home Magazine. Vol. VIII, No. 4*, April 1888, Wilbur H. Siebert Collection, State Library of Ohio.
9. Garrison, Wendell Phillips & Frances Jackson Garrison. *William Lloyd Garrison 1805-1879: The Story of His life Told by His Children, Vol. III*. The Century Co. New York. 1885, 191-193.
10. Garrison, Wendell Phillips & Frances Jackson Garrison. *William Lloyd Garrison 1805-1879: The Story of His life Told by His Children, Vol. III*, 193-194.
11. Laurence A. Glasco, *The W. Pennsylvania History of the Negro in Pittsburgh, Douglass letter August 20, 1847*. University of Pittsburgh Press. 2004, 193-194.
12. Garrison, Wendell Phillips & Frances Jackson Garrison. *William Lloyd Garrison 1805-1879: The Story of His life Told by His Children, Vol. III*, 195.
13. Johnston, Nathan Robinson, *Looking Back from the Sunset Land*, 399-401.
14. "The Kidnapping and Recovery of Frank Jackson Are Recalled by Old Timers," *New Castle News*, March 10, 1897, 8.
15. *The Liberator* (Boston, Massachussetts), July 27, 1855, 3.
16. *Anti-Slavery Bugle*, April 10, 1852, 1.
17. "Frank Jackson," *Anti-Slavery Bugle*, June 12, 1852, 3.
18. Durant, 34.
19. "The Kidnapping and Recovery of Frank Jackson Are Recalled by Old Timers," *New Castle News*, March 10, 1897, 8.
20. "Moore Superior Court," *Anti-Slavery Bugle*, September 18, 1858

21 *Greensboro Patriot* (Greensboro, North Carolina), September 3, 1858, 2.
22 "A Case of Kidnaping," *Semi-Weekly Standard,* Raleigh, North Carolina, October 13, 1858, 2.
23 *New Castle News*, March 10, 1897, 8.
24 *New Castle News*, February 13, 1903, 3.
25 "A Free Colored Man Rescued from Slavery," *Richmond Dispatch*, September 8, 1858, 1.
26 *The Liberator*, July 27, 1855, 3.
27 "Failure of a Speculation," *New York Tribune,* November 16, 1841, 1.

21

EX-SLAVES WHO CAME TO LAWRENCE COUNTY

JUDGE MAKES A HOME IN NEW CASTLE

JAMES M. FAULKNER, OR "Judge" was a former slave, born in Virginia. He came north after his emancipation and settled in New Castle. At one time he was married, and later widowed, with no indication of children.

Judge was known as an "aristocrat bootblack" and resided at 32 Bell Avenue for a time. He shined shoes in just about every barbershop and hotel in New Castle.

During the Civil War, Judge was a young slave on Major Marshall McCue's plantation at Mossy Creek in the Shenandoah Valley, 15 miles from Staunton. Major McCue was a member of the Confederate Congress and prominent enough to warrant a visit to his plantation from General Stonewall Jackson. Judge waited on the General's table and would later vividly describe Jackson in his recollections. Judge also served General Jubal A. Early when Early raided the Shenandoah Valley under pursuit from General Philip Sheridan.[1]

Judge always dreamt of returning to Virginia. Closing up shop for a few months one winter, he went "south" to East Liverpool, Ohio.[2]

As a result of failing eyesight, Judge's work began to suffer. He lost clients and had little income to support himself. For a time, he stayed in the City Home, before plying his trade in Mercer County, in Grove City and other localities there.[3]

He finally returned to New Castle and tried to revive his business. Each evening he would enter the City Building, walk downstairs to the bunk room (municipal lodging house), cover himself with a newspaper, and announce "this will be my last night here."[4]

As his health continued to fail, he complained to the police that he was going to die. He was ordered to the City Home, and taken out of the municipal building by force. After a short stay in the City Home, he again left, wandering the streets of New Castle.[5]

He went to Youngstown for a short time, but returned yet again, staying either at the City Home or on the streets. He asked the mayor to give him a sidewalk where he could shine shoes or enough money to realize his dream of returning to Old Virginia. The City decided to provide him those funds, but Judge died in October 1914, before action could be taken. He was buried on the grounds of the city home in Shenango Township.

VIRGINIA SLAVE SETTLES IN NEW CASTLE

ALEXANDER SCOTT WAS a mulatto slave, born in Warrenton, Virginia, the natural son of his master. His mother was sold when he was a boy not more than five years old.

His master moved to another plantation and forgot to take Scott. When he returned to claim his property, he found the boy asleep in bed with a big watchdog.

Scott's first mistress was very good to him and raised him as her own in all respects, except education. When he asked the minister at the Episcopal Sunday School he attended to teach him to read and write, the minister informed him it was against the law to teach Negroes. Angered by this unfairness, Scott resolved to someday escape.

At the age of 13, he was sold for $450. By this time he had been moved about so much that he no longer knew where his mother, brothers, sisters or other relatives were and never again learned their whereabouts.

One day in 1844 or 1845, his master ordered him to cut down poke stalks on the plantation. When he missed a few the master called him in to account for his neglect. Alexander could not control his rage. Within a few days he ran off to New York, where he took an active role in the Underground Railroad, assisting many slaves to freedom.

From New York he drifted to Boston and, shortly after the war broke out, enlisted as ward man's steward on the famous gunboat Kearsarge. After serving on numerous other vessels he was again transferred to the Kearsarge and was second gunner in the engagement with the rebel gunboat Alabama off Cherbourg, France.

After the War, he gained employment as a cook and steward for famous White Mountain hotels and resorts. After the deaths of his wife and children, he relocated to New Castle where he resided with Mrs. Melissa Johnston, (widow of Oscar) on North Shenango Street.[6]

George Washington Kincaid

GEORGE WASHINGTON KINCAID SCHOOL

GEORGE WASHINGTON Kincaid was born into slavery in 1854 in Morganton, Burke County, North Carolina. His mother, Louisa, was owned by William Kincaid and his father, William, belonged to William Kincaid's brother, Milton.

Kincaid received the rudiments of an education on the plantation. At some point he was removed from his mother and relocated. After the Civil War he moved to Tennessee and worked as a blacksmith and a puddler while studying at night. Encouraged by women working at the Freedmen's Mission, he entered the ministry of the A. M. E. Church.

Kincaid preached for 20 years at the largest colored churches of the country, including the Union Wesley, A.M.E. Zion Church in Washington, DC,[7] and the John Wesley A. M. E. Church on Arthur Street in Pittsburgh.[8]

He married his first wife around 1877[9] and claimed to be the first colored man in Tennessee to edit a newspaper, perhaps in Washington County where he resided in 1891.[10] Under the Harrison administration he held a government position.

On June 21, 1899, he married Miss Willie A. B. Smith of Lynchburg, Virginia.[11, 12] In June 1900 he was assigned to the pastorate at John Wesley Church in Chambersburg, Pennsylvania, and, in 1902,[13] became the pastor of Saint Luke's A.M.E. Church in New Castle, taking over from Pastor Duncunson.

During this period, he conceived an institute similar to the Tuskegee Institute established by Booker T. Washington.[14, 15] He professed that the colored man had to work his way upward in the economic and social scales. To Kincaid, the salvation of the Negro race lay in farming.

> "This is the only field of equality in which the Negro can enter the market and compete with the other fellow."[16]

With his vision in mind, he set to work. He located a 150 acre site on the on the Matthew S. Irwin farm, which bordered the Shenango River five miles north of New Castle, above the Harbor Bridge.

A number of prominent New Castle citizens took an interest in his plan, and the State Board of Charities agreed to recommend a $10,000 appropriation provided that a first mortgage be secured upon the farm by New Castle citizens.

The farm featured a stone house and a barn, but dormitories were needed for boys and girls. Each was estimated to cost $10,000. Local architects, S. W. Foulke & Son, prepared plans for an immense stone building to accommodate hundreds of children of both sexes.

By February 1903 the trustees were selected and organization completed.[17] The initial board of trustees is listed below.

President: Reverend G. W. Kincaid

First Vice President: Reverend H. S. Jordan

Second Vice President: John C. Jackson

Secretary and Treasurer: Captain Milton S. Marquis

Attorneys: S. P. Emery, Esq., C. H. Akens, Esq.

Trustees: W. D. Wallace, Charles Greer, P. J. Watson, Reverends L. J. Pollard and C. P. Hurrington, Peter M. Doup, W. D. Clinton, M.D., of Pittsburg, Reverend S. J. Caldwell, of Philadelphia, and G. W. Brown of Scranton.

Reverend C. P. Hurrington, Peter Doup, L. J. Pollard, W. Clinton, J. S. Caldwell, and George W. Brown were Black. Other trustees were prominent white New Castle businessmen.[18]

The institute was named the Western Pennsylvania Colored Industrial School for Farming and Domestic Science. Its facility received public endorsement from the New Castle Ministerial Association.[19]

State Representative Pomeroy sponsored a bill before the legislature, and Kincaid met with Governor Samuel W. Pennypacker, who gave assurances of his signature.[20] The demands of fundraising and running the institute were so great that Kincaid resigned his pastorate at Saint Luke's in late May 1903.

Several influential and wealthy state citizens voiced support for the facility. The Reverend and Mrs. J. H. Slater of Franklin, Pennsylvania were brought in to teach at the school in August 1903.[21]

A July 1904 article appeared in the Harrisburg Daily Independent indicating that Kincaid, in town to raise funds, possessed letters of recommendation from Lieutenant Governor William Brown, the Honorable W. D. Wallace, judge of the 53rd district, and Francis J. Torrance.

Unfortunately, fire destroyed the barn facilities. It was the hope of officers and trustees to reconstruct the outbuilding as quickly as possible. The loss was $5,000 with no funds in sight to meet it. The matter was laid before Andrew Carnegie, who promised, according to his established policy, to pay half the cost provided the other half was raised by the school. Kincaid came up $300 short of the amount necessary to meet the matching funds requirement.

On June 30th the Board of Trustees held its annual meeting. The Treasurer's report indicated that many localities in Pennsylvania and one in Youngstown had contributed, including Beaver, Sharon, Waynesburg, New Wilmington, New Brighton, Beaver Falls, Franklin, Erie, Johnstown, and others.

New officers were elected, as listed below.

President: George Washington Kincaid

First Vice President: W. D. Clinton

Second Vice President: D. S. Scott

Treasurer: P. M. Doup

Assistant Secretary: G. W. Johnson of Pittsburgh

Superintendent: C. P. Hurrington

Trustees: W. D. Wallace, Judge of 53rd District, Murray A. Verner, street railway magnate, J. K. Kean, Capitalist, Greenville, Pennsylvania, W. C. Lawton, President of Mortgage Banking Company, Pittsburgh, G. W. Gates Secretary and Treasurer of American Lumber Company of Pittsburgh, B. S. King, nephew of Andrew Carnegie, G. W. Brown of Scranton, Bishop J. S. Caldwell of Philadelphia, William T. Baker, Waynesburg, and J. W. Lee, Allegheny.[22]

Within a month the Sheriff seized the property through foreclosure proceedings, including the grain in the fields, farming implements, and other utensils about the place, in satisfaction of a judgment in the amount of $3,887.57 owed to Matthew S. Irwin.[23]

Kincaid went to Pittsburgh to raise $1,000 necessary to save the institution from foreclosure.

> "If the school is abandoned, nine Allegheny County colored children who are now happy farming will be returned to the Juvenile Court. Some are orphans, others are crippled. They are John Barnes, aged 15 years; James Kempjer, age 13; Harold Fisher aged 14; Levi Cross, aged 14; Robert Locket, aged 10; May Thornton aged 10; Raymond Pryer, aged 18; Jas. McGuire, aged 15 and Ralph Jackson aged 14."

Kincaid indicated that the 150 acre farm had many livestock and considerable produce. The farm could be saved for $3,000."

The money was not raised, and the farm was put up for sale on September 5th, 1904. Kincaid vowed that the school would continue, and that he would seek a smaller farm.[24] He soon indicated they would be moving four miles south of New Castle to a 50 acre farm.

The *Herald* stated that,

> "The financial affairs of the institution are being placed upon a more substantial basis than heretofore and the founder has great hopes."

According to Kincaid there were seven colored parole students from the Pennsylvania Reform School at Morganza in Allegheny County in his charge and being trained in the knowledge of useful occupations. The boys were being cared for by neighboring farmers.[25]

Kincaid continued his relentless efforts. In October 1904 a benefit was held at the old City hall in Pittsburgh to raise funds for the Western Pennsylvania Colored Industrial School. The benefit was presided over by Pittsburgh Judge, S. A. McClung, and Mayor James G. Wyman.[26]

A meeting of the Allegheny County Prison Board noted defects in the Juvenile court law. The Juvenile court of Allegheny County had sent a number of children to the farm without provision for their care. This had caused the school to go into debt, and Kincaid asked for $1,000 to pay the children's expenses. The Board felt this a deserving request and indicated application would be made for appropriations.[27]

Against all odds, Kincaid managed to relocate the school to the original farm. It happened that when the school first opened, Kincaid had secured a large supply of lumber from Lawrence County Lumber with a handshake and promise of future payment. Only a small payment was made before the farm went to sheriff's sale, including the lumber.

In order to protect itself from a major loss, Lawrence County Lumber purchased the farm. Kincaid went to their manager and told the officers of the great work which was going to be accomplished for his race, and his expectation of large sums of support from the likes of Andrew Carnegie. The company gave Kincaid another chance and allowed him back on the farm.[28]

Matching funds must have been obtained because in May 1905,[29] Andrew Carnegie issued a $2,500 check. Kincaid said the funds would be used for a dormitory to be named, Carnegie Hall for Colored Boys. Armed with this donation, Kincaid went to New York for a conference with J. Pierpont Morgan, noted financier and banker, in hopes of obtaining a like donation. He also planned on approaching the philanthropist, Henry Phipps, co-founder of Carnegie Steel.[30]

In November it was reported that the Western Pennsylvania Industrial School produced, among other things, three railcar loads of cabbage, purchased by and sent to Heinz's pickle factory in Pittsburgh. Heinz also provided an additional donation to the school.[31]

Kincaid's dogged pursuit paid off, and Carnegie agreed to contribute $20,000 toward the cost of erecting the buildings, as long as the Institute was able to raise money to match that amount. It was said that Carnegie took more than a passing interest in the school and was looking over the drawings left with him. Work on the buildings was expected to begin in April 1906. Kincaid represented that considerable money was available for the preliminary work.[32]

At the meeting of the Board of Trustees in February 1906 while Kincaid was away raising money, he was removed as President of his institute. The decision of the Board was announced by board member Peter M. Doup, a Black business owner in New Castle.

M. S. Marquis resigned at the same meeting. It was also decided to change the name from the Western Pennsylvania Industrial School to New Castle Normal School. A petition was filed with the court to allow a change in the number of directors from five to 15.

Opposition on the Board was due to the fact that Kincaid went on his money-collecting trip without calling the Meeting of the Directors, which should have been held during January.

> "It is also said that his popularity with the gentler sex has not been viewed with entire approval by those who were unfriendly to him."[33]

In September 1906, the then current pastor of A.M.E. Zion Church, Reverend P. K. Fonvielle, was elected as teacher in charge of the educational department. This was a change in operations. Previously inmates had been sent to the township schools, which caused many complaints from residents. At this time Kincaid was back on the trail, raising money and attempting to convince the legislature to fund girls' and boys' dormitories.[34]

As part of his efforts, Reverend Kincaid made application for a $25,000 appropriation from the Pittsburgh Board of Public Charities, $10,000 to be used for new buildings, and the balance for maintenance. The Board indicated it would recommend a $12,500 appropriation at an appropriate time.[35]

By November 27, 1907, Kincaid said there were 15 boys at the home, and he was unable to take on more. The New Castle News reported that a "four–year–old pickaninny," deserted by his Westmoreland County parents was toddling along the streets at Reverend Kincaid's heels. The child, Alex Moxey, had been sent to him by the Ladies' Aid Society of Westmoreland County, which was to bear the expenses of his education.[36]

The Advocate, a paper Kincaid edited, appeared in January 1908, with Kincaid's photo reportedly adorning its cover. Kincaid's opening editorial stated:

> "In introducing this paper to the public it is our purpose to publish a clean, wholesome, instructive paper, a paper that can enter any home or library, having for its object to place in the hands of each Negro a paper devoted to his race, morally, socially and politically."[37]

The *New Castle News* noted a good showing of business advertisements in the paper, including two breweries, six wholesale liquor establishments, and eleven retail liquor stores.

Things were not going well at the farm, however. In late February, James Shossner and his wife, Kincaid's sister, brought action against Kincaid for unpaid services. The Shossners, brought to the farm as assistant managers a few months prior, had been paid only 30 cents for their combined services.[38]

In May 1908, the New Castle and Youngstown Ministerial Associations, which had supported Kincaid's plan and recommended the project as worthy of support and financial aid, passed this resolution, published in all the local papers:

> "Whereas, your committee of March 1908, appointed for the purpose of investigating certain alleged wrongs and breaches of trust on the part of the superintendent of the proposed institution,
>
> Whereas, as your committee after careful investigation found these wrongs to exist in fact, and breaches of trust to be amazingly substantiated by credible witnesses, therefore,
>
> Resolved, that we express disapproval of the so-called superintendent of this proposed school, G. W. Kincaid, as a person morally unfit to train children in self control and self reliance and incapable of teaching farming and domestic science to children of any race. And be it further
>
> Resolved that we warn the people and the public generally to be aware of any collection of funds for this proposed school, or any solicitor or advertisements for the periodical called the "Advocate," the organ of the proposed school..."[39]

If contributions were slow coming in before the Ministerial Association action, they came to an abrupt halt afterward. The Institute's Board of Trustees issued a statement critical of the Ministerial Association's action and defended Kincaid and their cause.[40] The Secretary of the Board stated that he had audited the books and everything was in order. A payment of $2,500 had been put toward the purchase price when the farm was re–purchased but,

> "[t]he hard work had but begun. How to keep up expenses—how to pay taxes and meet payments when due was a serious problem. Reverend Kincaid had to meet these requirements. The board of trustees could afford him but moral aid and encouragement. So he had to travel from place to place begging for help to carry on the work. This took up practically all his time for contributions were slow and far between, and not being able to pay anyone to help on the farm his own children took up that end of the work and thus continued the struggling almost hoping against hope that the time would come when men who could, would sympathize and help."

The Board stated that it couldn't afford to pay Kincaid a salary, and he had fared worse than a day laborer for his untiring efforts over a seven year period. The Board directed Kincaid to file suit in Lawrence County Court against Ministerial Association resolution signatories.

The Institute had purchased the farm on an article of agreement with Lawrence Lumber, but by October 1908, had made only one small payment. Though Kincaid had made solicitations to pay the debt, it was reported that none of the money went to the Lumber Company, nor had it been spent on improvements at the farm.

The farm was in essentially the same condition as ten years before. The constable, armed with a landlord's warrant, went to the property to evict its occupants. The constable expected to find a small colony of children learning agriculture, but to everyone's surprise there was no school and only two boys in addition to Kincaid's son.

When Kincaid was being evicted, he said he hated to leave the place, but the landlord's warrant might be a blessing in disguise. He had had a call from the Republican national committee to make campaign speeches. The farm's sale relieved him of a burden of the responsibility, freeing him to go on the campaign trail.[41]

Reverend Kincaid subsequently founded an agricultural school in Fayette County, Pennsylvania. On a visit to New Castle in 1911, Kincaid boasted he had been successful at obtaining legislation to fund an industrial school in Jumonville, providing he could raise an equal amount of $10,000, which, he said, was not a problem.

On a subsequent visit to New Castle in October 1917, he told the *New Castle News* he was the head of a big industrial school at Jumonville, the former Jumonville Soldiers' Orphan's Home. The new school had 300 acres, 13 buildings and more than 200 colored students learning scientific farming and various trades. He said it was second only to Booker T. Washington's school.[42]

A *United Press* article in August 1911 reported that the school, an institution for Negroes patterned after the famous Tuskegee Normal and Industrial School, would formally open September 22, the 49th Anniversary of the Emancipation Proclamation.[43]

The *Pittsburgh Courier* ran an editorial about Kincaid's efforts to gain money for his school. The editorial indicated that Kincaid was being true to his reputation and that a conditional appropriation had been made by the State to foster his arrangement.

> "While we are always in accord with any and all movements tending to elevate the race, yet with the past experience of Reverend Kincaid fresh in our minds, it must be shown by the brother before we can pledge our support to or approve of his latest institution. They passed when Negroes can travel the country over soliciting money for fakes under the guise of 'industrial institutions for Negroes' Reverend Kincaid collected and spent more than enough money to purchase that home and school he once fathered near New Castle and until he makes a satisfactory account to the public, he may expect little or no support in his new project. Brother, we will have to be shown."[44]

In 1915 the U.S. Department of the Interior, Bureau of Education, performed a study of private and higher schools for colored people in the United States. They visited "Dunbar Camp [aka Jumonville] Agricultural, Industrial, and Mechanical School," solicitor, G. W. Kincaid.

Its report provides:

> "No such school exists, but the solicitor, who claims to be the founder, has conducted an extensive advertising campaign. The visit to Jumonville in July 1915, disclosed the fact that the property claimed does not belong to him. At one time a purchase of the school for orphan children of soldiers and sailors

was considered. The president used the photographs of these buildings and grounds as those of his 'school.' Among his claims are 'good foundation for departments of agriculture, live-stock raising, dressmaking, millinery and other departments.' The amount of money that has been raised in the name of the school could not be ascertained. A few years ago the State legislature made an appropriation of $10,000 on condition that an equal sum be raised by the school. While much money was raised the conditions were not fully met and the appropriation never became available.

Recommendation:—That all donations be withheld.

Date of Visit: July 1915"[45]

By 1920 Kincaid was divorced and living in Pittsburgh. He remarried Catherine B., a woman 26 years younger than him. The Reverend's daughter, Ethel E., married Reverend Oden in 1908. It is believed Kincaid had at least one other daughter and a son.

In 1934, while living in Roslyn Height, Carnegie, Pennsylvania, Kincaid fell ill. With him were Georgia Elizabeth Oden, M.D. of Yonkers, New York, a graduate of Howard University and Freedman Hospital, Mrs. Ethel Oden of Yonkers, New York, Dr. P. L. Kincaid of Braddock, and Mrs. Bertha Whittington from Goldsboro, North Carolina.[46]

Kincaid died in 1938 and is buried in Carnegie.

FIRST AFRICAN AMERICAN WESTMINSTER GRAD

JOHN F. QUARLES WAS born a slave April 8, 1846 to the Reverend Frank and Martha Quarles in Caroline County, Virginia.[47] In the 1850s, he and his father, mother and sister, Sarah, were moved to Georgia[48] when their owner, Ephraim G. Ponder, retired from his plantation to Atlanta with a young wife and numerous slaves.

Ponder built a new mansion and ventured into manufacturing, using his slaves who were trained in mechanics.[49] Ponder's marriage soon turned sour, as his wife was reportedly a drunkard and adulteress. He filed for divorce in October 1861.[50]

He left his mansion and his slaves with his wife, who in essence ignored them. Neither Mrs. Ponder, nor the guardian of the estate, who lived in another city, bothered much with their slaves.[51]

At least one of Ponder's mechanics was permitted to hire out and accumulate some wealth. John's father, Frank, an educated man, was given enough freedom that he was able to become a minister at the First Baptist Church in Atlanta. He was ordained in 1863, two years prior to emancipation.

No doubt educated by his father, John was able to read and write. When he requested Mrs. Ponder's permission to teach the slave children, even though it was illegal in Georgia, she acquiesced. The woodshop became Quarles' schoolhouse in the evening hours.

One of his students, Henry Flipper,[52] would become the first Black cadet at West Point. Just before Sherman entered Atlanta in September 1864, Mrs. Ponder and her slaves fled by train to Macon, Georgia, where it appears they stayed until the war ended in April, 1865.[53] Ponder's mansion was all but destroyed in Sherman's attack.[54]

In 1866 Quarles was given the opportunity for an education at Geneva Hall, the predecessor of Geneva College, then located in Northwood, Ohio. The Synod of the Covenanter Church in Ohio established the school to give talented colored persons preparatory training for the work of teaching their brethren and preaching the Gospel of Christ.[55] Over half of its

Reconstruction Era enrollment consisted of freed slaves.⁵⁶

The following is a description of Quarles upon his entry at Geneva:

> "John Franklin Quarles. Son [of] a colored clergyman and of Scotch–Indian–African descent. Color: dark yellow, features good, not striking; good head. Peculiarity of talent: good memory, lover of history and elocution. Moral character: unquestioned."⁵⁷ As envisioned by Geneva, Quarles moved on to the United Presbyterian institute's Westminster College, in New Wilmington, Pennsylvania entering into its theology program. Nathan Robinson Johnston, a minister and professor at Geneva made this observation: "One thing at least was made manifest, that the Negro has brains. Mr. Quarles, an emancipated slave and one of the most brilliant of all the students, had gone on to Westminster to finish his studies."⁵⁸

Westminster College, located in Lawrence County, was formed by the Shenango and Ohio Presbyteries of the Associate Presbyterian Church. It received its charter in March 1852 from the legislature.

In 1858 the college and its property was transferred to the First Synod of the United Presbyterian Church, an organization formed by the union of the Associate and Associate Reformed Presbyterian churches.⁵⁹ Reverend R. A. Browne, a well–known and highly respected Lawrence County Presbyterian Minister, and former Chaplain of the 100th Pennsylvania Volunteer Regiment (Roundheads), was President of Westminster.

> "Dr. Browne (president of the College) described him as 'a bright mulatto,' and on that point turned the story he told me of the young man's ready repartee. In his turn he gave a speech in the 'morning hall.' It was a good one and well delivered, and the Doctor in remarking on it before all said, 'That was an excellent speech, Mr. Quarles, a credit to your race.' 'Which one?' he responded instantly."⁶⁰

Quarles is said to have been sent to Westminster College under the patronage of U.S. Senator Charles Sumner, (R–Mass.), an Anti–slavery leader. A radical Republican, Sumner devoted his energies to destroying "Slave Power," or what the party perceived as the efforts of slave owners to take control of the Federal Government and thereby ensure the survival and expansion of slavery.

On May 19 and 20, 1856, Sumner gave a bitter speech.⁶¹ In "The Crime Against Kansas," he denounced the Kansas–Nebraska Act and conducted a personal verbal attack on South Carolina Senator Andrew Butler, calling him an imbecile and stating that he had "chosen a mistress. I mean the harlot, slavery."⁶²

After the speech he was sitting at his desk in the Senate chambers when South Carolina Congressman Preston Brooks burst in and beat him bloody with a cane. Brooks was supposedly defending the honor of his cousin, Senator Butler.

Ironically, Lawrence, Kansas, was sacked the next day, an event considered by many as the start of the Civil War. After the war, Sumner continued to be a champion of the Black cause, fighting for equal civil and voting rights.

John Quarles began theological studies on December 10, 1868.⁶³ In 1869 he was empowered by the faculty at Westminster to visit colored churches, conventions and conferences in the South to gather support for the National Reform Movement that sought to amend the Constitution to provide for a Christian Government.⁶⁴ Consequently, he travelled to Washington, D.C., in the summer of 1869.⁶⁵

A man of many firsts, Quarles holds the distinction of being the first Black student to graduate from Westminster College. It was also said that he graduated at the head of his class.⁶⁶

> "Only a few years ago he had been a slave. The sword had been God's instrument to cut his chains. Give

the millions of freed–people a fair opportunity and erelong they will rank high in the scale of education."[67]

Perhaps it was during his trip to Washington that Quarles became interested in politics and law. He gave up theology and entered Howard University Law School.[68, 69] During his time at Howard, Quarles also managed to teach school in Augusta, Georgia.[69]

In June 1872 Howard Law graduated its first class, and Quarles was among them. Senator Sumner, under whom Quarles is said to have studied law,[71] was requested to provide a commencement address. Sumner had a previous engagement at Harvard, but realizing the significance of this class, cancelled his appearance there and spoke at Howard.

In January 1873 Quarles was admitted to the bar in Georgia, its first colored lawyer.[72] That same month, he wrote to President Grant applying for the position of Consul at Antwerp Belgium, noting that Georgia had no one in the Consular Service.

U.S. Representative Richard H. Whiteley of Georgia, endorsed his request:

> "I regard Mr. Quarles as one of the most promising and worthy young men of his race in our State or in the South, and commend him to your favorable consideration."

Henry Wilson, U.S. Senator from Massachusetts, also endorsed him. Quarles did not receive his desired post, but on February 18th President Grant appointed him Consul at Port Mahon on the Island of Minorca with a pay of $1500 per annum.[73]

After three years in service, Quarles was recalled due to Congress' failure to make the "usual appropriations." He reapplied to President Grant on December 7, 1876 for a position to Basel, Switzerland, that would enable him to rejoin his family.

Frederick Douglass wrote to Grant on Quarles' behalf asking:

> "... that he be reinstated in the Consular service for the following reasons: That Quarles, is the only person from his state, Georgia, holding a position in this branch of the consular service, ... and that he is endorsed and recommended by the Republications of the entire State, that Mr. Quarles, is the only colored man holding such a position in this branch of the foreign service and thus he not only represents his state, but we regard him in a peculiar sense as the representative of the colored people of the country in this branch of the public service."

Quarles survived the political wind change, and on June 21, 1877, was appointed U.S. Consul at Malaga by President Hayes.[74] He served for a period of three years. While in Malaga he married a granddaughter of General Jaqueminot, one of Napoleon's Marshals.

In 1880, he returned to the States and established a practice in New York City. He was admitted to practice before the New York Supreme Court on May 13, 1880, the first colored applicant in the state. The motion for his admission was made by the Honorable Algernon S. Sullivan, a Democrat.[75, 76]

On January 28, 1885, John F. Quarles, died of pneumonia at the age of 38.[77] This brilliant man spoke six languages.[78]

OLD MOSE, AN ICON AT MCCONNELL'S MILL

MOSE WHARTON WAS BORN into slavery in Winston-Salem, North Carolina on May 30th, 1860. His mother Sarah, and his father William, were owned by a Dr. Wharton and when freedom came, they assumed their former master's last name. Mose

Mose Wharton came to Lawrence County about 1878 where he worked for a few different families.

In 1880 Captain Thomas McConnell took him to McConnell's Mill in Slippery Rock Township, to work at what was then an operating grist mill.[79, 80] For a time he was the only black man seen in the area. He reportedly was one of the shiftiest "leather pushers" (boxer) during his early days.

Returning home to McConnell's Mill one evening he and a companion were stopped on a lonely spot on the road by two men who grasped the horses and demanded their money or their blood. "…but as revolvers were soon brought into play the highwaymen proved to be practical jokers."[81]

Well known throughout the area, Mose delivered flour to almost every store from New Castle to Butler. His mother Sarah was born about 1842 and was raised in the cotton and tobacco fields of the Carolinas. After the war she moved to Indianapolis, Indiana where her eldest son William also resided. Her husband died about 1903 and in 1911 she came to Lawrence County and assisted her son Mose in taking care of the mill. Sarah died here in 1928.[82]

After Captain McConnell's son, Thomas', death in 1928, Mose continued in the employ of Thomas Hartman who took over ownership of the mill. In 1929 Wharton had the unfortunate experience of finding a frozen body when he went to the barn to get hay for his cow. He discovered the corpse when his pitchfork stuck in the body under the hay.[83]

Mose continued to work and greet all those who visited the Mill until he was 92 years of age, and his health failed. After a hospitalization he entered the County home in March 1952. "Old Mose" as he was affectionately referred to, died December 11, 1954. He was survived by only one sister, Nora Wade Bacon, New Rochelle, NY.[84]

He and his mother are buried in Portersville Presbyterian Cemetery.

Chapter Notes

1. "'Judge' Dies At City Home," *New Castle News*, October 26, 1914.
2. *New Castle News*, November 26, 1912.
3. "'Judge' Now At Poor Farm," *New Castle News*, May 22, 1913.
4. "'Judge' Tries To Come Back," *New Castle News*, January 28, 1914, 4.
5. "'Judge' is in Sorry Plight," *New Castle News*, March 30, 1914, 1.
6. "Very Eventful Life," *New Castle News*, April 6, 1898, 1.
7. *The Washington Bee* (Washington, DC), January 24, 1899, 5.
8. "Hopes to Save the Industrial Farm," *New Castle News*, August 24, 1904, 12.
9. United States Census, 1930.
10. Tennessee, Enumeration of Male Voters, 1891. Ancestry.com
11. *Richmond Planet* (Richmond, Virginia), July 1, 1899, 1.
12. Virginia, Select Marriages 1785-1940. Ancestry.com
13. *Harrisburg Daily Independent,* Harrisburg, Pennsylvania, June 19, 1900, 5.
14. "$2,500 Check for Industrial School," *New Castle News*, May 17, 1905
15. *New Castle Weekly Herald* (New Castle, Pennsylvania), November 26, 1902, 4.
16. "Addressed Colored People," *The Scranton Republican*, Scranton, Pennsylvania, February 2, 1917.
17. *New Castle Weekly Herald*, February 4, 1903, 1.
18. *New Castle Weekly Herald*, November 26, 1902, 4.
19. "Ministers Endorse Industrial School," *New Castle News*, March 2, 1904, 4.
20. "Pastor of Local Church Had Interview with Pennypacker on Industrial School," *New Castle News*, March 18, 1903, 5.
21. "Rev. Kincaid, Pastor Local Church, Resigns," *New Castle News*, May 27, 1903.
22. "Education is the Negro's Only Hope" *Harrisburg Daily Independent*, July 12, 1904, 1.
23. "Sheriff's Property," *New Castle Weekly Herald*, August 17, 1907, 1.
24. "School to Continue," *New Castle Weekly Herald*, September 7, 1904, 7.
25. "Secured a New Site," *New Castle News*, September 14, 1904, 1.
26. "For Benefit of Industrial School," *New Castle Weekly Herald*, October 26, 1904.
27. "To Revive The School," *New Castle Weekly Herald,*, November 10, 1904, 6.
28. "OUSTED," *New Castle News*, October 6, 1906, 1.
29. "$2,500 Check for Industrial School," *New Castle News*, May 17, 1905, 5.
30. "Will Morgan Stand Minister's Touch?" *New Castle News*, August 16, 1905.
31. "Has Sold Three Carloads of Cabbage," *New Castle News*, November 22, 1905.
32. "Carnegie to Contribute," *New Castle News*, December 20, 1905.
33. "Rev. G. W. Kincaid Loses Presidency of Industrial School Which He Founded," *New Castle News*, February 7, 1906.
34. "Will Teach the Common Branches," *New Castle News*, September 12, 1906.
35. "Is Confident of An Appropriation," *New Castle News*, December 5, 1906.
36. "Deserted boy Gets Home on Kincaid Farm," *New Castle News*, November 27, 1907.
37. *New Castle News*, January 7, 1908, 8.
38. "30 Cents Salary for Month's Work," *New Castle News*, February 21, 1908, 1.
39. "Kincaid to Educate Negroes with New Paper," *New Castle News*, May 4, 1908, 8.
40. *New Castle News*, May 6, 1908, 8.
41. "OUSTED," *New Castle News*, October 6, 1908.
42. "Kincaid is Head of A Big School," *New Castle News*, October 25, 1917; "Reverend Kincaid Heads Industrial School," *New Castle News*, September 13, 1911.
43. "Another Colored School to Open," *New Castle Herald*, August 21, 1911, 8.
44. "We must be shown," *Pittsburgh Courier*, Pittsburgh, Pennsylvania, August 26, 1911, 4.
45. "Kincaid is Head of A Big School," *New Castle News*, October 25, 1917; "Reverend Kincaid Heads Industrial School," *New Castle News,* September 13, 1911.
46. "Carnegie, Pa.," *The Pittsburgh Courier,* Pittsburgh, Pennsylvania, January 20, 1934.
47. Freedman's Bank Records, 1865-1871 – Ancestry.Com; Registers of Signatures of Depositors in Branches of the Freedman's Savings and Trust Company, 1865-1874. Washington, DC.
48. Cathcart, William D. D., *The Baptist Encyclopedia: A dictionary of Doctrines, Ordinances. Vol. 2*, 1881, 952.
49. "Flipper at Home," *Auburn Daily Bulletin*, July 14, 1877, fultonhistory.com
50. Cusic, Don, *The Trials of Henry Flipper, First Black Graduate of West Point*, 9.

51 Cusic, Don, *The Trials of Henry Flipper, First Black Graduate of West Point*, 7.
52 Cusic, Don, *The Trials of Henry Flipper, First Black Graduate of West Point*, 11.
53 Ibid.
54 See Barnard's Photographic Views of the Sherman Campaign, ca. 1866 "Potter's House" (sic) at http://dlg.galileo.usg.edu/hargrett/barnard/jpgs/plate38.jpg
55 Johnston, Nathan Robinson, *Looking Back from the Sunset: Or People Worth Knowing*, 384-385.
56 Balmer, Randall Herbert, *Encyclopedia of Evangelicalism*, 2004, 286.
57 *Westminster College Magazine*, Winter 2005, 22. (www.westminster.edu)
58 Johnston, Nathan Robinson, *Looking Back from the Sunset: Or People Worth Knowing*, 417.
59 *A History of Higher Education in Pennsylvania, Volumes 902-904*, Haskins & Hull, 1902, 267.
60 *Westminster College Magazine*, Winter 2005, 22, quoting from student paper Holcad.
61 *The Record-Argus*, Greenville, Pennsylvania, February 5, 1885, 2.
62 Sumner, Hon. Charles, "Crime Against Kansas," Speech in the Senate of the United States, May 19, 1856, 3. Openlibrary.org
63 Sproull, John W. et. al. *The Reformed Presbyterian and Covenanter, Volume 8.* 1870, 121, 234.
64 Sproull, John W. et. al. *The Reformed Presbyterian*, 243.
65 Sproull, John W. et. al. *The Reformed Presbyterian*, 254.
66 *The Record-Argus*, Greenville, Pennsylvania, February 5, 1885, 2.
67 Johnston, Nathan Robinson, *Looking Back from the Sunset: Or People Worth Knowing*, 402.
68 Langston, John Mercer, *From the Virginia Plantation to the National Capitol, John Mercer Langston, 1894 or the First, and only Negroe*, American Publishing Company. 1894, 303-307.
69 "Georgia's Colored Consul," *New York Times*, June 21, 1877, 3.
70 Quarles, John F. *Freedman's Bank Records, 1865-1871.* Georgia.
71 *The Record-Argus*, February 5, 1885, 2.
72 "Personal Intelligence," *Daily Era* (Raleigh, North Carolina), January 30, 1873, 1.
73 Langston, John Mercer, *From the Virginia Plantation to the National Capitol*, 307.
74 *The Holton Recorder* (Holton, Kansas), June 21, 1877.
75 *The Pantagraph* (Bloomington, Illinois), May 14, 1880, 1.
76 *Richmond Dispatch*, May 17, 1880, 2.
77 "Miscellaneous," *The National Tribune*, February 5, 1885, 8.
78 *The Brooklyn Daily Eagle* (Brooklyn, New York), October 21, 1883, 2.
79 "Mose is Booster in Hospital Drive," *New Castle News*, January 24, 1948, 1.
80 "Wharton Funeral Time," *New Castle News*, December 13, 1954, 2.
81 "McConnell's Mills", *New Castle News*, June 22, 1904.
82 "Aged Colored Woman at McConnell's Mills Expires After Illness," *New Castle News*, December 20, 1928, 19.
83 "Find Frozen Body Under Straw Stack During Morning," *New Castle News*, February 9, 1929, 1.
84 Mose Wharton Obituary, *New Castle News*, December 11, 1954, 4.

22

OTHER EX–SLAVES

SIMON ARNOLD

SIMON ARNOLD WAS BORN about 1826 in South Carolina and was sold as a slave to a family in Georgia. While enslaved, he had a wife and two children, but they were separated from him and sold. He never learned what became of them. He must have escaped slavery or was somehow freed, as he served in the Union Navy during the Civil War, and was reportedly a brave sailor.

Arnold settled in New Castle about 1878, and was employed for many years by William Patterson, President of the National Bank of Lawrence County and one of the most prominent citizens in the county. Arnold lived on Green Street in Snake's Rest, west New Castle. A deacon of Mount Zion Baptist church,[1] he would frequently preach to the small congregation in the city.

In 1897 Arnold was put in charge of a Gentlemen's Driving Park at the fairgrounds,[2] where he was to live and take care of the grounds. In December, 1898,[3] he died in New Castle. His little Snake's Rest cottage was turned into a city infectious disease facility, originally used for smallpox.[4]

ISAIAH MILLER

BORN IN 1844 AS A SLAVE in Virginia, Isaiah Miller was sold and living in Georgia during the early Civil War years. He escaped in 1863 and joined General George Henry Thomas at Chattanooga and served as a Union soldier in Company I, 23rd Regiment, U.S. Colored Troops until the end of the war.[5]

By 1870, Miller was living with his wife Rachel, and a daughter in New Castle. He was a member of the Second Baptist Church, and is listed as a teamster in the 1889 City Directory. From then until his death he resided with his family at 273 North Mercer. In 1891, he owned real estate assessed at $100. He had three more children and had become a highly respected citizen of the city.

> "On October 16, 1896,[6] Isaiah Miller died. Surviving him were two sons, Isaiah Howard, and Harry C., and his wife, Rachel, who lived until 1921."[7]

Miller was buried at Greenwood Cemetery.

CHARLES TILDEN

CHARLES TILDEN WAS born in 1818, supposedly in Pennsylvania. At some point he may have been sent south, as his obituary states that he arrived in New Castle some 30 years prior to his death and had been a slave for many years. We know from City Directories that he worked as early as 1872 as a laborer for Cunningham & Co., founders and machinists in New Castle. In 1886 he was a coachman for noted Abolitionist, R. W. Clendenin.

Tilden resided at 24 South Mill in 1886, at 114 North Beaver in 1888, and 166 West Lincoln in 1896. He was a member of the Saint Luke's A. M. E. Zion church and was said to be devoted to the cause.

In March 1898, Tilden died, leaving behind his wife, Nellie, the daughter of Hamilton Parish, and five children, Annie, Mary, Lydia, Elmira and Charles.

Tilden was buried at Greenwood Cemetery.[8]

NANCY JOINER

NANCY JOINER WAS born a slave and lived in Winston, North Carolina after the war. She is believed to have had at least five children, John, William, Berry, Mrs. John Ward, and Alex Oakes.

After the War, her son, John, his sister, and half–brother, Alex Oakes left North Carolina and settled in New Castle, where John believed

> "... the colored man had a chance as well as his white brother and would be not be lorded over as an inferior being."

Nancy's daughter married John Ward and took up residence on Phillips Hill in New Castle. When she received word that her mother was in need, she and her siblings scraped enough money together to bring their dear mother to join them in New Castle. She arrived in September 1894 to a joyous reunion.

Nancy told a pitiful story of the impositions practiced on the Blacks in her section of the South. Though she had been a slave before the Civil War, her master had treated her kindly. Afterward she remained with him for a few years, but then decided to live an independent life.

According to Nancy, Negroes were treated even worse after the war than before. Prior to that, they were valuable property and well taken care of to ensure their masters' investment. After the Civil War, Blacks were worked harder than in slavery days. They received only 25–30 cents for a day's labor. As a general rule Blacks did not own land and rented their cabin and little garden from the white man who employed them. If they refused to work at any price the landlord set, they would be evicted.

Some Negroes worked farms on the shares, giving the landowner two–thirds of the gross proceeds. Even then Blacks were often cheated. Negroes were usually so poor that they were forced to ask for help from their landlord at various times during the year. The landlord would usually keep the laborers' crop share as payment.

One of Nancy's sons remained in North Carolina, where he farmed a large and unusually fine tobacco crop. Before the plants had even matured, he was offered $150 a bushel for it, and refused, knowing that it would be worth several hundred dollars at harvest. But it was not to be. His white landlord took the entire crop on account of assistance amounting to a few dollars extended to Nancy's son through the winter.

An added insult was that Black children were forbidden to attend white schools, and no provision was made by the state for their education. In order to obtain instruction, Blacks had to pay a subscription and could only be taught by a Black teacher.[9]

ALEXANDER OAKES

Alexander Oakes, born March 5, 1839 in North Carolina, remained in New Castle until his death. He worked at the Reis Brothers Steel mill prior to its bankruptcy in 1883.[10]

Described as a "stalwart Negro," Oakes worked for many years in the steel industry. He was a member, deacon, and one of the original founders of the Second Baptist Church on West

Falls Street, and a member of the Order of Odd Fellows.

His wife's name was Harriet A. Warwick, born February 4, 1852, in Virginia to John Warwick and Sarah Walsh. She passed away on November 24, 1908, while living at 210 Green Street.[11, 12] Children included Miss Annie M. Oakes, Mrs. A. D. Thomas, both in New Castle, Mrs. Mary Wright of Homestead, and Mrs. Josephine Vanwicker of Chicago.[13]

JOHN JOINER

In 1889, John Joiner lived behind Keystone Rink, located on Beaver Street near Washington Street. One night he found a warning pinned to his door that if he did not mend his ways, and go to work, he would be subjected to the cruelest tortures. The notice stated that Mr. Joiner did not take proper care of his children.[14]

John's wife, Mary, filed for divorce in July of 1897, claiming he had deserted her and their six children in 1895.[15] Shortly after the filing, their four year old son, Herbert, met with a horrible accident. He and some friends were playing with a "Jackson cracker," and Herbert lit it.[16] The explosion nearly severed his hand. Mary married James Lee and the family lived on Croton Avenue in the 1900 census, which lists John's children as Edith, William, Johnny, Edna, Herbert, and Rhubert.

In 1902, John was living in the rear of 14 Croton Avenue, and his fourteen year old son, Johnny, was a parolee from Morganza, a mental health hospital and reform school established in the mid–1870s near Canonsburg, Pennsylvania. In 1902, Johnny worked at the Hazel Glass House in Canonsburg. During the July 4th holiday he was handling a pistol when a cartridge exploded, nearly severing his hand. He died of lockjaw.[17, 18]

PETER M. DOUP

PETER DOUP WAS BORN in Winston, North Carolina, between 1862 and 1865. His mother, Lucinda, later married James Eckles (Eccles) and appears to have followed Peter to New Castle.

Peter established the New Castle Steam Carpet Cleaning Works, at No. 70 South Mercer Street, in 1882. In 1890, he took in his half–brother, John A. Eckles, as a partner. The firm made, laid, scoured and refit carpets, repaired and upholstered furniture, renovated feathers, cleaned houses, and hung wallpaper. The firm employed 12 assistants.

Doup also catered, and furnished waiters for evening receptions. He was a member of New Castle Lodge of the United Grand Chapter of the Holy Royal Arch Masons, and the Most Worshipful Grand Lodge of Free and Accepted Masons of the state of Pennsylvania. He was elected Vice President of the Western Pennsylvania Afro–American Republican League. His business was highlighted in the 1898 Industrial Souvenir Edition of the Courant.

In 1903, Doup was on the Board of Trustees for the Colored Industrial School established by the Reverend Kincaid. He was also a member of the Bethel A. M. E. Church where the Hall bore his name.

When Doup, considered a leader in the Black community, attempted to buy a sandwich and a cup of coffee at a restaurant in New Castle, he was charged $.25 instead of the customary $.10. Doup held his ground, offering only ten cents. The police were called. The owner explained that while the law demands he serve all who apply, no price is fixed, leaving him free to charge three times or more to colored people. This was done without any special antagonism to the colored people, the owner said, as white people did not

Doup Business Office

extensively patronize restaurants where colored peopled were served.

> "It is merely to protect himself in his business. Other restaurant keepers adopt similar tactics, it is said."[19]

Doup went to the police station, paid his ten cents, and left.

In 1903, the city had a crackdown on chartered clubs. Police claimed that the clubs' advancement of culture, music, science, and the fine arts, made them no better than speakeasies. Doup was the proprietor of The Majestic Club on South Mercer Street. His was one of four clubs that were shut down.[20]

In 1908, Doup opened an employment bureau on South Mill Street, promising to find employment for both white and colored.[21] Two white girls, aged 16 and 18, who had sought work at his place of business, accused Doup of trying to hire them to do nothing but "be friends" to a man in town and another in Cleveland for upwards of $50 a week.[22] Charges were brought and he was held on $500 bail, but nothing more is known on the outcome of those charges.

At some point afterwards Doup moved to Youngstown and set up his carpet business there. In March 1913 he was arrested by Youngstown detectives after having been under investigation for some time as a large scale white slave dealer. Doup had sent a 16 year old office girl to a man to collect bills that he told the girl were owed to Doup's business. He had previously made arrangements with the man to provide him with a white slave.

Convicted of criminal assault and procuring girls for immoral purposes, he was sent to the Ohio penitentiary for a term of 4 to 25 years. He was released prior to 1925 and was spotted by New Castle residents visiting Hollywood, California, where he was employed as a street sweeper. He was also working as a pastor.

Doup died in Los Angeles on 21 August, 1931.

Chapter Notes

1. "Rev. Moore In Jail." *Daily City News*, New Castle, Pennsylvania, December 23, 1889, 3.
2. "Gentlemen's Driving Park," *Daily City News*, New Castle, Pennsylvania, August 24, 1887, 3.
3. "Simon Arnold Passes Away After a Lingering Illness," *New Castle News*, December 21, 1898, 2.
4. "Smallpox is Now A Dead Letter," *New Castle News*, April 9, 1902; *New Castle News*, May 14, 1902, 10.
5. Miller, Isaiah, *Record of Burial Place of Veteran, Commonwealth of Pennsylvania Department of Military Affairs* (Ancestry.com). Date of Death: October 16, 1898.
6. *New Castle News Weekly*, October 21, 1896, 1.
7. *New Castle News*, July 11, 1921.
8. *New Castle News*, March 2, 1898.
9. *New Castle News Weekly*, September 4, 1894.
10. "Like Finding It," *New Castle News Weekly*, March 25, 1891.
11. *New Castle News*, November 25, 1908.
12. Pennsylvania Death Certificate 106345.
13. *New Castle News*, August 10, 1921, 2.
14. "White Caps Once More," *The Daily City News*, February 7, 1889, 3.
15. *New Castle News*, July 14, 1897, 5.
16. *New Castle News*, July 28, 1897, 1.
17. "Died From Lockjaw," *The Daily Notes*, Canonsburg, Pennsylvania, July 7, 1902, 3
18. *New Castle Weekly Herald*, July 9, 1902, 1.
19. "Color Line Brawn," (sic), *New Castle News*, November 8, 1905, 14.
20. "War Declared on Chartered Clubs," *New Castle News*, June 24, 1903, 19.
21. "Charges Against Doup Sensational," *New Castle News*, March 2, 1908, 1.
22. "Peter Doup is Held for Court," *New Castle News*, March 6, 1908, 2.

23
MYTHS & LEGENDS

OVER THE YEARS, a variety of myths and legends have been perpetuated about a variety of locations assumed to be part of the Underground Railroad. At the same time, other stories have been lost. Here we try to confirm or disprove commonly believed stories and support new ones.

Thomas Berry House

LOCAL LEGEND CREDITS Joseph White for secreting escaping slaves in the Thomas Berry House on the northwest corner of Grant Street and North Jefferson. This is not fully supported by the evidence.

The Thomas Berry House was built by the free African American barber sometime after he moved to the city in 1841. Included in the southwest corner of the house was a hidden cellar, suggesting that members of the Berry family were the first to hide fugitives.

> "The only entrance to the cellar, which is in good state of preservation, is by trap door in the floor of a small first floor bedroom, opening from the dining room. Many occupants of the house have not known of the existence of the cellar, the trap door making no break in the even appearance of the floor."

Joseph S. White is generally credited for utilizing the house as an Underground Railroad Station, but

> "[t]his house was built by Thomas Berry, a colored barber who is remembered by many citizens. It was he who constructed the cellar."[1]

Thomas and Mary are not mentioned as being Conductors in most articles available from the 1880s and 1890s. That may have been due to prejudice or public sentiment at the time, but it seems obvious that Thomas would not have built a secret cellar if he had not planned to use it. Joseph White's son, J. Crawford, reportedly stated,

> "The truth was, the station had been built for a special purpose, to secrete fugitive slaves

Thomas Berry House

hoping and trying to make the land of freedom, when pursued closely by their masters."

The house would indeed become an Underground Railroad Station when Joseph White owned it after 1857, but White's own letters state that his early Underground Railroad experiences were at his father's house on the east side of North Jefferson Street, not at the Berry House.

Rumors that tunnels ran from the Berry House to the river and/or beneath N. Jefferson Street were refuted by J. Crawford White.

> "I was informed of the open eyed wonderment of the scholars of Martin Gantz school, at the stories told them by their teachers, about New Castle's station on the same side of Jefferson Street, and that, beginning at the Shenango River, then used as the Erie and Pittsburgh canal, there was an underground tunnel that led eastward to the aforesaid station!
>
> "Tho' I couldn't endorse that, it made quite an interesting story."[2]

Furthermore, Joseph White never mentions using tunnels or secret cellars in any of his letters or newspaper articles. A *New Castle News* article written before the house was demolished states that no evidence of a tunnel connecting the house to the river was found.[3]

KURTZ HOUSE

RUMORS HAVE PERSISTED for decades that the Kurtz House, once located at the southeast corner of East Washington and Croton Avenue, was part of the Underground Railroad. The story was accompanied by additional rumors of tunnels leading to the Neshannock Creek.

The house dated to the 1840s when it was owned by Robert Cochran. Cochran operated a store on the southeast side of the Diamond near 16–18 East Washington Street, selling dry goods, groceries, hardware, queensware, boots, shoes, hats, caps and bonnets.[4]

In 1846, Thomas Berry's barber–shop was located on Mill Street over Cochran's store. If Cochran was an Abolitionist, he gave no indication. He did not join the Free Presbyterian Church, but was a member of the First Presbyterian Church and even helped erect the church edifice in 1849.[5] There is no indication that he participated in the Underground Railroad.

Kurtz House

Stories that an underground tunnel ran from the river to the house were probably a result of the Riverside Livery Stables at 7 Croton Avenue abutting the river directly across the street from the Cochran/Kurtz house. Most likely a feature of the livery was mistaken for a tunnel. It has been reported that the business possessed

> "an underground stable, the floor of which is below the river level."[6]

Even Isabella Kurtz has stated that the homestead had no historical significance.[7]

replacing a previously structure at that location. Clearly, the current house could not have been a part of the Underground Railroad, as it was built too recently. But what of the prior home?

Christian was a member of the Evangelical German Lutheran Church, and the Genkinger name has not been associated with Abolitionist connections, activities, or churches, making it doubtful that the previous home was a station on the Underground Railroad. A family historian, Ms. Evelyn Genkinger of New Castle, confirms that there is no family connection to the Underground Railroad.

Christian Genkinger House

CHRISTIAN GENKINGER HOUSE

The beautiful Second Empire Victorian house standing at the bend on Butler Avenue and Paul Street is rumored to be connected with the Underground Railroad. The most common tales speak of secret tunnels beneath the home, or leading to the house across the street.

Christian Genkinger was born in Germany and came to New Castle in 1853, where he set up a distillery on Butler Avenue.[8] He built the existing home between 1877 and 1890,

COURTHOUSE

A courthouse might be the last place one would suspect fugitive slaves to hide, but there is some evidence that the Lawrence County Courthouse cellar was used for just this purpose. The cellar was more crawlspace than basement when the building was erected in the early 1850s.

> "Except for a small basement section in the rear of the courthouse building, there is no cellar under the courthouse at all. Several small tunnels run under the building."[9]

to public office included School Directors R. W. Clendenin and J. N. Euwer in 1853, Councilman R. W. Clendenin in 1856 and 1857, Assistant Assessor Joseph S. White in 1858, and S. W. Mitchell, Overseer for the Poor in 1859 and 1862.[12]

EUWER BUILDING

THE BUILDING LOCATED at 210 East Washington Street houses Main Street Clothiers today, but was originally Euwer's Clothing Store.

The pre–Civil War building was lost to a fire in 1873, but rebuilt with five stories at the same location.[13] The Euwers

> "…very frequently would have a number of runaway slaves secreted in his stables and cellars."[14]

Lawrence County Courthouse

A 1910, a *New Castle News* article printed a story about the courthouse basement being used to store confiscated kegs of beer.

> "The place is what is known as the 'dungeon' and has been very little used since it was abandoned as a station for the Underground Railroad before the war. The dungeon is located almost underneath the Prothonotary's office…"[10]

Is it possible that the courthouse would have been used? It appears that Abolitionists had access to the building. Before the Free Presbyterian Church had its own building, meetings were held at the courthouse, supplying their own coal and light, and paying the janitor.[11]

Dr. Charles Whippo, Associate Judge for the county, was an Abolitionist, and held Anti-Slavery meetings with the Free Soil party at the courthouse in 1853. Other Abolitionists elected

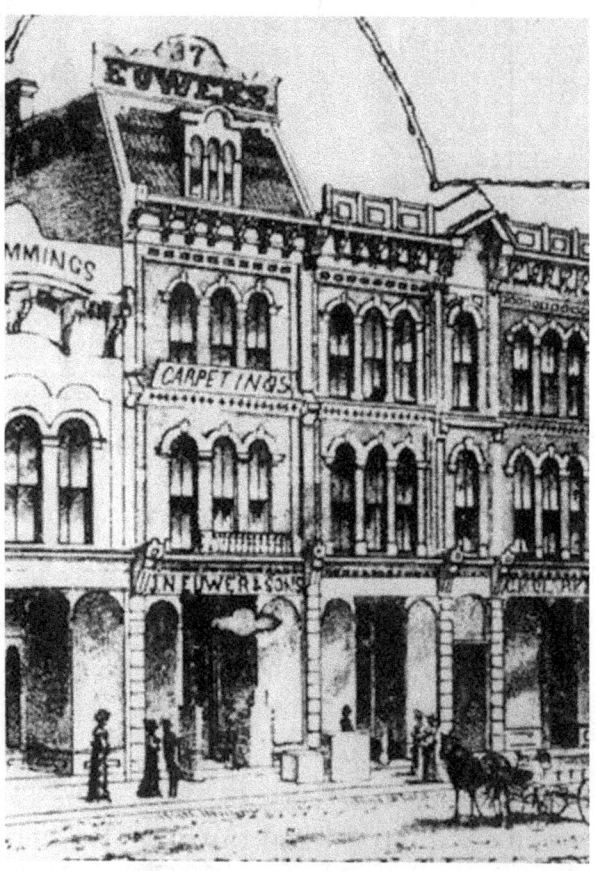

Euwer Clothing Store

It is reasonable to deduce that the original Washington Street cellar was used for this purpose. Is the cellar under the present building the original cellar? Antique square-headed nails in the basement's stone walls suggest it could be. Also, the cellar entrance is built into the floor in a fashion identical to a door in the Reinholdt building at 41 North Mercer Street that was built before 1855.

"The interesting thing about this part of the basement is that it shared a chimney with the upstairs fireplace so it wouldn't look fishy to people searching for runaway slaves in the cellar, and word soon passed that this was a safe stop, as the documents on the lobby walls indicate."[15]

Unfortunately, the evidence available does not strongly support this assertion. Construction of the house began in 1849. In 1850, Seth Poppino was single and living with George Clark and his

Poppino Home

NEW WILMINGTON TAVERN

LOCAL LEGEND HAS IT that The Tavern built by Dr. Seth Poppino was part of the Underground Railroad. A *Pittsburgh Press* article stated the house was built in the late 1840s or early 1850s, and its basement was used as a safe house for fugitive slaves traveling from New Castle to Mercer or Sharon.

Mary Ellen Durrast–Connelly recalled that when her parents were renovating the house to create their restaurant, they found a hidden kitchen in the basement.

family.[16] The home was therefore completed around the time the Fugitive Slave Act passed in 1850. The doctor and his family would have been subject to prosecution, a large fine, and imprisonment if caught harboring escaped slaves. Also, Conductors from the period observed that the number of slaves arriving declined after the Act's passage. It seems likely that the existing network of Stations could have handled the flow.

Dr. Poppino was not identified by other Conductors as a member of the Underground Railroad. Joseph S. White wrote of delivering fugitives to the Young farm at Indiana Run north of New Wilmington, but made no mention of Poppino. New Wilmington resident Robert Ramsey's obituary named conductors in Erie, but not Dr. Poppino. Mrs. Angeline Quinby of Trumbull County, Ohio, wrote of receiving fugitives from John and David Young of New Wilmington, but not Dr. Poppino.[17]

Nor does Dr. Poppino's obituary[18] mention his involvement with the Underground Railroad, and his wife's obituary also fails to disclose a connection.[19] Additionally, Mrs. Poppino's biography in the *20th Century History of New Castle and Lawrence County* does not describe any Abolitionist views or activities that might suggest she or her home was part of the Underground Railroad. No newspaper articles were found connecting the family to the Underground Railroad until the 1970s, more than 100 years removed from the events.[20]

The assumption that a basement kitchen must have been constructed for fugitives is similarly unsupported. In 18th century England when the kitchen was inside the house, it was commonly downstairs. Williamsburg features several examples of basement kitchens.[21] A brick–floored kitchen is located in the basement the 19th century Hosmer's Inn in Mumford, New York,[22] and a Neshannock home built in 1833 by Frederick Zeigler was equipped with a basement kitchen. This home, on Maitland Lane, was later owned by George Reynolds. The chimney still stands today.[23]

Rumors abound that tunnels connected the Tavern to other points in New Wilmington, but Jay Behm, who purchased the Tavern in 2004, scoured the basement and did not find evidence of such passageways. Poppino's grandson, Dr. James H. Spencer, M.D. did write a booklet, "The Tavern: Then and Now," for a special Issue of *Just Reminiscing*, Spring 1982 in which he states,

"My memory of this is vague, but I recall my grandmother telling me that they harbored slaves escaping from the South and on their way to freedom in Canada. They were sheltered in the cellar, and the Tavern thus qualifies as a way station on the underground railroad." (p. 13)

Another relative, Martha Spencer, has questioned Dr. Spencer's vague memory. She does not believe that her ancestors were Conductors. She did confirm that Seth was an Abolitionist and copies of the *Luminary* and the *Promulgator* were among his possessions.[24]

Mary Elizabeth Junkin married Dr. Seth Poppino about 1856. Her father was Benjamin Junkin, a distinguished jurist in Venango County who served as Associate Judge. Her mother was Maria (Agnew) Junkin.

Mary was the third from youngest daughter in a family of nine children, three girls and six boys. Five brothers served in the Civil War.[25]

Benjamin Junkin, Mary (Junkin) Poppino's father, was present at the Presbyterian General Assembly meeting where Anti–Slavery Presbyterian minister, Reverend Bushnell, and others broke away because of the Assembly's failure to condemn slavery. Benjamin and his brother, George, listened to Bushnell for a while, but remained with the Pro-Slavery Presbyterian Church.[26]

Dr. George K. Junkin was a strong pro–slavery minister. In 1843, as President of Miami University in Cincinnati, he delivered a lengthy speech entitled, "The Integrity of Our National Union, vs. Abolitionism: An Argument from the Bible, in Proof of the Position that Believing Masters Ought to be Honored and Obeyed by their Own Servants, and Tolerated in, Not Excommunicated from, the Church of God."[27]

The speech was not well received in the Ohio press, which described him as "a Pro–Slavery, narrow minded bigot… [who] would hold salves with great unction."[28]

Junkin became President of Lafayette College in Easton, Pennsylvania before accepting the same position at Washington (and Lee) College in Lexington, Virginia. Robert E. Lee became Junkin's successor there.

One of Junkin's daughters married Stonewall Jackson, and another married Confederate General Preston.[29, 30] George's son, William, also a minister, joined the Confederacy, married into a prominent Virginia family, and read the eulogy at Stonewall Jackson's funeral.[31]

Reverend D. X. Junkin remained in New Castle.

"[L]ike his brother, [he] had been pro–slavery, and he was a strong opposer of the National Reform movement."[32]

NEW BEDFORD'S SECOND MANY–SIDED HOUSE

PULASKI TOWNSHIP IS HOME to unusually-shaped houses. William W. Walker, Abolitionist and Conductor, owned one of them, a 10-sided structure on Marr Road. There is little doubt of its involvement in the Underground Railroad.

The second home, a 12–sided brick structure on State Route 208, has also been rumored to have been part of the Underground Railroad. This house was supposedly connected by tunnel to W. W. Walker's ten–sided house nearly a mile away.

According to the Donaldson family history,

"James H. Donaldson was a farmer, sold farm machinery and owned and operated a sawmill. He and his family lived in a log house, one mile west of Pulaski, Pa., on what is now Route 208, until later in 1860 or early 1870 when the house burned down. He and several other farmers dug the clay, made the moulds and burned sufficient brick to build the… octagon shaped… Donaldson eight–room house."

James H. Donaldson was born in 1833 and resided in Neshannock Township in 1850.[33] In 1854, James' father, Ebenezer Donaldson, purchased from William Byers the property on which the "octagonal" house was built. Since the Donaldsons built the home, it could not have been constructed until after 1854 when Ebenezer

Donaldson House

purchased the property. Ebenezer remained on his farm in Neshannock and sold the property to Joseph Brown on June 30, 1862. Brown retained it until 1877.

James Donaldson was a supporter of the New Castle–Kansas Aid Society. A John Donaldson was a member of the Free Church in New Wilmington. Nothing else has been discovered to connect Ebenezer or James H. Donaldson to the Underground Railroad or to identify them as Abolitionists.

It should be noted that in a recent history of New Wilmington the authors connected the Captain James Brown house on State Route 208 and this "octagonal house" with the family of the famous Abolitionist, John Brown.[34]

While Captain James Brown was Joseph Brown's brother, and Joseph once owned this twelve-sided house, a concerted effort to unearth a connection between this family of Browns and Abolitionist John Brown yielded no results.

The Pulaski Browns were Pennsylvania–born for a number of generations, while Abolitionist John Brown came from Connecticut and a long line of ancestors living in New England, dating back to the Mayflower.[35] John Brown's grandfather was Captain John Brown of the 18 Connecticut Regiment in the Revolutionary War.[36]

MYSTERY HOUSE

NEW CASTLE HOUSES known to have been used as Underground Railroad stations have long since been demolished. Only a few pre–Civil War structures remain. Could one of these buildings have been used to hide fugitive slaves? The following entry was transcribed from an October 25, 1893 *New Castle News* article.

> "On a prominent residence street of this city stands a large brick house, apparently not remarkable for anything but its age. It is a two–story building, and was built in the childhood of some of the oldest citizens.
>
> The house possesses an interesting history, and has connected with it a very remarkable feature, long forgotten, but recently brought again to light. A short time since, the present occupants were engaged in house cleaning, and when the carpet on a small first–floor bedroom was removed, a small trap door, which had long passed unnoticed, was detected in the floor. Upon opening it was found to lead to a small cellar, which had no communication with the main cellar, being separated from it by several feet of earth. No stairway or ladder led down to the floor, and a lantern was lowered into it. It was found to be about ten feet square, with no window or opening of kind excepting the trap door. The floor was not paved in any way, but the ground was nicely leveled and packed tightly down. The cellar contained nothing but an old stool, a battered candlestick, and a mildewed shoe."

A quiet investigation was instituted, and at last there was found an old citizen who explained the mystery of the long forgotten cellar. In the days before the war when the Anti–Slavery agitation was at its height, the house was owned by a lady who was a member of a secret society having for the object not only the abolition of slavery, but the aiding of escaped slaves to freedom.

Many times the pursuit of the unfortunate Blacks was so close that the society found it difficult to make sure their escape. It was as a hiding place for use in such cases, that the cellar was excavated, and many a slave was quartered in it for days, and sometimes weeks, and cared for by the charitable lady of the house.

> "Until shortly before the war the New Castle branch of the society continued operations, but as the membership was small, the organization was easily dissolved, breaking up when the hostilities between the north and south began. The trap door was fastened down, and the house being sold when the lady died, over a quarter of a century ago, the existence of the cellar was forgotten, and until a few months ago the trap door passed unnoticed. The old gentleman from whom the information was obtained told some interesting stories regarding

the unfortunates who had been hidden in the cellar. One poor Black who had escaped from his cruel owner, who for some distance had pursued him with bloodhounds, was so weakened by sickness brought on by privation and exhaustion that he died shortly after being placed in the benevolent lady's care, and at night was buried in Neshannock Township not far from the city limits. Not only did the runaways have to be guarded against their owners but also had to be kept out of sight of northern people so far as possible, on account of the laws and the rewards offered by their masters. The cellar will probably be filled up as it can be put to no use, and the tenants of the house have kept its existence a secret to all except a few friends fearing annoyance from the curiosity which would be aroused should its locality be made public. The gentleman who gave the history of the cellar says that he is one of the two surviving members of the society which in a quiet way extending such efficient help to the escaping bondmen."

Is it possible to solve this mystery? We have the following clues:

1) lady of the house was member of a "small secret society" and died about 1868

Since the organization was small, the woman was probably either the widowed wife of a known Conductor or a single Abolitionist acquainted with other Conductors. The list below includes wives and/or founding members of the Free Presbyterian Church and a few others. Potential suspects are marked with asterisk.

*Althea Whippo: The Whippos were active Abolitionists. Charles died in 1858 and Althea in 1865.

Catherine Emery: Both she and husband were still living in 1860.

Sarah McMillen: Sarah and husband were both alive in 1870.

Catherine Mitchell: Died before 1850

Mrs. Amzi (Mary McMillen) Semple: Died before 1850

*Annie Semple: She was widowed by 1850, died between 1860 and 1870.

Mrs. Mary Jane (Mitchell) Davies: Died in 1911.

Martha Semple: She was still living in 1870.

Mrs. Eli (Eliza) Semple: She remarried and was still living after 1870.

Miss Jane Tidball: living with sisters before she died in 1858.

Adaline White: Ded in 1907.

Elizabeth White: Died in 1875.

Mary Ann Berry: Died in 1900.

Judith Euwer: Died in 1878.

Isabella Henderson: Her husband was still alive in 1860.

*Fanny Wilson: She was a single African American woman who died between 1860 and 1870. Although not listed as an Abolitionist, she shared her home with several young people, including the Davis family, whose son was born in Canada, suggesting they may have had connections with slaves escaping to Canada.

2) two–story brick house in prominent neighborhood

Althea Whippo: The Whippo house was not brick, so Althea Whippo can be eliminated as a possible person.

Fanny Wilson: Fanny had no property listed on the 1855 map, so we assume she rented a house. Using the 1850 and 1860 census to identify her neighbors, we concluded that she lived in the southwestern part of the city, in the vicinity of South and County Line Streets, on the west side of Jefferson Street.

The mystery house would have been on both the 1855 map, and on the 1893 map, when the news story was written. Some brick homes in the area in question may have survived until 1893, but because so many residents in the neighborhood rented at that time, it is difficult to determine which houses may have been important. Was this an area with "prominent residences?" Fanny's neighbors included mill laborers, including boilers, tinners, nail cutters, puddlers, and iron heaters. There were also hotel porters, merchants, blacksmiths, and grocers. It seems doubtful this neighborhood would have been considered prominent. Fanny Wilson is probably not the lady in question but cannot be entirely ruled out.

Annie Semple: Since Annie wasn't listed on the 1855 map as owning a home, she must have been renting. Using the 1850 census when she lived with Eli Semple, a known Conductor, and the 1860 census when she was head of household, we estimated the location of her neighborhood.

Her home would have been in the area bounded by North Jefferson and North Mill Streets, and East Falls Street and East Washington. This neighborhood could be classified as having "prominent residences," housing residents employed as carpenters, marble cutters, tobacconists, clerks, printers, milliners, attorneys, shoemakers, ministers, teachers and painters.

Using 1894 Sanborn Fire maps that indicate which buildings were brick, we determined a number of buildings that would have existed pre–Civil War, and in 1893. We then identified brick buildings that might have been rented.

These include a house owned by J. Leslie on North Mercer, G. Robinson on North Mercer, the Reinhold buildings on North Mercer, and two houses owned by Joseph S. White on a lot at the corner of Mercer and North Streets.

Joseph S. White was a Conductor on the Underground Railroad.

3) house sold after the woman died around 1868

Joseph S. White sold the house on the corner of North Mercer and North Street to William Shaffer in July of 1868.[37] The house at the eastern end of the property was sold to Mary Ann Berry in 1869.

4) trap door discovered before October 25, 1893

Dr. William G. Wilson, of Pulaski, gave notice that he would be moving to New Castle in April 1893.[38] He purchased Joseph White's house on North Mercer Street and used it as a residence and office.

It seems more than a coincidence that Joseph S. White sold the property about the time the lady died, and Dr. Wilson moved in just before the trap door discovery.

5) trap door in small first floor bedroom opened into a ten foot square separate cellar

The house at the corner of North Mercer and North Street still stands as the All in a Nut Shell clothing store, 102 North Mercer Street. According to the maps, it was expanded twice, once after 1855 to create an L–shaped footprint, and again around 1900 to make it square.

Is there any indication of a trap door in the floor? Yes. A section of flooring between two support beams above the first basement addition has been patched. This could have been the trap door if the current square basement was not completed until after the second addition was constructed.

6) history came from older man, one of two remaining from society.

When the "older man" was interviewed, Joseph S. White, who was known for his Underground Railroad work, was alive. If he was had owned the house, he would be well acquainted with its history. That may be why the "older man" was familiar with so many details.

While we cannot positively conclude that the building located at the corner of North and Mercer Streets is the mysterious house, evidence does point in that direction.

Chapter Notes

1 "Progress Eliminates Site of Underground Railroad," *New Castle News*, May 29, 1957.
2 "J. Crawford White relates Early Days at Martin Gantz," *New Castle News*, May 28, 1928.
3 "Progress Eliminates Site of Underground Railroad," *New Castle News*, May 29, 1957.
4 McCleary, T. Jefferson, *Early History of New Castle*.
5 *Biographical Sketches of Leading Citizens Lawrence County Pennsylvania*, 17.
6 "A Sea of Raging Water," *New Castle News*, March 30, 1898.
7 "Kurtz Homestead Proposed Lot Site Stirs Interest as Landmark in City," *New Castle News*, May 4, 1963.
8 "Do you Remember," *New Castle News*, July 27, 1939.
9 "Needs of Courthouse Again Brought to Fore," *New Castle News*, March 19, 1932.
10 "County Officials are Scarcely Able to Work," *New Castle News*, July 13, 1910.
11 "Church of the Week," *New Castle News*, February 13, 1971, 6.
12 Hazen, 78-84.
13 Hazen, 750.
14 *Pittsburgh Press*, August 14, 1991.
15 J. N. Euwer Obituary, *Lawrence Guardian*, November 11, 1878.
16 United States Census: Pennsylvania, Lawrence County 1850.
17 Quinby, Angeline, "Route from New Wilmington to Warren, Trumbull Co.," February 21, 1896. Wilbur H. Siebert Collection, State Library of Ohio.
18 Seth Poppino Obituary, *The Guardian*, January 8, 1876.
19 Mary Poppino Obituary, *New Castle News*, January 20, 1917.
20 Hazen, 611.
21 http://www.history.org/foundation/journal/summer07/kitchens
22 https://www.gcv.org/Historic-Village/19th-Century-Food
23 *Atlas of Lawrence County*, M. K. Hopkins and Co. Philadelphia. 1872, 85.
24 Personal discussions between Jay Behm and Martha Spencer.
25 Hazen, 611.
26 Johnston, Nathan Robinson, *Looking Back from the Sunset Land*, 393.
27 https://archive.org/details/integrityofourna00junk
28 "The General Assemblies," *Anti-Slavery Bugle*, June 2, 1855, 2.
29 Thompson, Robert Ellis & Wharton Barker, *The American: A National Journal, Vol. 4-5*, June 3, 1882, 119.
30 Allan, Elizabeth Preston, *The Life and Letters of Margaret Junkin Preston*. New York. 1903, 345.
31 Wilkins, J. Stevens, *All Things for Good: The Steadfast Fidelity of Stonewell Jackson*. Cumberland House. Nashville, Tennessee. 2004, 262.
32 Johnson, Nathan Robinson, *Looking Back from the Sunset Land*, 393.
33 United States Census: Pennsylvania, Lawrence County 1850.
34 DeWitt, H. Dewey et al. *The History of New Wilmington, Pennsylvania 1797-2003: The Story of A Small Town*. New Horizons Publishing. 2004, 453.
35 Redpath, James & John Brown, *The Public Life of Capt. John Brown, with an Auto-Biography of His Childhood and Youth*. Thayer and Eldridge. Boston. 1860, 13-21.
36 *Biographical Sketches of Leading Citizens, Lawrence County Pennsylvania*, 366.
37 *Lawrence County Deed Book 16*, 239.
38 "About People," *New Castle News*, April 26, 1893.

Name Index

A

Adair, James 112
Adaline (Pollack) 77
Adams, Asa 98
Adams, James 128
Adams, John Quincy 44
Adams, Rachel 104
Agnew, Maria 180
Aiken, Alexander 104, 128
Aiken, Andrew 104
Aiken, David 104
Aiken, Emmaline 104
Aiken, Erskine E. 104
Aiken, Glenn 104
Aiken, Isaiah Henderson 104
Aiken, James 48, 104
Aiken, James (s) 104
Aiken, James (s2) 104
Aiken, Joseph 128
Aiken, Margaret 104
Aiken, Margaret (d) 104
Aiken, Martha 104
Aiken, Mary 104
Aiken, Rachel 104. *See also* Adams, Rachel
Aiken, Robert 104
Aiken, Susannah 104
Aiken, Trisha 104
Akens, C. H. 157
Alford, Thomas 48
Allen, Ephraim W. 3
Allen, G. 54
Allison, Elizabeth 117
Allison, John 50
Allsworth, William 48
Alsworth, James 99
Alsworth, William 99
Anderson, Alexander 49, 115
Anderson, George 10
Anderson, Jane 115
Anderson, Lavina. *See* McBride, Lavina
Anderson, Mary 117
Anderson, Samuel 115
Anderson, William 115
Angel, John 91
Armstrong, John 122
Arnold, Simon 169
Arnold, William 10
Atchison, David R. 57
Aughenbaugh, Philip 85
Auld, James 29
Ault, Daniel 113

B

Bacon, Nora Wade 165
Bailey, Anna Jane 114
Bailey, David 112
Bailey, Samuel R. 46
Baker, Frances 17
Baker, Isaac 9, 17
Baker, William T. 158
Barker, D. R. 49
Barnes, John 158
Bascom, Oliver 82
Bedford, Nathaniel 112
Beecher, Henry Ward 29, 55
Beecher, Lyman 61
Beer, John 85
Behm, Jay 180
Belnap, Gilbert 138
Berry, Charles 14
Berry, Emma 12, 13
Berry, Frank 12
Berry, Fremont 12
Berry, Isabelle 15
Berry, Lizzie 12
Berry, Margaret 12
Berry, Mariah 12
Berry, Mary Ann 11, 12, 13, 16, 175, 183, 184
Berry, Mary (d) 12
Berry, Mary L. 16. *See* Long, Mary
Berry, Mary M. 12, 13
Berry, Oliver 12
Berry, Plympton Ross i, 12, 13, 14, 15, 16
Berry, P. Ross. *See* Berry, Plympton Ross
Berry, Thomas 12, 14
Berry, Thomas D. 11, 12, 14, 16, 73, 77, 78, 175, 176
Best, T. M. 31
Bevington, Margaret 93
Bigham, Ebenezer 32
Bigham, J. C. 29, 31, 32, 33, 108
Bigham, William 32
Birney, James G. 44, 46
Black, James 112
Black, Thomas 112
Blackwood, James 67
Blair family 107

Blakely, C. 70
Blanchard, Mr. 41
Blatchley, Miller 76
Boggs, George 67, 73
Boggs, John 28
Bogguess, Abel 144. *See also* Garlick, Charles A.
Bogguess, Elijah 144
Bogguess, Richard 144
Bonaparte, Napoleon 164
Bonnell, William 70
Book, Jacob 49
Book, John C. 95
Book, Mary 95
Bootman, L. M. 117
Boyd, Daniel 28
Boyd, Dorcas. *See* McWilliams, Dorcas
Boyd, Elizabeth 129
Boyd, John 129
Boyd, John (s) 129
Boyd, Nancy 129
Boyd, Samuel 29
Boyd, William 129. *See* Boyd, John
Boyd, Wilson 129
Boyles, Emma 70
Boynton, Joseph S. 117
Bradford, Arthur B. iii, 28, 29, 31, 32, 33, 37, 39, 42, 49, 51, 54, 55, 69, 70, 118, 124, 132
Bradford, Elizabeth. *See* Wicks, Elizabeth
Bradford, Governor William 37
Bradford, O. B. 39
Breckenridge, John 26
Brooks, Preston (State Rep.) 163
Browne, R. A. 49, 54, 55, 93, 163
Brown, George Washington 53, 55, 56, 57, 58, 157, 158
Brown, James (Captain) 182
Brown, John 53, 58, 182
Brown, John (Captain) 182
Brown, John Jr. 58
Brown, Joseph 132, 182
Brown, William (Lieut. Governor) 158
Bryan, George 2
Bryan, J. D. 50
Buchanan, James 44
Burgess, John 31
Burk, Ned 10
Burleigh, C. C. 43, 44, 147
Burnside, John 128
Burnside, Robert 128
Bushnell, Alexander 38
Bushnell, Captain 96

Bushnell, Eleanor. *See* Hannen, Eleanor
Bushnell, Sarah. *See* Wells, Sarah
Bushnell, Wells 8, 10, 26, 27, 29, 31, 32, 33, 38, 39, 67, 69, 73, 75, 99, 116, 145, 180
Bushnell, Wells (s) 67
Butler, Andrew (Senator) 163
Byers, Ebenezer 132
Byers, William 113, 181

C

Cadwallader, Amy 92, 94, 95
Cadwallader, Eli 47, 92, 94
Cadwallader, Elizabeth 92. *See also* Hawley, Elizabeth
Cadwallader, Joseph 46, 47, 92
Cadwallader, Lydia 92
Cadwallader, Mary 92
Cadwallader, Samuel 92
Cadwallader, Sarah 92. *See also* Dallas, Sarah
Cadwallader, Sarah (d) 92
Cadwallader, Septimus 47, 92, 94, 115
Cadwallader, Septimus (s) 92
Cairns, Nancy 27
Cairns, William 25, 27, 122, 125
Caldwell, J. S. (Bishop) 157, 158
Caldwell, S. J. 157
Calvin, John 7
Calvin, John P. 95
Cameron, Alex 14
Carey, William 10
Carlisle, William S. 14
Carman, L. 48
Carnahan, D. 29
Carnahan, David 138
Carnegie, Andrew 158, 159
Carothers, Charles 70
Carpenter, Warren 47, 48
Carr, John 81
Carroll, Charles 2, 6
Carson, John 48, 99
Caruthers, Robert 113
Chenowith, Arthur 7, 132
Chenowith, John 132
Chesney, John 128
Chew, Amos 145
Chew, Benjamin 101
Christy, Andrew (Lieutenant) 93
Clapp, J. M. (Captain) 69
Clark, Clement 99
Clarke, John 98
Clarke, Walter 7, 98

Clark, George 140, 179
Clark, James B. 48
Clark, John 49
Clark, Samuel D. 28, 48
Clark, Sara Jane 39
Clark, S. D. 99
Clark, W. D. 51
Clark, William 124
Clark, William F. 11, 41, 42, 49, 148
Clay, Henry 44
Clendenin, Belinda 70. *See* Pollock, Belinda
Clendenin, Mrs. 46
Clendenin, Robert W. 67, 68, 169, 178
Clendenin, William 68
Clifton, Joseph 70
Clinton, W. D. 157, 158
Cloud, Thomas 98
Cochran, Robert 176
Coffin, Levi 1
Colvin, John Sr. 7
Condict, Jacob 70
Condict, Ruth 70
Cooley, Hannah 115
Coovertt, Joanna 129
Coovertt, John (Colonel) 129
Cotton, Alexander 113
Cotton, Hugh 9
Cotton, James 54
Cotton, Josiah 28
Cotton, William 31, 54
Cowden, Isaac 140
Cowden, John P. 48, 103, 129
Cowens, Diana 10
Cozad, William 31
Craig, David 70
Craven, Richard 10
Crawford, A. L. 138
Crawford, David 54
Cremer, Jacob 92
Cross, Levi 158
Crowley, Thomas 22
Crowl, Philip 82
Crowl, Phillip 138
Cuff, Edward 14
Cunningham, E. W. 54
Cunningham, R. W. 47, 70
Curry, Emma. *See* Berry, Emma
Curry, William 13
Curtis, Lawden 10
Curtis, William 21

D

Dallas, Sarah 92
Daniels, Daniel 128
Daniels, Thomas 128
Davidson, John 39, 99
Davidson, Mary 89
Davids, Tice 1
Davies, Agnes 135
Davies, Alex 135
Davies, Anna 135
Davies, Charles 135
Davies, Harry 135
Davies, Mary 135
Davies, Mary Jane 135. *See also* Mitchell, Mary Jane
Davies, Robert 135
Davies, William 135
Davies, William (s) 135
Davis, Alexander 13
Davis, A. T. 54
Davis, Captain 146
Davis family 183
Davis, James 10
Davis, Levi 9
Davis, Lewis 9
Davis, Mary J. 70
Davis, Millie 146
Davis, Mrs. 146
Davis, Robert 124
Dawson, Nancy 115
Dennison, Sarah. *See* Nighten, Sarah
Dennison, William T. A. 14
Dickson, Isaac 70
Dickson, James 48
Dinsmore's, Watson 66
DiRisio, Elizabeth Hoover i
Dobbins, Lawrence 98
Dobbins, Robert B. 27
Donaldson, Ebenezer 181, 182
Donaldson, James H. 54, 111, 181, 182
Donaldson, John 31, 182
Douglass, Frederick 4, 37, 61, 94, 146, 147, 164
Doulton, S. D. 55
Doup, Lucinda 171
Doup, Peter M. 157, 158, 159, 171, 172
Douthett, J. 70
Duncan, James 33
Duncunson, Pastor 157
Dunlap, Elizabeth 76
Dunn, Freeman 49
Durand, William 138

Durrast-Connelly, Mary Ellen 179

E

Early, Jubal A. (General) 155
Eccles. *See* Eckles
Eckles, James 171
Eckles, John 128
Eckles, John A. 171
Edgar, John 98
Edgar, Mr. 128
Elliot, Moses 26
Elliott, C. 99
Elliott, Cordon 31
Emery, Catherine 54, 70, 183
Emery, Emily 54
Emery, Jeremiah 54
Emery, John N. 54, 70, 72, 73
Emery, Joseph 48
Emery, Luke 54
Emery, S. P. 157
Emory, Catherine 69
Emory, John 69
Enos, George 73
Enos, Ruth 73
Espy, William 98
Euwer, Daniel 72, 73, 75
Euwer, Daniel (s) 72
Euwer, Isabella 73
Euwer, James 72
Euwer, John N. 46, 54, 70, 72, 75, 124, 178
Euwer, John (s) 72
Euwer, Joseph 72
Euwer, Judith K. 73, 183. *See also* Henderson, Judith K.
Euwer, Nancy 72
Evans, Alvira 143
Evans, Jackson 67, 143
Everett, Charles D. 11

F

Fairbanks, Calvin 1
Falls, Henry C. 54
Falls, Wilson 70
Faulkner, James M. 155
Fetter, David 128
Fetter, Randolph 128
Fillmore, Millard 33, 44
Finney, Charles G. 61
Fisher, Eva 34
Fisher, Harold 158
Fitzhugh, James 10
Fitzhugh, Thomas 10
Flipper, Henry 162
Fonvielle, P. K. 159
Forney, John W. 21, 65
Foster, Abby. *See* Kelley, Abby
Foster, Judy i
Foster, Stephen Symonds 43, 147
Fox, Peter 127
Francis, William M. 27
Franklin, Thomas 132
Frazier, Pompey 8
Frazier, Tamar 8
Freemen, D. W. 55
Fullerton, James 7

G

Gaily, Robert 9
Galloway, John 138
Gantz, W. 70
Gardiner, Richard 49
Garlick, Anson Kirby 145
Garlick, Charles i
Garlick, Charles A. 39, 144, 145
Garrison, Abijah 3
Garrison, William Lloyd iii, 3, 4, 29, 37, 39, 43, 61, 94, 146, 147
Gates, G. W. 158
Gealey family 107
Genkinger, Christian 177
Genkinger, Evelyn 177
Gentz, M. 70
Gibson, Abner 31
Gibson, Charles 31
Gibson, Francis 31
Gibson, Hiram 31
Gibson, Isaac M. 31
Gibson, John 122
Gibson, Robert 67
Gibson, William 81
Gibson, William M. 31
Gibson, William Wiley 31, 70
Giddings, Joshua R. 39
Gilbert, John 112
Gilleland, James 48, 70
Gilliland, Robert 54
Girley, John 46
Glass, Philetus Sr. 138
Glass, W. A. 148
Glenn, Robert 54
Gold, M. H. 9

Goodwillie, David 49
Gordon, Alexander 34
Gordon, Elizabeth 36, 116
Gordon, George 29, 33, 34, 35, 36, 78, 116
Gordon, John 34
Gordon, Joseph 28, 29, 33, 34, 36, 41, 49, 116, 118
Gordon, Peter 10
Gormley, Robert 81, 83
Gormley, Samuel 81
Graham, Robert 128
Grant, Ulysses S. (President) 164
Green, John 81
Greer, Charles 157
Greer, George 77
Griffing, Charles S. 43, 70
Griffing, Josephine 43, 70

H

Hale, James 10
Hall, David 10, 17
Hall, John 10
Hall, Lewis 10
Hall, Mr. 103
Hallowell, J. N. 41
Hall, Sarah 10
Hall, Thomas 9, 21
Hamilton, Isabella W. 54
Hamilton, Robert 138
Hamilton, Samuel 54
Hamilton, William 21
Hanna, R. 47
Hanna, Thomas 26, 67, 75. *See also* Hannay, Thomas
Hannay, Thomas 66, 67, 73, 104
Hannen, Eleanor 38, 70, 73
Hannen, Elizabeth. *See* Richards, Elizabeth
Hannen, John 27, 38
Harrah, T. H. 82
Harris, John 9, 10
Harrison, William Henry (President) 157
Hart, A. M. 117
Hart, Ambrose 96
Hartman, Thomas 165
Hasley, Mrs. James 135
Hatchman, Josiah 48, 49, 70
Hawley, Elizabeth 92
Hawthorne, Alexander S. 69, 70
Hawthorne, Eliza J. 69
Hawthorne, James 69
Hawthorne, Joseph 69
Hawthorne, Mary. *See* McMurray, Mary

Hayden, William 122
Hayes, Rutherford B. (President) 164
Hayes, Seth 145
Haymond, Captain 23
Hays, William 45
Hazlep, James 137
Hefflin, William 144
Heinz, Henry John 159
Henderson, George 48, 73
Henderson, George (s) 73
Henderson, Hugh 73
Henderson, Isabella 73, 183. *See* Euwer, Isabella
Henderson, John 73
Henderson, Judith K. 72
Henderson, Kate 73
Henderson, Margaret 73
Henderson, Mary 73
Henderson, Mr. 128
Henderson, Nancy 73
Henderson, Susan 70
Hendrickson, Cornelius 131, 132
Hendrickson, Daniel 131
Hendrickson, David 65
Herbert, George 128
Hewitt, Mr. 128
Higgins, O. 128
Hill, Jacob 14
Hindman, Dr. 137
Hise, Daniel 34
Hodge, William 137
Hogue, Sarah 116
Holtin, Andrew 70
Homer, Julia A. 10
Hoover, Abraham 92
Hoover, Peter 92
Hopper, Esther 99
Hopper, James W. 31
Hopper, Robert 99
Horner, John 70
Houston, Martha 74
Howe, William 146
Humes, George F. 41
Hurrington, C. P. 157, 158
Hutchman, Josiah 49, 128

I

Inbody, Daniel 112
Irwin, Matthew S. 157, 158
Irwin, Robert 122

J

Jackson, Andrew 44
Jackson, Daniel 9
Jackson, Elijah 9, 148
Jackson, Elijah Jr. 22, 148
Jackson, Frank 148, 149, 150, 151
Jackson, "General" 151. *See also* jackson, Frank
Jackson, John C. 157
Jackson, Ralph 158
Jackson, Sarah 10, 148
Jackson, Stonewall (General) 155, 181
Jaqueminot, General 164
Jefferson, Thomas 11, 44
Johnson, G. W. 158
Johnson, Harry 10
Johnson, H. U. 30
Johnson, Ida G. 13
Johnson, Jane 151
Johnson, Mary 74
Johnson, Mary L. 12, 70
Johnson, Thomas 12
Johnson, Thomas W. 12, 22
Johnston, Anna 17
Johnston, Frances 9
Johnston, Henry 9
Johnston, James R. 31
Johnston, J. S. 10
Johnston, Melissa 17, 156
Johnston, Nathan Robinson 163
Johnston, Oscar L. 9, 17, 21, 156
Johnston, Peggy 7, 8
Johnston, Robert 17
Johnston, Thomas 21
Johnston, William J. 31
Joiner, Alex 170
Joiner, Berry 170
Joiner, Edith 171
Joiner, Edna 171
Joiner, Herbert 171
Joiner, John 170, 171
Joiner, Johnny 171
Joiner, Mary 171
Joiner, Nancy 170
Joiner, Rhubert 171
Joiner, William 170, 171
Jones, Benjamin S. 43
Jones, J. Elizabeth Hitchcock 43
Jones, Jessie 128
Jones, Samuel 128
Jordan, Henry 8
Jordan, H. S. 157
"Judge" 155. *See also* Faulkner, James M.

Judy, James 111
Junkin, Benjamin 180
Junkin, D. X. 181
Junkin, George K. 180, 181
Junkin, Maria. *See* Agnew, Maria
Junkin, Mary Elizabeth 140, 180
Junkin, William 181
Justice, Elizabeth 99
Justice, Esther 99. *See also* Hopper, Esther
Justice, Esther (d) 99
Justice, James 99
Justice, Margaret 99
Justice, Stephen M. 70

K

Kean, J. K. 158
Keith, George 2
Keller, Jonathan 65
Kelley, Abby 39, 43, 147
Kempjer, James 158
Kidwalader. *See* Cadwallader
Kincaid, Catherine B. 162
Kincaid, Elma Sharpless 95
Kincaid, Ethel E. 162
Kincaid, George Washington 156, 157, 158, 159, 160, 161, 162, 171
Kincaid, Milton 156
Kincaid, P. L. 162
Kincaid, William 156
King, B. S. 158
King, Elias 33
King, Melissa 116
Kingsbury, Deacon 138
King, V. M. 29
Kirk, A. C. 49
Kirk, A. G. 49
Kirk, James Y. 31
Kirk, Joseph 30
Kirkpatrick, Ann 26
Kissick, J. 54
Knight, Johnson 129
Knox, Elizabeth 116. *See* Gordon, Elizabeth; *See also* Gordon, Elizabeth
Knox, John 31, 32, 35, 36, 116, 117
Kuester, D. G. 51
Kurtz, Isabella 177

L

Landrum, Sarah 18
Landrum, Tyrone 17, 18, 21

Lane, James 146
Lane, James H. (Colonel) 56, 59
Larimer, William Jr. 46
Lawton, W. C. 158
Leasure, Daniel 41, 53, 54, 55, 70
Leasure, Edith 54
Leasure, George 54
Leasure, Isabella. *See* Hamilton, Isabella W.
Leasure, James 54
Leasure, John 54
Leasure, Mary 54
Leasure, Milo 54
Leasure, Rachel 54
Leasure, Samuel 54
Lee, James 171
Lee, J. B. 113
Lee, J. W. 158
Lee, Robert E. (General) 181
Lemoyne, Francis J. 46
Leonard, John 10
Leopold II (King) 23
Leslie, J. 184
Leslie, James 122
Leslie, Mary C. 135. *See also* Davies, Mary
Lewis, Alvira 67, 143
Lewis, Andrew 67, 143
Lightner, Anges 9
Lightner, John 9, 10
Lightner, Rachel 10
Lincoln, Abraham 3, 34, 35, 44, 58
Littleford, John 7
Lloyd, Frances Maria 3
Locke, Cynthia 69
Locket, Robert 158
Lodge, George 47
Logan, Peter 10
Long, Mary 16. *See* Johnson, Mary L.
Lostetter, James 116
Lostetter, John 116
Love, John 104, 128
Lovejoy, Elijah P. 55
Lowell, James Russell 61
Lumsden, William 31
Lundy, Benjamin 3

M

Madison, James 44
Magaffin, H. 151
Magaffin, James 151
Magee, George Hamilton 10, 75, 102, 104, 129, 144

Magee, John H. 73, 103
Magee, Nancy 104
Magee, Sarah 104
Magee, Thomas 104
Marquis, Milton S. (Captain) 157
Marquis, M. S. 159
Marshall, Samuel 39, 145
Mason, James Murray (Senator) iii
Matthews, Betsy 8
Matthews, Samuel 21
Mayberry, John 70
May, Charles 148
McBride, James M. 115, 116
McBride, Jane 116
McBride, Lavina 115
McBride, Newell 115
McBride, Robert K. 48, 116
McBride, Samuel 7
McCandlish, William 27
McClelland, Alex 140
McClelland, Joseph 99
McClintock, Eli C. 77
McClung, S. A. 158
McClymonds, Elizabeth 104
McClymonds, John 104
McClymonds, Margaret 104
McClymonds, Mary 104
McClymonds, Mary (d) 104
McClymonds, William 54, 55, 70, 104
McCombs, Mrs. 70
McCombs, William W. 132
McConahy, John 116, 117
McConahy, Martha. *See* Smith, Martha
McConahy, Mary V. 117
McConahy, Zenas W. 117
McConaughy, Ann (Nancy) 74
McConnell, Thomas (Captain) 165
McConnell, Thomas (s) 165
McCowin, James 85
McCracken, Elizabeth. *See* Mowry, Elizabeth
McCready, Absalom 31
McCready, Mr. 26
McCrumb, Robert 31
McCrum, John 137
McCue, Marshall (Major) 155
McCulhan, C. W. 48
McCullough, Robert 112
McCune family 107
McDowell, George 132
McElevy, John 70
McFadden, Agnes 117

McFarland, John 33
McFate, William 92
McGee, Roy i
McGilvray, Catherine 66
McGlathery, John P. 48
McGuffey, Jane 134
McGuffin, Lawrence L. 26, 70
McGuffin, Robert 10, 70
McGuire, James 158
McIntyre, Tom 144
McKee family 107
McKee, James 26
McKeever, Thomas 145
McKinley, William (President) 139
McLain, D. H. A. 47
McLean, Samuel A. 28, 29, 32, 118
McMaster, Mr. 128
McMillan, G. Riley 124, 128
McMillan, J. L. 54
McMillan, Robert 128
McMillen, Anna 73
McMillen, Belinda 73
McMillen, Clarissa 73
McMillen, Ella 73
McMillen, Joseph 73
McMillen, Mary 69, 70, 73, 74, 76, 183
McMillen, Sarah 183
McMillen, Sarah E. 69, 70, 73
McMillen, Travis 73
McMillen, White 8, 48, 69, 70, 73, 75, 116
McMurray, Mary 69
McNabb, George 117
McNeal, Alison i
McNeath, D. N. 70
McNickel, John 48, 82
McWhorter, John 65
McWilliams, Dorcas 129
McWilliams family 91
McWilliams, Robert 122
Mendenhall, George C. 149
Mercer, William 31
Michaels, James 21
Miller, Isaiah 169
Miller, Nancy 31
Miller, Rachel 169
Minich, James 78. *See* Minick, James
Minick, James 30
Minick, John 31, 78
Minnick, Daniel 124
Mintz, William 99
Mitchell, Catherine 73, 183. *See* Raney, Catherine

Mitchell, Clementa 73
Mitchell, Dr. 78
Mitchell, George 8
Mitchell, John F. 117
Mitchell, Joseph 73
Mitchell, Martha 73
Mitchell, Mary 73
Mitchell, Mary J. 69, 70
Mitchell, Mary Jane 135, 183
Mitchell, Mary Semple 69
Mitchell, Samuel Jr. 73
Mitchell, Samuel W. 9, 69, 70, 73, 75, 135, 178
Mitchell, William 73
Mitchell, Wilson 31
Moffatt, James 70
Moffett, Frances I. 70
Moffett, William J. 70
Mohawk, Sam 18
Monroe, James 11, 44
Montgomery, Samuel 54, 70
Moore, Adam 54
Moore, Andrew 85
Moore, James S. 33, 48
Moore, Sampson 112
Moorhead, Amanda 70
Moorhead, Harriet 70
Moorhead, James 42, 54, 70
Moorhead, William 42
Morehead, Rachel 77
Morehead, William 7, 26
Morgan, G. C. 70
Morgan, George C. (Colonel) 149, 150, 151
Morgan, J. Pierpont 159
Morris, Thomas 46
Morrow, Gennie V. 26
Morse, Thomas 70
Mowry, Elizabeth 66
Mowry, Peter 112
Moxey, Alex 160
Murray, Matthew 102

N

Neal, James 111
Neil, John 9
Nellie (slave woman) 8
Nelson, D. 70
Nesbit, Francis 98
Nesbit, William 113
New Castle, PA 2
Nichols, John i

Nicholson, James 8
Nighten, Ariana (Ann) 14
Nighten, Charles W. 14, 21
Nighten, Sarah 14
Norman, Evan 13
Norman, John H. 9, 12
Norman, Margaret. *See* Berry, Margaret
Norwood, David 122

O

Oakes, Alexander 170
Oakes, Annie M. 171
Oden, Ethel 162. *See also* Kincaid, Ethel E.
Oden, Georgia Elizabeth 162
Oden, Reverend 162
Offutt family 107
Offutt, John 109
Offutt, Mrs. W. A. 132
Oliver, John 103
Oliver, R. W. 49
Ormes, Barzeal 9
Ormes, William 9

P

Paden, Elizabeth 116
Paden, Thomas 116
Park, James 132
Park, John 132
Park, William 132
Park, William, Jr. 132
Patterson, James 112
Patterson, Samuel 49
Patterson, William 16, 169
Pattison, Alex 134
Pattison, David 67, 134
Pattison, David (s) 134
Pattison, Ginett 134
Pattison, Jane 134. *See also* Stewart, Jane
Pattison, Mary 134
Pattison, Robert 134
Pattison, William 134
Patton, Hugh B. 81
Patton, William 81
Pearson, Bevan 69
Pearson, Henry 69, 70
Pearson, Jane T. 69, 70
Pearson, S. 70
Pearson, Warner 69
Peebles, Robert 10
Pennsylvania 2

Pennypacker, Samuel W. P. (Governor) 157
Perrine, Jesse R. 47
Perry, Commodore 117
Phillips, J. N. 48
Phillips, Thomas W. 9
Phillips, Wendell 39, 61
Phipps, A. W. i
Phipps, Henry 159
Pillsbury 147
Piper, John 113
Plannett, J. W. 49
Plumb, Ralph 145
Pollard, L. J. 157
Pollock, Adaline 67
Pollock, Belinda 67
Pollock, Joseph 26, 67, 77
Pomeroy, William 26
Pomeroy, William C. (State Rep.) 157
Ponder, Ephraim G. 162
Ponder, Mrs. 162
Poppino, Anna Mary 140
Poppino, Charles W. 140
Poppino, Hatti 140
Poppino, James J. 140
Poppino, Martha P. 140
Poppino, Mary Elizabeth 180. *See also* Junkin, Mary Elizabeth
Poppino, Sarah 140
Poppino, Sarah L. 140
Poppino, Seth 140, 179, 180
Poppino, Seth L. 140
Porter, John M. 33
Porter, Mary H. 31
Porter, Nathaniel 28
Porter, William 137
Potter, Theodore 10
Powers, Theodore 138
Preston, General 181
Pryer, Raymond 158

Q

Quantrill, William 58, 59
Quarles, Frank 162
Quarles, John Franklin 162, 163, 164
Quarles, Martha 162
Quinby, Angeline 180

R

Rainbow, John 39, 145
Ramage, Almira. *See also* Seavey, Almira

Ramage, Anna 86
Ramage, Benjamin i, 86, 88, 89
Ramage, Charles 86
Ramage, Emma 86
Ramage, James 86
Ramage, Martha 86
Ramage, Mary 86
Ramage, Samuel 86
Ramsey family 107
Ramsey, John 139
Ramsey, Prudence 139
Ramsey, Robert 138, 139, 180
Randolph, J. 51
Randolph, John 128
Raney, Catherine 73
Raney, James 91
Raney, John 91
Raney, William 26
Rankin, John 29
Reece, Michael iii
Reed, Horace Greely 95
Reinhold, Frederick 69
Reynolds, George 180
Reynolds, John 48, 55
Reynolds, Judge 149
Reynolds, Robert 50, 70
Rhodes, Henry 26
Richards, Elizabeth 38
Richardson, John R. 54, 70
Ritner, Joseph (Governor) 45
Robert 104
Robert, John H. 81
Robinson, G. 184
Robinson, George P. 70
Robinson, John E. 31
Robinson, Margaret 99
Robinson, S. 55
Robison, David 10
Robison, William 85
Rogers, W. S. 27
Rose, Marcus H. 47
Rouse, Margaret 15
Rowland, Elizabeth 116. *See also* Allison, Elizabeth
Rowland, William Jr. 116, 117
Rowland, William Sr. 116, 117

S

Sample, Angeline 26
Sample, Ann. *See* Kirkpatrick, Ann
Sample, Artamisa 74
Sample, Caldwell 74
Sample, Catherine 74
Sample, Cintha 74
Sample, Desmona 74
Sample, Eli 74, 116
Sample, Eliza 26
Sample, Florinda 26
Sample, John 74
Sample, Kirk 26
Sample, Manurva 26
Sample, Martha 74
Sample, Martilla 26
Sample, Mary 74
Sample, Nancy 26
Sample, Nancy (d) 74
Sample, Robert 25, 26, 27, 125
Sample, Samuel 26, 69, 74
Sample, Smiley 74
Sample, Thomas 45
Sample, Uriah 74
Sample, Zenesta 26
Sampson, Irwin 139
Sampson, Sarah 139
Sanders, Abraham 93, 122
Sankey, C. C. 70
Sankey, Charles C. i
Sankey, Ezekiel 132
Satterfield, Elijah 9
Sawer, John 8
Scott, Alexander 155, 156
Scott, Dred 4, 5
Scott, D. S. 158
Scott, George 49, 67
Scott, William 46, 49, 104
Seavey, Almira 86, 89
Selby, John F. 43
Semple, Amzi C. 46, 68, 69, 73, 74, 75, 116
Semple, Anna 73, 74, 75. *See also* Semple, Annie
Semple, Annie 69, 70, 183, 184
Semple, Carrie 74
Semple, Eli 73, 74, 75, 184
Semple, Eliza 183. *See* Woodard, Eliza
Semple, Elizabeth 74
Semple, Eliza W. 69, 70
Semple, Lewis 74
Semple, Martha 69, 70, 74, 183
Semple, Mary 74
Semple, Mary Johnson. *See* Johnson, Mary
Semple, Mary McMillen 73. *See also* McMillan, Mary
Semple, Oliver 74
Semple, Robert. *See* Sample, Robert

Semple, Scott 74
Semple, Sidney 74
Semple, Thomas. *See* Sample, Thomas
Semple, William 74
Shaffer, William 184
Sharpless, Abbe 95
Sharpless, Amy 94. *See also* Cadwallader, Amy
Sharpless, Benjamin 47, 92, 93, 94, 95
Sharpless, Edwin A. 95
Sharpless, Eliza 95. *See also* Williams, Eliza
Sharpless, Elizabeth 92
Sharpless, Ellonor 95
Sharpless, Franklin 95
Sharpless, Isaac 92
Sharpless, Laura 95
Sharpless, Mifflin 95
Shaw, Alexander 31
Shaw, George 128
Shaw, James 48
Shaw, William H. 55
Sheakley, John 7
Sheal, Maggie 70
Shearer, Mr. 132
Sherer, Lydia J. 70, 81
Sheridan, Philip (General) 155
Sherman, William Tecumseh (General) 162
Sherriff, Magaret Harriet 116
Shields, Mary 83
Shields, William 31
Shivers, Vince i
Shoemaker, Peter 9, 10
Shossner, James 160
Siebert, Professor. *See* Siebert, Wilbur
Siebert, Wilbur 1, 94, 114, 115, 132
Silliman, Jemima 89
Silliman, Maggie 89
Silliman, Mary. *See* Davidson, Mary
Silliman, Thomas 48, 87, 88, 89
Skaggs, Larkin M. 58, 59
Slater, Mrs. J. H. 157
Smedley, R. C. 1
Smedly, Ephraim 138
Smedly, James 138
Smiley, J. S. 11
Smith, Garrett 46
Smith, Martha 117
Smith, Miss Willie A. B. 157
Smith, Peter 9, 10
Snowdon, John 10
Somerville, David 26
Sommerville, Eleanor 116
Sommerville, Margaret Harriet. *See* Sherriff, Margaret Harriet
Sommerville, William 116
Speer, John 55, 56, 58
Speer, John Jr. 58
Speer, Joseph L. 55
Speer, Mary. *See* Shields, Mary
Speer, Robert 58, 67, 83
Speer, Robert (probably Thomas) 81
Speer, Thomas 82, 83, 104, 128, 129
Speer, William 59
Spencer, James H. 180
Spencer, J. H. 140
Spencer, Martha 180
Sprott, John 85
Sprott, Samuel 85
Sproull, Margaret 66
Stafford, Cornelius 122
Stanley, Andrew 128
Starks, Daniel 9, 10
Stephenson, Eliza 70
Stephenson, James 69, 70
Stephenson, Margaret J. 69
Stephenson, Sarah E. 70
Stephenson, William 151
Sterling, J. M. 31
Stevenson, Elisha M. 92, 112, 115, 132
Stevenson, E. M. (s) 115
Stevenson, James 115
Stevenson, Nancy. *See* Dawson, Nancy; *See also* McBride, Lavina
Stevenson, Nancy (d) 115
Stevenson, Rebecca 115
Stevenson, Silas 74
Stevenson, Thomas D. 115
Stewart, Alexander 81
Stewart, Anna J. 70
Stewart, Calvin 104
Stewart, Charles 15, 23, 93, 96, 112
Stewart, Deacon 146
Stewart, Eliza 15
Stewart, Emma 15
Stewart, Eugene 15
Stewart, George 15
Stewart, Henry 15
Stewart, Isabelle. *See* Berry, Isabelle
Stewart, James R. 53
Stewart, Jane 134
Stewart, John A. 54
Stewart, John Carlysle 65
Stewart, Lemuel A. 15, 16

Stewart, Lemuel B. 15, 16
Stewart, Leonard A. 21
Stewart, Margaret 15, 16. *See* Rouse, Margaret
Stewart, Mary (Margaret) (d) 15
Stewart, Matilda 104
Stewart, Matthew 102, 104, 128
Stewart, Matthew (s) 104
Stewart, Nathan 104
Stewart, Philo M. 26
Stewart, Robert 46, 55, 102, 151
Stewart, Roberta 15
Stewart, R. W. 70, 76
Stewart, Samuel 15, 21
Stewart, Sarah 104
Stewart, Sarah (d) 104
Stewart, William 23, 149, 151
Stewart, William A. 15, 16, 17, 21, 53
Stewart, William R. 15
Stewart, Zachariah 15
Stickle, Samuel 128
Stone, J. M. 27
Stone, Lucy 61
Stoner, John 128
Stowe, Harriet Beecher 5, 29
Stright, Rachel 70
Strongfellow, William 21
Stuart, Matthew 49
Stuart, S. P. 96, 115
Sullivan, Algernon S. 164
Summerville. *See* Sommerville
Sumner, Charles (Senator) 163, 164
Swan, Frederick W. 150
Sykes, Joseph L. 47

T

Taft, Alphonso 23
Taft, William Howard 23
Tappan, Arthur 61
Tappan, Lewis 61
Taylor, Addie 87
Taylor, Ann 87
Taylor, Charity 87
Taylor, Daniel W. 87
Taylor, Elena 17
Taylor, Enos M. 87
Taylor family 107
Taylor, George 17
Taylor, George (s) 17
Taylor, Harriet J. 87
Taylor, Isabelle 9
Taylor, John 70
Taylor, John P. 87
Taylor, Joseph I. 87
Taylor, Lee 87
Taylor, Lucretia 87
Taylor, Martha E. 87
Taylor, Matilda 87
Taylor, Nathaniel 61
Taylor, Samuel 86, 87, 88, 89
Taylor, Samuel S. 87
Taylor, Thomas C. 87
Taylor, William M 87
Taylor, Zachary 44
Telford, James 41
Thomas, E. M. 70
Thomas, George Henry (General) 169
Thomas, Mrs. A. D. 171
Thompson, Captain 93
Thompson, John 71
Thornton, May 158
Tidball, David 46, 69, 70
Tidball, Jane 69, 70, 183
Tidball, John 81
Tidball, Margaret 69
Tidball, Mary 69
Tilden, Annie 170
Tilden, Charles 169, 170
Tilden, Elmira 170
Tilden, Lydia 170
Tilden, Mary 170
Tilden, Nellie 170
Tindall, Zachariah 122
Torrance, Francis J. 158
Torrence, J. W. E. 29
Townsend, Edith. *See* Ware, Edith
Townsend, Elizabeth 94
Townsend, Francis 92
Townsend, Milo A. 94, 147
Townsend, Rachel 92
Townsend, Talbot 47, 92, 94
Travis, Richard 7, 8
Trotter, B. C. 31
Tubman, Harriet 4, 5

U

Underwood, Sarah 140

V

Van Buren, Martin 44
Van Fleet, David 116

Van Fleet, George W. 116
Van Fleet, Phoebe 116
Van Fleet, Richard 116
Van Fleet, Sarah 116. *See also* Hogue, Sarah
Vanwicker, Mrs. Josephine 171
Vashong, J. B. 145
Veigart, F. 70
Verner, Murray A. 158
Vogan, John 54

W

Waddington, Benjamin 82
Waddington, John 82
Waddington, Wilkes 82
Walker, Agnes. *See* McFadden, Agnes
Walker, Anna Jane 114. *See also* Bailey, Anna Jane
Walker, Beveridge 113
Walker, Hughston (Houston) 113
Walker, James 111, 116, 117
Walker, John 114, 115
Walker, John. A. 117
Walker, John G. 113
Walker, Robert 117
Walker, Robert (s) 117
Walker, William Jr. 114
Walker, William W. 36, 39, 112, 114, 115, 132, 181
Wallace family 107
Wallace, Mrs. Robert 134
Wallace, Robert 131
Wallace, Sarah 70, 132
Wallace, W. D. 157, 158
Wallis, Robert 7
Walsh, Sarah 171
Ward, John 170
Ward, Mrs. John 170
Ware, Edith 94
Warner, Althea 71
Warnock, Elizabeth 70
Warnock, W. S. 70
Warwick, Harriet A. 171
Warwick, John 171
Washington, Booker T. 157, 161
Washington, William 156
Watson, Hiram 31
Watson, Lot 48
Watson, P. J. 157
Watson, William 31
Waugh, David D. 70
Waugh, James 137
Waugh, John 137

Weigert, F. 70
Weir, Frederick 128
Weld, Theodore D. 61
Well, Sarah 38
Wesley, John 156
Westerman, James 70
Wharton, Dr. 164
Wharton, Mose 164, 165
Wharton, Sarah 164, 165
Wharton, William 164
Wharton, William (s) 165
Whippo, Althea 71, 183. *See* Warner, Althea
Whippo, Charles T. 8, 69, 70, 71, 178, 183
Whistler, C. W. (Captain) 150, 151
White, Ada 77
White, Adaline 13, 69, 70, 73, 75, 76, 183
White, Alice 77
White, Amanda 76
White, Arthur 77
White, Benjamin 124
White, Carrie 77
White, Crawford 8, 26, 65, 66, 73, 74, 76, 77, 92
White, David 26, 76
White, Dunlap 73
White, Edward 104
White, Elizabeth 183. *See* Dunlap, Elizabeth
White, Elizabeth Ann 76
White, Eva 77
White, Frederick 77
White, James 76
White, James D. 76, 132
White, J. C. 47
White, J. D. 124
White, John 77
White, John Crawford 76, 77, 78, 144, 175, 176
White, Joseph Semple 13, 14, 30, 34, 48, 54, 65, 66, 67, 69, 70, 73, 74, 75, 76, 77, 78, 116, 132, 143, 144, 175, 176, 178, 179, 184
White, Josiah C. 48, 70, 76
Whiteley, Richard H. (U.S. Rep.) 164
White, May Belle 77
White, N. 70
White, Sarah M. 70
Whitham, John D. 29, 33, 39, 40, 48
Whitren, Reverend 39. *See* Whitham, John D.
Whitten, James 128
Whittier, John Greenleaf 61
Whittington, Bertha 162
Wicks, Captain 37
Wicks, Elizabeth 37
Wick, William 138

Wiggans family 18
Wigle, Abraham 128
Wilbur Siebert 113
Wilder, Ebenezer 54
Wilder, Shubael 70
Willard, Eugene S. 77
Williams, Albert 124
Williams, Charles 124
Williams, Eliza 95
Williams, Ellen 23
Williams, George Washington 15, 23
Williams, Henry 55, 122, 124
Williams, James 124
Williams, Mary 124
Williams, Mary (d) 124
Williamson, Passmore 151
Williamson, Sarah 31
Williams, Robert 124
Williams, Thomas 23
Williams, William Margaret 124
Willis, Kathyrn H. i
Wilson, Fanny 9, 17, 183
Wilson, Henna 129
Wilson, Henry (Senator) 164
Wilson, Jacob 129
Wilson, Jemima 129
Wilson, John 8
Wilson, John C. 70
Wilson, John G. 70
Wilson, John R. 31
Wilson, Margaret 83, 129
Wilson, Patrick 113
Wilson, Rachel 83, 129
Wilson, Robert 21
Wilson, Samuel 26
Wilson, Thomas 83, 104, 128, 129
Wilson, William G. 184
Wolf, J. D. 49
Woodard, Eliza 74
Wood, Hugh 65
Wood, John 65
Woods, James H. 31, 70
Woods, James R. 70
Woods, Robert 99
Wood, William 98
Wright, Alexander III 93
Wright, Alexander Jr. 93, 94, 96, 112
Wright, Alexander Sr. 93
Wright, Edward (Major) 97
Wright, Elizabeth 93, 94, 96
Wright, Elizur Jr. 61

Wright, Isaac 93
Wright, John 47, 93
Wright, John P. 113
Wright, Joseph 92, 93, 94, 132
Wright, Mrs. Mary 171
Wright, Samuel 10, 104
Wyman, James G. (Mayor) 158

Y

Young, Amanda 129, 134
Young, Caroline 129
Young, David 10, 112, 132, 134, 180
Young, Elizabeth 104
Young, Hannah 134
Young, Jane 134. *See also* McGuffey, Jane
Young, Joanna 129. *See also* Coovert, Joanna
Young, John Jr. 11, 27, 30, 36, 49, 148, 149
Young, John Sr. 7, 8
Young, Marcus 129
Young, Margaret 104
Young, Mary 70, 104
Young, Mary (d) 104
Young, Matilda 104, 129
Young, Matthew 127, 129
Young, Mrs. David 112, 132
Young, Phillip 128
Young, Robert 104, 127
Young, Samantha 129
Young, Sarah 134
Young, Sarah Jane 129
Young, Sylvester M. 129
Young, William 132, 134
Young, William H. 129
Yrajer, Bump 9

Z

Zeigler, Frederick 180

www.ingramcontent.com/pod-product-compliance
Lightning Source LLC
Chambersburg PA
CBHW080401170426
43193CB00016B/2780